LEARNING FROM
GREAT LEADERS

INSPIRING
LEADERSHIP

JOHN ADAIR

D0317998

THORO**GOOD**

111449047

Published in 2002, reprinted 2003 and 2005
Thorogood Publishing Ltd
10-12 Rivington Street
London EC2A 3DU

Telephone: 020 7749 4748 • Fax: 020 7729 6110
Email: info@thorogood.ws
Web: www.thorogood.ws

Books Network International In
3 Front Street, Suite 331
Rollinsford, NH 30869, USA

Telephone: +603 749 9171 • Fax:
Email: bizbks@aol.com

A CIP catalogue record for this book is available
from the British Library.

ISBN HB: 1 85418 261 7
ISBN PB: 1 85418 207 2

Designed by Driftdesign.

Printed in India by Replika Press.

For Thea

Contents

Introduction   **1**

PART 1

ONE Leadership Through Knowledge   **4**

Socrates – A Leader of Ideas   6

The Case of the Aspiring General   7

The Case of the Young Cavalry Commander   8

Knowledge – The Key to Leadership   11

Are Knowledge and Experience Enough?   13

A Leader in Action   17

Chapter Review   20

TWO Leadership Skills   **24**

The Case of Nicomachides   25

Human Needs and Leadership Functions   28

A Leader in Estate Management   30

Are Leaders Born or Made?   33

Chapter Review   34

THREE **The Servant-Leader**   **37**

The Teaching of Lao Tzu   39

The Tao of Leadership   40

Jesus and His Disciples   44

Servant Leadership in Perspective   47

The Japanese Contribution   53

Chapter Review   55

FOUR **The Ability to Give Direction**   **58**

What's in a Word?   59

The Shepherd and His Flock   61

Interlude: The Three Circles   66

Alexander the Great   67

Creating Unity and Teamwork   69

Caring for Individuals   71

Chapter Review   74

FIVE **Making the Right Decisions**   **77**

Thinking to Some Purpose   78

From Ideas to Responsible and Decisive Action   85

Case-study: Chairing the Cabinet   90

Intuition and Imagination   94

Calmness Under Pressure   99

The Value of Humour   103

Chapter Review   105

SIX **The Art of Inspiring While Informing**   **108**

The Effective Communicator   109

The Art of Inspiring Others   110

The Relevance of the Second World War   114

Case-Study: The Forgotten Army   115

Case-study: Montgomery   124

The Effects of Telecommunications   129

Chapter Review   133

PART 2

SEVEN **The Roots of British Tradition**   **138**

Eagles of Rome   138

The Tribal Legacy   145

Alfred the Great   148

Chapter Review   154

EIGHT **The Gentleman Leader**   **156**

The Impact of Education   158

Leadership Qualities   162

Machiavelli and Leadership   169

The Great Rebellion   172

The American Experience   176

George Washington   182

Chapter Review   185

NINE **Nelson**   **187**

Early Life   188

The Man and the Legend   189

Achieving the Task   194

Bringer of Harmony   197

Meeting Individual Needs   198

Nelson's Legacy   204

Chapter Review   205

TEN **Polar Explorers**   **207**

Captain Robert Falcon Scott   208

Sir Ernest Shackleton   211

Gino Watkins   213

Chapter Review   218

ELEVEN Leadership in a Changing World 220

The New Climate of Change in the Nineteenth Century 221

How Progress Happens 225

Captains of Industry 227

Management Through Leadership 232

A Factory of Democratic Leaders 234

Slim on Leadership 243

Managers or Leaders? 246

Chapter Review 249

PART 3

TWELVE Charisma 254

The Rediscovery of Charisma 255

Leadership: A Gift from Above? 256

Case-study: Alexander the Great 261

Case-study: Lawrence of Arabia 268

Chapter Review 273

THIRTEEN Women as Leaders 276

The Western Tradition 277

Leadership in Marriage 282

Great Social Reformers 287

Women as Manager-Leaders 291

Case-study: Margaret Thatcher 293

Chapter Review 301

FOURTEEN Styles of Leadership   **303**

Greatness	303
Abraham Lincoln	306
Charles de Gaulle	309
Adolf Hitler	315
Mahatma Gandhi	322
Nelson Mandela	328
Chapter Review	333

FIFTEEN Leaders for Tomorrow   **335**

Not Followers But Companions	338
An Invitation to Greatness	338
Chapter Review	344

Picture Acknowledgements	346
Select Bibliography	347
Index	349

Introduction

'Visit the past in order to know the present'

The purpose of this book is to review some of the great leaders in history, and to identify the main lessons of leadership that can be learnt from them. What emerges is a concept of leadership that is highly relevant to the needs of the world today. This is not surprising, for human nature does not change over the centuries and part of the greatness of great leaders stems from their deep understanding of people.

The importance of good leadership today hardly needs to be stressed. For it is widely recognised that a democratic society cannot work effectively without it. Leaders are needed in all fields and at all levels to give direction, create teamwork and inspire people to give of their best.

Here, then, are the timeless and yet timely truths which are the pillars of leadership. Each chapter concludes with a brief *summary*, a list of *key concepts* and some suggestions for *further reflection*. These are designed both to help you to identify clearly the foregoing principles or lessons, and also to stimulate your own further thinking. My hope is that by this means the book will become for you what the Romans called a *vademecum*, 'go with me' in Latin, a companion book on your own journey as a leader. The path of leadership can be 'steep and thorny' at times and you may well find it worthwhile to revisit these pages. My hope is that you will always finding something here to refresh, to encourage and inspire you on your way to becoming an inspirational leader.

My warmest good wishes go with you.

John Adair

PART 1

ONE
Leadership Through Knowledge

'It is a fact that some men possess an inbred superiority which gives them a dominating influence over their contemporaries, and marks them out unmistakably for leadership.' So an eminent churchman Dr Hensley Henson, Lord Bishop of Durham, told his audience at the University of St Andrews. 'This phenomenon is as certain as it is mysterious,' he continued. 'It is apparent in every association of human beings, in every variety of circumstances and on every plane of culture. In a school among boys, in a college among students, in a factory, shipyard, or a mine among the workmen, as certainly as in the Church and in the Nation, there are those who, with an assured and unquestioned title, take the leading place, and shape the general conduct.'

These words were spoken in 1934, the year, incidentally, that Adolf Hitler became Head of State in Germany with the title of *Führer*. The Bishop believed, as most people thought then, that leadership was a form of 'inbred superiority' – in other words, you are either born with it or not. The born leader will emerge naturally as the leader because he (note the assumption that leaders are men) has innate qualities which give him that 'assured and unquestioned title.' Such a leader could presumably lead in any circumstance or situation.

It may come as a surprise that Scotland's oldest university, St Andrews, instituted lectures in leadership in 1930. Sponsored by a local Scottish family, the Walker Trust series of leadership lectures was inaugurated by John Buchan, Lord Tweedsmuir, with a lecture on 'Montrose and Leadership'.

There were twelve lectures in all, spread over a period of some thirty years. They included lectures by Montgomery and Wavell. The tradition of thinking about leadership, however, is much older than this century, and its roots lie outside Britain. The story begins in ancient Athens, among the group that gathered around the philosopher of practical reason – Socrates.

Socrates. Apart from being himself a leader of ideas Socrates was the first person to ask some of the key questions about the nature of leadership.

Socrates – A Leader of Ideas

Socrates lived in the fourth century BC. In early life he is said to have been a sculptor. As a citizen-in-arms he served with distinction in at least three campaigns, but the greater part of his life he devoted to philosophical discussion. Socrates set himself the task of clarifying for himself and other men current issues of political and moral life. The method he used was so distinctive of him that we still describe it as 'Socratic'. Briefly, Socrates pretended ignorance in order to encourage others to express their views fully. When he had drawn them out by cross-examination he gently exposed their inconsistencies by the same process. It was not an approach that made him popular in all quarters – Socrates was no respecter either of persons or of hallowed beliefs in his quest for truth. In 399 BC Socrates' enemies accused him, quite wrongly, of impiety and of corrupting the young. In spite of an eloquent self-defence at his trial, they condemned him to death by forcing him to drink hemlock.

The Parable of the Ship's Captain

The sailors are quarrelling over the control of the helm... They do not understand that the genuine navigator can only make himself fit to command a ship by studying the seasons of the year, sky, stars, and winds and all that belongs to his craft; and they have no idea that, along with the science of navigation, it is possible for him to gain, by instruction or practice, the skill to keep control of the helm whether some of them like it or not.

Plato, *The Republic*

Socrates wrote no books. Our main sources of information about him are Plato's *Dialogues*, Xenophon's *Memorabilia* and Aristophanes' satirical picture in *The Clouds*. It is uncertain how far Plato and Xenophon attribute their own opinions to their common master. When it comes to the theme of leadership it is especially difficult to determine how much goes back to Socrates. Xenophon himself was both a leader and a thinker about leadership. Did he put his own views into the mouth of Socrates? He certainly wrote in the form of Socratic dialogues, with Socrates as one of the speakers.

Or, when as a young man he heard Socrates cross-examining various would-be leaders, did he take notes? These questions cannot be answered with any degree of confidence, but at least we know of one core idea in Xenophon which does go back to Socrates – that leadership is tied to situations and depends largely upon the leader having the appropriate knowledge: we know this because Plato also takes up that theme. But Xenophon's own experience and reflections must have led him to develop the seeds of ideas thrown out by the 'The Thinker' (as he and his fellow students nicknamed Socrates). Xenophon's own military interest, for example, comes over clearly in the two following dialogues.

The Case of the Aspiring General

One of the young Athenians around Socrates announced that he wished to stand in the annual election of ten generals in the city's army. Socrates encouraged him to attend the classes of an itinerant teacher called Dionysodurus, who had recently arrived in Athens and advertised a course in generalship. When the young man returned he had to endure some good-humoured banter from Socrates and his friends.

'Don't you think, gentlemen,' said Socrates, 'that our friend looks more "majestic" as Homer called Agamemnon, now that he has learned generalship? For just as he who has learned to play the harp is a harper even when he does not play, and he who has studied medicine is a doctor even though he does not practise, so our friend will be a general for ever, even if no one votes for him. But an ignoramus is neither general nor doctor, even if he gets every vote. Now', he continued, turning to the young Athenian, 'in order that any one of us who may happen to command a regiment or company under you may have a better knowledge of warfare, tell us the first lesson he gave you in generalship.'

'The first was like the last,' the young man replied: 'he taught me tactics – nothing else.'

'But that is only a small part of generalship,' replied Socrates. By question-and-answer he then led the young man into a much fuller understanding of the knowledge and abilities required for a successful military leader. A general must be good at administration, so that the army is properly supplied with military equipment and provisions. Moreover, as Xenophon knew from his own experience, a general should ideally possess a number of person qualities and skills:

> 'He must be resourceful, active, careful, hardy and quick-witted; he must be both gentle and brutal, at once straightforward and designing, capable of both caution and surprise, lavish and rapacious, generous and mean, skilful in defence and attack; and there are many other qualifications, some natural, some acquired, that are necessary to one as a general.'

Even on the all-important subject of tactics, Socrates found the instruction given to his young friend by Dionysodurus to be deficient. Did Dionysodurus give no advice on where and how to use each formation? Was *no* guidance given on when to modify deployments and tactics according to the needs of the many different kinds of situations one encounters in war? The young man insisted that this was the case. 'Then you must go back and ask for your money back,' said Socrates. 'For if Dionysodurus knows the answers to these questions and has a conscience, he will be ashamed to send you home ill-taught'.

The Case of the Young Cavalry Commander

One day Socrates met a newly-elected cavalry commander. Socrates asked him first why he had sought that office. The young many agreed that it could not have been because he wanted to be first in the cavalry charge, for the mounted archers usually rode ahead of the commander into battle, nor could it have been simply in order to get himself known to everyone – even madmen achieve that. He accepted Socrates' suggestion that it must be to leave the Athenian cavalry in better condition than when he found it. Xenophon, both a renowned authority on horsemanship and the author of a textbook on commanding cavalry, had no difficulty in explaining what needs to be done to achieve that end. The young commander, for example, must improve the quality of the cavalry mounts; he must school new recruits – both horses and men – in equestrian skills and then teach the troopers their cavalry tactics.

'And have you considered how to make the men obey you?' continued Socrates, 'Because without that horses and men, however good and gallant, are of no use.'

'True, but what is the best way of encouraging them to obey, Socrates?' asked the young man.

'Well, I suppose you know that under all conditions human beings are most willing to obey those whom they believe to be the best. Thus in sickness they most readily obey the doctor, on board ship the pilot, on the farm the farmer, whom they think to be most skilled in his business.'

'Yes, certainly,' said the student.

'Then it is likely that in horsemanship too, one who clearly knows best what ought to be done will most easily gain the obedience of the others.' Xenophon captures here a very distinct theme in Socrates' teaching on leadership. In harmony with the rest of the doctrine of Socrates (for, despite his pose of ignorance, Socrates had ideas of his own), it emphasises the importance of *knowledge* in leadership. People will obey willingly only those whom they perceive to be better qualified or more knowledgeable than they are in a particular situation.

Xenophon. Besides being a successful military leader himself
Xenophon also taught leadership through his books.

Knowledge – The Key to Leadership

Socrates clearly taught that professional or technical competence should be a prerequisite for holding a position of leadership responsibility. 'You must have noticed,' said Socrates to another man, 'that if he is incompetent, no one attempts to exercise authority over our harpists, choristers, and dancers, nor over wrestlers? All who have authority over them can tell you where they learned their business.'

The tendency of people to follow a leader who knows what to do is strengthened in a time of crisis. In a discussion with Pericles, son of the famous statesman, which took place when an army from the Greek state of Boeotia was threatening Athens, Socrates made the additional point that such a crisis should be more to an effective leader's liking than a period of ease and prosperity, for it is easier to make things happen. He illustrated this point with a favourite analogy, the behaviour of sailors at sea:

> 'For confidence breeds carelessness, slackness, disobedience: fear makes men more attentive, more obedient, more amenable to discipline. The behaviour of sailors is a case in point. So long as they have nothing to fear, they are, I believe, an unruly lot, but when they expect a storm or an attack, they not only carry out all orders, but watch in silence for the word of command like choristers.'

There are three main forms of authority in human affairs: the authority of position or rank, the authority of personality, and the authority of knowledge. Socrates clearly emphasised the latter. It is the man or woman who knows what to do and how to do it who will be obeyed, especially in times of crisis. Now, if that were the whole story about leaders, then the right to lead would be acquired with technical or professional knowledge. When the soldier learns tactics, the doctor studies medicine, the sailor acquires knowledge of navigation and the farmer becomes experienced in agriculture, then they would also be qualifying as leaders. For they are accumulating the necessary knowledge and experience which will incline those more ignorant than themselves to obey, at least in their own field. For Socrates and his school, as exemplified by Plato, knowledge is the main gateway to leadership. We can trace here the beginnings of a major theme in the Western tradition of leadership. The desire for educated rulers, governors or leaders – men and women with an authority based on knowledge and experience rather than those who relied upon birth, title or position – would encourage the establishment of schools and universities. It was a rivulet in the tradition which the Renaissance transformed into a mighty river.

But is having relevant knowledge and experience to the situation – the general working field or the particular situation of crisis – the *whole* of leadership? Xenophon knew that it was not so. From his close observation of men in action, he made a distinction between those leaders who won *willing* obedience from their subordinates and colleagues, as compared to those who merely extracted compliance from them either out of fear or a grudging acceptance of the authority of knowledge.

A man of the moment

Apparently against the advice of Socrates, Xenophon enlisted in a Greek army which the Persian prince Cyrus the Younger hired in a bid to replace his brother Artaxerxes II on the throne of Persia. In 401 BC a decisive battle was fought at Cunaxa, not far from ancient Babylon. The 10,400 Greek hoplites – heavy armoured spearmen – acquitted themselves well on the day, but Cyrus lost both the battle and his life.

After the battle of Cunaxa, the Persians offered the Ten Thousand (as the Greeks were later known) surrender terms if they stayed where they were, but threatened to attack if they moved from their camp. One of their six generals, a Spartan named Clearchus, took it upon himself to act as spokesman for his fellow generals to the Persian emissaries, but gave no indication to anyone what he was going to say. After sunset he summoned a meeting of the officers, briefly reviewed the options and then told them what they must do. They must head northwards that very night on the first stage of a long march to safety on the shores of the Black Sea, which lay some 800 miles away. As Xenophon records in *The Persian Expedition* everyone sensed that only Clearchus could lead them out of mortal danger:

'On receiving their instructions the generals and captains went away and carried them out; and from then on Clearchus was in command, and they were his subordinates. This was not the result of an election, but because they realised that he was the one man who had the right sort of mind for a commander, while the rest of them were inexperienced.'

A Greek foot soldier, crouching behind his shield, meets a charging Persian horseman. Providing they kept their good order Greek spearmen had little to fear from cavalry.

Are Knowledge and Experience Enough?

Clearchus, the Spartan general who saved the day after Cunaxa, is a good example of such a limited leader. We can recognise men of his stamp again and again in military history. The Roman army depended upon men such as he. Their type would resurface in latter armed forces: the Prussians of Frederick the Great, the British Royal Navy in Georgian times, the German *Wehrmacht* in the Second World War, and the American Army in Vietnam.

Clearachus was about fifty at the time of his death. He had spent much of his life at war, acquiring by hard experience a sound knowledge of his profession. But, as Xenophon noted, Clearchus never won the hearts of men. He had no followers who were there because of friendship or good feeling towards him. Xenophon continued:

> *'As for his great qualities as a soldier, they appear in the facts that he was fond of adventure, ready to lead an attack on the enemy by day or night, and that, when he was in a awkward position, he kept his head, as everyone agrees who was with him anywhere. It was said that he had all the qualities of leadership which a man of his sort could have.*

He had an outstanding ability for planning means by which an army could get supplies, and seeing that they appeared; and he was also well able to impress on those who were with him that Clearchus was a man to be obeyed. He achieved his result by this toughness. He had a forbidding appearance and a harsh voice. His punishments were severe ones and were sometimes inflicted in anger, so that there were times when he was sorry himself for what he had done. With him punishment was a matter of principle, for he thought that any army without discipline was good for nothing; indeed, it is reported that he said that a soldier ought to be more frightened of his own commander than of the enemy if he was going to turn out one who could keep a good guard, or abstain from doing harm to his own side, or go into battle without second thoughts.

So it happened that in difficult positions the soldiers would give him complete confidence and wished for no one better. On these occasions, they said that his forbidding look seemed positively cheerful, and his toughness appeared as confidence in the face of the enemy, so that it was no longer toughness to them but something to make them feel safe. On the other hand, when the danger was over and there was a chance of going away to take service under someone else, many of them deserted him, since he was invariably tough and savage, so that the relations between his soldiers and him were like those of boys to a schoolmaster.'

It is tempting to conclude that while Clearchus had great abilities as a soldier, and also as what we would now call a manager (planning and controlling), he fell far short as a leader. One reason why people today often react so negatively to the idea of military leadership is because they assume that all military leaders are cast from the same mould as Clearchus. This is certainly not the case.

Xenophon's last point, that Clearchus treated his soldiers like a pedagogue (literally in Greek a 'leader of children') is illuminating. The Greeks prided themselves on the belief that they were the most intelligent people on the face of the earth; they were deeply conscious, too, of their tradition of equality and democracy. They did not like being bullied or treated as children.

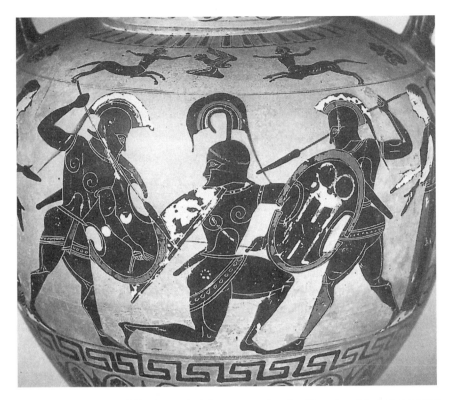

A Greek vase depicting spearmen in action. Through such individual combat Greek warriors won the glory and renown for which they craved.

Xenophon, aged twenty-six, was elected as one of the successors to Clearchus and the other five Greek generals whom the Persians butchered in an act of treachery not long after Cunaxa. Having been taught leadership by Socrates, what style of leadership would Xenophon display? Doubtless he thought hard about that question. Obviously he did not want to be another Clearchus, nor did he want to err too far in the opposite direction of courting popularity and appearing weak. Xenophon tells us that Proxenus the Boeotian, one of the other murdered generals, had made that mistake. It was he, incidentally, who had first invited Xenophon to go on the Persian expedition, and so they were probably friends. Proxenus was a very ambitious young man and had spent much money on being educated by a celebrated teacher called Gorgias of Leontini. 'After he had been with him for a time,' wrote Xenophon, ' he came to the conclusion that he was now capable of commanding an army and, if he became friends with the great, of doing them no less good than they did him; so he joined in this adventure planned by Cyrus, imagining that he would gain from it a great name, and great power, and plenty of money.' Yet, with all these ambitions, Proxenus made it clear to all that he wanted to get these things in a fair and honourable way or not at all. He liked to be liked, however, which led him into the mistakes of appearing soft and of courting popularity for its own sake:

> 'He was a good commander for people of a gentlemanly type, but he was not capable of impressing his soldiers with a feeling of respect or fear for him. Indeed, he showed more diffidence in front of his soldiers than his subordinates showed in front of him, and it was obvious that he was more afraid of being unpopular with his troops than his troops were afraid of disobeying his orders. He imagined that to be a good general, and to gain the name for being one, it was enough to give praise to those who did well and to withhold it from those who did badly. The result was that decent people in his entourage liked him, but unprincipled people undermined his position, since they thought he was easily managed. At the time of his death he was about thirty years old.'

It could be said that Proxenus was not right for the military situation, and he could not establish the right relationship with soldiers. But probably he would have been as ineffective in non-military spheres of leadership as well. For Proxenus's very virtues created a certain lack of firmness or toughness which can lead to a loss of respect. Without respect, leadership is fatally impaired. A weak leader exposes himself to exploitation by his more unscrupulous subordinates. Bad leadership of this kind looks remarkably the same whatever the field or area of human enterprise.

Xenophon, who sat at the feet of Socrates, the western world's first great teacher of leadership, now shows us what he meant by leadership.

The Mountainous country of southern Turkey through which Xenophon and the Ten Thousand made their famous march to the Black Sea.

A Leader in Action

Imagine yourself on a sun-baked, stony hillside on the southern edge of Kurdistan (on the borders of what is now Iraq and Turkey) watching this scene unfold before you. It is about noon; the sky is clear blue, except for a line of white clouds almost motionless above a distant mountain range. Marching through these foothills comes the advance guard of the Ten Thousand. The hot sun glints and sparkles on their spears, helmets and breastplates. They are hurrying forward, eager to reach the safety of the mountains in order to be rid of the Persian cavalry snapping like hunting dogs at their heels. But first they have to cut their way through the Carduci, the warlike natives of the region. Across the pass you can see a strong contingent of these tribesmen already occupying the lower heights of a steep hill which commands the road. Now the Greek advance guard has spotted them, too, and it halts. After some hurried deliberations you can see a messenger running back. A few minutes later a horseman – it is Xenophon – gallops up to the commander of the advance guard, a seasoned Spartan captain named Chirisophus. Xenophon tells him that he has not brought up a reinforcement of the light-armed troops that had been urgently requested because the rearguard – still under constant attack – could not be weakened. Then he carefully studies the lie of the land. Noticing that the Carduci have neglected to occupy the actual summit of the hill, he puts this plan to his Spartan colleague:

> 'The best thing to do, Chirisophus, is for us to advance on the summit as fast as we can. If we can occupy it, those who are commanding our road will not be able to maintain their position. If you like, you stay here with the main body. I will volunteer to go ahead. Or, if you prefer it, you march on the mountain and I will stay here.'

> 'I will give you the choice,' replies Chirisophus, 'of doing whichever you like.'

It would be an arduous physical task, Xenophon points out, and he tactfully says that being the younger man he would be the best one to undertake it. Having chosen some 400 skirmishers, armed with targets and light javelins, together with 100 hand-picked pikemen of the advance guard, he marches them off as fast as he can go towards the summit. But when the enemy see what the Greeks are doing, they too begin to head for the highest ground as fast as they can go.

> 'Then there was a lot of shouting, from the Greek army cheering on its men on the one side and from Tissaphernes' people cheering on their men on the other side. Xenophon rode along the ranks on horseback, urging them on. "Soldiers," he said, "consider that it is for Greece you are fighting now, that you fighting your way to your children and your wives, and that with a little hard work now, we shall go on the rest or our way unopposed."

> Soteridas, a man from Sicyon, said: "We are not on a level, Xenophon. You are riding on horseback, while I am wearing myself out with a shield to carry." '

As the commander, Xenophon had several options open to him. He could have ignored the man. Or he could have threatened him. Or he could conceivably have had him arrested and punished later. Xenophon took none of the courses. Writing of himself in the third person he told us what happened next:

> 'When Xenophon heard this, he jumped down from his horse, pushed Soteridas out of the ranks, took his shield away from him and went forward on foot as fast as he could, carrying the shield. He happened to be wearing a cavalry breastplate as well, so that it was heavy going for him. He kept on encouraging those in front to keep going and those behind to join up with them, though struggling along behind them himself. The other soldiers, however, struck Soteridas and threw stones at him and cursed him until they forced him to take back his shield and continue marching. Xenophon then remounted and, so long as the going was good, led the way on horseback. When it became impossible to ride, he left his horse behind and hurried ahead on foot. And so they got to the summit before the enemy.'

Note that it was the other soldiers who shamed Soteridas into taking back his shield. Although Xenophon, burdened with a heavy cavalry breastplate, eventually fell back behind the ranks as the men rushed up the hill, yet he encouraged the men forward and urged them to keep their battle order. Eventually he remounted and led his soldiers from the front, at first on horse and then again on foot.

Once the Greeks had gained the summit the Carduci turned and fled in all directions. The Persian cavalry under Tissaphernes, who had been distant onlookers of the contest, also turned their bridles and withdrew.

Then Chirisophus's men in the vanguard of the army were able to descend through the mountain pass into a fertile plain beside the Tigris. There they refreshed themselves before facing the fearsome rigours of a winter march amid the snow-covered Armenian highlands. Eventually, in the summer of the following year, the army reached the safety of the Hellespont, the narrow straits dividing Europe from Asia. They owed much to Xenophon who, not long afterwards, became the sole commander of the Ten Thousand.

Anyone reading this story will recognise that in it Xenophon acted as a leader. He led by example. That is a universal principle or theme in the story of leadership. It is especially important where people face hardship or danger: they expect their leaders to run the same risks and shoulder the same burdens as themselves, or at least show a willingness to do so.

The story of Xenophon's assault on the Carduci illustrates another cardinal principle of leadership. Leaders encourage people. They renew spirits, giving others fresh courage to pursue the common course of action. Xenophon's words and deeds infused the Greeks with new confidence and resolution. His brave example inspired them.

Leadership Through Knowledge

CHAPTER REVIEW

Summary

It was Socrates who first taught that leadership tends to be exercised by the person who knows what to do in a given situation. Consequently, he placed much emphasis upon the need to acquire the appropriate technical competence and experience if one wished to lead others. But knowledge is not the whole story. There are people who are technically competent and highly specialised in their fields, yet they are not recognised as leaders. Something more is required. As the experience of Xenophon suggests, a good leader gives direction, sets an example, shares danger or hardship on an equal footing, and wins the willing support of others. He or she should win respect without courting popularity. Are these more general leadership abilities transferable from one field to another? Could they be learned?

Key Concepts

- Socrates did not write any books, but two of his circle – Xenophon and Plato – independently give us in his name the teaching that leadership flows to the person who knows what to do in the given situation. The situational approach, as it has later been called, dates back to Socrates.

- People are most willing to obey those who know what they are doing.

- As the experience of Xenophon himself and his observations of other generals suggests, a good leader gives direction, sets an example, and shares danger or hardship on an equal footing. He or she should win respect without courting popularity.

- There is a difference between managing – administration, planning and controlling – and leadership. A good leader does those things but transcends them: he or she has the secret of arousing the willing and enthusiastic support of others to the common task at hand.

- The story of Xenophon's assault on the Carduci illustrates another cardinal principle of leadership. Leaders *encourage* people. They renew spirits, giving others fresh courage to pursue the common course of action. Xenophon's words and deeds infused the Greeks with new confidence and resolution. His brave example inspired them.

Further Reflection

Xenophon mentions more than once in this opening description the personal *qualities* required in a General. In the *Cyropaedia* he listed the qualities of an ideal ruler as:

- temperance
- justice
- sagacity
- amiability
- presence of mind
- tactfulness
- humanity

- sympathy
- helpfulness
- courage
- magnanimity
- generosity
- considerateness.

Aristotle, Plato's greatest pupil, suggested just four qualities of leadership:

1 justice
2 temperance
3 prudence
4 fortitude.

Field Marshal Montgomery quoted them with approval.

Lord Slim also taught four qualities, but they are different:

1 courage
2 willpower
3 initiative
4 knowledge.

What qualities do you think a business leader requires?

It is helpful first to distinguish *qualities* of personality and character from *knowledge* in the technical or professional sense that Socrates had in mind. Then, think in terms of levels of qualities. As a start, a leader should possess or exemplify the qualities expected or required in their working groups or organisations.

- Look back on the last chapter and list the five core qualities of a good soldier, regardless of rank. Keep it by you, and amend it as you read the rest of the book.

- In your business what qualities of personality and character do you expect everyone to have? Do you – by common consent – exemplify those qualities? (These qualities, you should note, are *necessary* but not *sufficient*: – they won't make you a leader, but you cannot be one without them.)

There are some more generic qualities associated with leadership, in any field, such as enthusiasm, integrity (the quality that makes people trust you), energy, toughness or being seen and accepted as a leader. Using this brief list, and adding to it as you read on, identify your own strengths and weaknesses in terms of leadership qualities.

Having read these lists and the other attributes mentioned above, what do you think at present are the five or six key qualities or characteristics of a good leader today? What other qualities can you foresee becoming important and so joining your list in the next ten years? (You may like to revise this, your 'first thoughts' list, when you have finished reading the book.)

TWO
Leadership Skills

'There is nobody who cannot vastly improve his powers of leadership by a little thought and practice.'

LORD SLIM

The question of leadership transferability had a special importance in Athens in the days of Socrates. The various offices in the Athenian army and navy, including the generalships (which were roughly equivalent to the commands of large territorial infantry battalions today), were open to all citizens by election. To secure one of these commands was a first step for any ambitious young man aspiring to become a political leader in Athens. There were other offices, too, such as being choir-master of one of the city's choirs. Like the regiments, these choirs were based upon the old tribal structure of Athens. The Greeks were extremely competitive, and a choir that won the prize in competition brought much credit to its tribe and its choir-master.

Therefore Socrates and Xenophon had a contemporary reason for being interested in the question of whether or not any transferable or personal skills existed, as distinct from professional ones (which would equip a young man to lead in business or politics, in the arts, such as music, or in the Athenian army or navy). Athenians were essentially civilians. Like Socrates, when Athens went to war they had to fight in the phalanx of spearmen or pull an oar in the navy's warships. For the notion of having professional officers or soldiers was alien to the Greek states, except for Sparta – a nation of soldiers.

In the following discussion Socrates explored the issue of transferability by arguing provocatively that a successful business man will make an effective general. During the course of it, incidentally, Socrates became the first person in history to identify what today would be called leadership functions.

The Case of Nicomachides

Once on seeing Nicomachides returning from the elections, Socrates asked him, 'Who have been chosen generals, Nicomachides?'

'Isn't it like the Athenians?' he replied; 'They have not chosen me after all the hard work I have done since I was called up, in the command of company or regiment, though I have been so often wounded in action.' (Here he uncovered and showed his scars.) 'They have chosen Antisthenes, who has never served in a marching regiment nor distinguished himself in the cavalry and understands nothing but money-making.'

'Isn't that a recommendation,' said Socrates, 'supposing he proves capable of supplying the men's needs?'

'Why,' retorted Nicomachides, 'merchants also are capable of making money, but that doesn't make them fit to command an army!'

'But,' replied Socrates, 'Antisthenes also is eager for victory, and that is a good point in a general. Whenever he has been choir-master, you know, his choir has always won.'

'No doubt.' Conceded Nicomachides, 'but there is no analogy between the handling of a choir and of an army.'

'But you see,' said Socrates, 'though Antisthenes knows nothing about music or choir training, he showed himself capable of finding the best experts in these activities. And therefore he finds out and prefers the best men in warfare as in choir training, it is likely that he will be victorious in that too; and probably he will be more ready to spend money on winning a battle with the whole state than on winning a choral competition with this tribe.'

'Do you mean to say, Socrates, that the man who succeeds with a chorus will also succeed with an army?'

'I mean that, whatever a man controls, if he knows what he wants and can get it he will be a good controller, whether he controls a chorus, an estate, a city or an army.'

Really, Socrates,' cried Nicomachides, ' I should never have thought to hear you say that a good business man would make a good general!'

By his familiar method of patient cross-examination, Socrates won agreement from Nicomachides that successful business men and generals perform much the same functions. Then Socrates proceeded to identify six of these functions or skills:

- selecting the right man for the right job;

- punishing the bad and rewarding the good;

- winning the goodwill of those under them;

- attracting allies and helpers;

- keeping what they have gained;

- being strenuous and industrious in their own work.

'All these are common to both,' Nicomachides accepted, 'but fighting is not.'

'But surely both are bound to find enemies?'

'Oh yes, they are.'

'Then is it not important for both to get the better of them?'

'Undoubtedly; but you don't say how business capacity will help when it comes to fighting.'

'That is just where it will be most helpful,' Socrates concluded. 'For the good business man, through his knowledge that nothing profits or pays like a victory in the field, and nothing is so utterly unprofitable and entails such heavy loss as a defeat, will be eager to seek and avoid what leads to defeat, prompt to engage the enemy if he sees he is strong enough to win, and, above all, will avoid an engagement when he is not ready.'

A modern full-size replica of a Greek warship being rowed by three tiers of oarsmen. To create good teamwork among the oarsmen called for inspiring leadership.

The amazement expressed by Nicomachides at Socrates' line of argument in this dialogue rings true. For the teaching of Socrates, that people will only follow leaders who have the authority of knowledge relevant to a given situation, must have been well-known in Athens. Moreover, in that city, as in Britain during much of this century, business men were held in low social regard. Young gentlemen from good Athenian families would seek military and political careers, but they did not become merchants. Of course the scale of commerce and industry before the Industrial Revolution was relatively small and the scope for leadership was correspondingly limited. Armies and navies, by contrast, remained the largest and most important forms of common human enterprise until relatively recent times. In the mid-eighteenth century, for example, the Royal Navy was the largest industry in Western Europe.

Socrates did challenge this Athenian snobbery that has cast such a long shadow in history. 'Don't look down on business men, Nicomachides,' he said towards the end of their discussion. 'For the management of private concerns differs only in point of number from that of public affairs. In other respects they are much alike, and particularly in this, that neither can be carried on without men, and the men employed in private and public transactions are the same. For those who take charge of public affairs employ just the same men when they attend to their own; and those who do understand how to employ them are successful directors of public and private concerns, and those who do not, fail in both.'

Human Needs and Leadership Functions

Because of his observation that men are common to both armies and business, Socrates (or is it Xenophon?) focused on leadership as the ability to supply the men's needs. He made this point early in the conversation with Nicomachides, and it is repeated in other dialogues. A good leader meets the needs of his men, just as a good shepherd looks after his flock. The thought, too, that leadership is essentially about helping people to achieve a better life does strike a chord in our own age. It suggests a theme, destined to be taught later by Jesus of Nazareth, that leadership is a form of service to one's fellow men and women.

Within the compass of human needs in working groups, we can now distinguish clearly three distinct but overlapping or interacting areas of need: to achieve the common *task*, to be maintained as a *team*, and the needs of which *individuals* as such bring with them by virtue of being human. If the common task has sufficient value for them, people in enterprises, organisations and groups experience a need to accomplish it successfully, and they look for leaders who will help them to do so. They also need to be built up and held together as a working team. Such social cohesiveness is more than physical; it is a matter of harmony between minds and spirits. Individual needs include the basic ones for food and for shelter, for care when wounded or sick, and for security in time of danger. But we are personal as well as human, and so we seek the social acceptance and esteem which comes from recognition by others of our personal contribution to the common task or the common good. The Greeks differed from other contemporary nations in their heightened sense of being individuals. It flowed from, and also fed on, competitive desire for the fame or renown that comes from some notable act or achievement. They thirsted for individual recognition.

In order that the common task can be achieved and the group held together as a team, certain key *functions* have to be performed. Someone, for example, has to define the task, to ensure that plans are drawn up to accomplish it, to control or monitor progress, and to review performance so that it can be improved. Someone has to create and maintain the team. Perhaps the most important function in that particular area is the one that Socrates mentioned: selecting the right person for the right job. That implies a certain amount of professional or technical knowledge, but also the more general ability of having good judgement. Poor judgement of people is often the 'Achilles heel' of an otherwise successful leader. Lastly, someone has to ensure that individual needs are met, a cluster of activities which range from administration to rewarding and admonishing, encouraging and praising.

These functions can properly be called leadership functions, although that does not imply that the leader does them all personally. They are more transferable. If a leader does move into a different field, his or her success would depend largely upon having the ability to acquire the necessary technical knowledge quickly. As the advance of technology and the complexity of modern work may make transfer more difficult, an important corollary is that organisations will increasingly have to grow their own leaders.

People are basically the same, and they respond in similar ways to good leadership. They look first for a leader who can enable them to accomplish their task and who will occasionally work with them as a team member on an equal footing. Such a leader will share their hardships and encourage them in times of difficulty or adversity. He or she will show an awareness and practical concern for their needs as individuals. These personal qualities and skills of leadership are indeed transferable from one field to another. For in all organisations the needs to achieve the common task and to work together as a team are present, together with the needs of individuals as such.

A Leader in Estate Management

When Xenophon was not campaigning, he exercised leadership among the farm labourers on his estates. He returned to the theme of leadership in his most influential book, the *Cyropaedia*. In later centuries it became the text book on leadership for many of the great leaders of Rome. As the strange-sounding title suggests, the *Cyropaedia* is a philosophical dialogue about the education of Cyrus the Great, who in fact does little more than lend his name to an ideal king ruling an ideal state. In it, Xenophon advocated that a leader should demonstrate that in summer he can endure the heat, and in winter the cold; and he should show that in difficult times he can endure the hardships as well as, if not better than, his men. Moreover, a leader should rejoice with them if any good befell them, and sympathise with them if any ills overtook them, showing himself eager to help in times of stress. 'It is in these respects that you should somehow go hand-in-hand with them,' wrote Xenophon. 'All this contributes to the leader being loved by his men.' Xenophon added the interesting observation that it was actually easier for the leader to endure heat and cold, hunger and thirst, want and hardship, than his followers. 'The general's position, and the very consciousness that nothing he does escapes notice, lightens the burden for him.'

The same principle, Xenophon held, would apply in all areas of human work, simply because men and their needs are the same. In another of the books he wrote, on his estates at Scillus, the *Oeconomicus* – the book of estate management – he put across this distinctive view with characteristic style and compelling vigour. It reflected his own experience running these estates under the shadow of Mount Olympus. Much of the book is concerned with technical farming matters and the organisation of the estates. But Xenophon urged upon his readers the importance of leadership on large farm estates. 'Nobody can be a good farmer,' he said, 'unless he makes his labourers both eager and obedient; and the captain who leads men against an enemy must contrive to secure the same results by rewarding those who act as brave men should act and punishing the disobedient. And it is no less necessary for a farmer to encourage his labourers often, than for a general to encourage his men. And slaves need the stimulus of good hopes no less, nay, even more than free men, to make them steadfast.'

The Parthenon and other buildings on the Acropolis, built on the site of the ancient fortress of Athens.

This general leadership ability, as relevant to agriculture as to politics or war, was often absent, he noted, in those who held positions of authority. Xenophon instanced the Greek warships of his day, which were rowed by free men and not by slaves:

> 'On a man-of-war, when the ship is on the high seas and the rowers must toil all day to reach port, some rowing-masters can say and do the right thing to sharpen the men's spirits and make them work with a will. Other boatswains are so unintelligent that it takes them more than twice the time to finish the same voyage. Here they land bathed in sweat, with mutual congratulations, rowing-master and seamen. There they arrive with dry skin; they hate their master and he hates them.'

Xenophon's mind ranged back to the generals he had known, who also differed widely from one another in this respect. 'For some make their men unwilling to work and to take risks, disinclined and unwilling to obey, except under compulsion, and actually proud of defying their commander: yes, and they cause them to have no sense of dishonour when something disgraceful occurs. Contrast the genius, the brave and skilful leader: let him take over the command of these same troops, or of others if you like. What effect has he on them? They are ashamed to do a disgraceful act, think it better to obey, and take a pride in obedience, working cheerfully, everyman and all together, when it is necessary to work. Just as a love of work may spring up in the mind of a private soldier here and there, so a whole army under the influence of a good leader is inspired by love of work and ambition to distinguish itself under the commander's eye. Let this be the feeling of the rank and file for their commander, then he is the best leader – it is not a matter of being best with bow and javelin, nor riding the best horse and being foremost in danger, nor being the perfect mounted warrior, but of being able to make his soldiers feel that they must follow him through fire and in any adventure. So, too, in private industries,' Xenophon continued, 'the man in authority – bailiff or manager – who can make the workers keen, industrious and persevering – he is the man who gives a lift to the business and swells the profits.'

Are Leaders Born or Made?

For Xenophon, this kind of leadership is quite simply 'the greatest thing in every operation that makes any demand on the labour of men.' If leaders are made in the sense that they can acquire the authority of knowledge, are they born as far as the capacity to inspire is concerned? It is tempting to conclude so. The ability to give people the intellectual and moral strength to venture or persevere in the presence of danger, fear or difficulty is not the common endowment of all men and women. Xenophon, however, did believe that it could be acquired through education, though not 'at sight or at a single hearing.' He was not specific about the content or methods of such an education for leadership, but Socratic discussion must have been one strand in it.

As Xenophon implied, some degree of leadership potential has to be there in the first place. Many people possess it without being aware of the fact. Given the need or opportunity to lead, some encouragement and perhaps a leadership course or programme, most people can develop this potential. Those with a greater amount of natural potential can correspondingly become greater leaders within their spheres, providing that they are willing to work hard at becoming leaders.

Learning about leadership happens when sparks of relevance jump in between experience or practice on the one hand, and principles or theory on the other hand. One without the other tends to be sterile. It is a common fallacy that leadership is learned only through experience. Experience only teaches the teachable, and it is a school which charges large fees. Sometimes people graduate from it when they are too old to apply the lesson. Leadership is far better learned by experience *and* reflection or thought, which, in turn, informs or guides future action. Other people, as examples or models, teachers or mentors, have an important part to play in this process. Socrates, for example, most probably acted as Xenophon's own mentor.

The belief that theories or principles, imbibed from books or courses, can by themselves teach a person to lead, is equally a half-truth. All the academic study of leadership does is to teach one *about* leadership, not how to lead. It is certainly useful for people to clarify their concepts of leadership, either as a prelude or as an interlude in the practical work of leading others.

But leadership is learnt primarily through doing it, and nothing can replace that necessary cycle of experiment, trial-and-error, and success and failure, followed by reflection and reading. Following this path of self-development, a person may become so effective as a leader that others will say 'He or she was born to it.' Little will they know the work it took!

Leadership Skills

CHAPTER REVIEW

Summary

The path to leadership is open to all. A person is a true leader in so far as he or she meets – or enable others to meet– three areas of need in groups or organisations:

1   to achieve the common task

2   to work in harmony as a team

3   to satisfy each individual's needs.

Socrates listed some of the activities to those ends which in business or war characterise an effective leader:

- selecting the right people

- gaining their goodwill and inspiring their willing obedience

- building good relations with colleagues

- setting a personal example of energy and industry.

With this analysis he foreshadowed the functional approach to leadership. Through education and experience, the Greeks first led us to believe, a person with potential for leadership can develop over a lifetime his or her awareness, understanding and skills as a leader. Such a person needs enough success to keep despair at bay, but enough failure to preserve humility, that essential ingredient in all great leadership today.

Key Concepts

- Apart from the *qualities* approach – what you have to be – and the *knowledge* approach – what you have to know – there is a third *functional* approach to leadership which centres on what you have to do in order to lead.

- The debate about transferability – would a businessman make a good general – led Xenophon into foreshadowing the functional approach as we know it today. He identified these common skills:

    - selecting the right individuals (judgement of people)

    - rewarding and disciplining (justice)

    - winning the goodwill of those under you (motivating)

    - building good relations with colleagues, allies and suppliers (team building)

    - setting a personal example of hard work (energy).

- The objection of Nicomachides – that businessmen know nothing about fighting – is apparently dismissed here because Xenophon is emphasizing the other side of the coin. In reality, *both* knowledge related to the field or situation *and* skill in these more general leadership functions is required of a leader and your *qualities* will colour or give your personal stamp to the actions you take as a leader.

- Although Xenophon did perceptively see leadership as a means of meeting the human needs of groups and individuals, he was not systematic about this insight. The three-circles model of needs – task, team and individual – repairs that deficiency. It enables us to relate *functions* more closely to needs.

- Again, Xenophon, by his word and example on his estates, reminds us of the gulf that lies between exercising coercive power over people and using the inner power that stems from firm leadership and personal example. He demonstrated, too, that leading from the front had the same effect upon farm labourers as it had upon soldiers in battle. Human nature does not change – that is one message of this book.

Further Reflection

- In Athens, according to Pericles, 'What counts is not membership of a particular class, but the actual ability which man possesses'. Education of the few who possessed this natural leadership talent, both to develop them as whole men and later to enable them to acquire the technical or professional knowledge in their chosen departments of civic life, was central to the Greek way of life. Good leadership, they knew, is essential for a democratic society. As Plato said, 'What a country honours will be cultivated there. Do we place a similar value on leadership?

- The Greeks certainly believed that leadership could be learnt, whatever your level of natural aptitude. Both Alexander the Great and Julius Caesar read Xenophon's books. Another Greek writer, Plutarch, wrote the first book of leadership case studies for the benefit of the Romans. In the middle of the Second World War, Winston Churchill said that 'Every prospective officer should follow General Gordon's recommendation and read *Plutarch's Lives.*' After the Renaissance, largely inspired by Plato's Republic, schools and universities sprang up like mushrooms to equip people to be leaders, not as a consequence of birth or social rank but because they had the personal qualities, appropriate knowledge and transferable skills of leadership. Do you think schools and universities are still fulfilling that original social purpose?

- In classical education up to modern times the place of 'theory' in leadership development was supplied by such authors as Xenophon, Plato, Plutarch, Caesar and Cicero, all read in their original Greek or Latin. How should we now convey the philosophy or principles of good leadership – and leadership for good – in school and university?

THREE
The Servant-Leader

'Let the greatest among you become as the youngest, and the leader as one who serves.

JESUS OF NAZARETH

We are not accustomed to thinking of leaders as servants. We tend to emphasise position rather than responsibility. Leaders in our society are paid more than others; they enjoy the other rewards of privileges and status. Leadership stands for power and dominance over others. That is not unlike the pattern of leadership that Jesus saw both among the Gentiles and within Israel in his day: rulers who lorded it over their subjects, intent upon subservience and hungry for public recognition.

True, Socrates had identified the common element of service in all leadership, by insisting that the core responsibility of leaders is to meet human needs. Xenophon had found that it worked in practice. If you came down from your height – literally in the case of a mounted commander and metaphorically in that of a landowner – and worked among people, this action would inspire willing obedience. The Roman leaders who followed his example and teaching found that the same principle worked for them. Both Greeks and Romans were essentially pragmatists. By the exercise of practical reason, they sought to discover what works in leadership, and to a large measure they did so.

Jesus clothed much the same message with his religious authority. By so doing, however, he altered for all time the moral climate of leadership. The deepest flaw in leadership is usually arrogance. The root of arrogance is an inflated pride which makes a person in a position of leadership act in an excessively determined, overbearing, or domineering way. This insistence on being dominant is always based upon a real or an assumed superiority. Because of an exaggerated sense of self, and excessive pride in wealth, station, learning or achievements, the arrogant person takes upon himself more power or authority than is rightly his.

Jesus, as seen in a medieval sculpture standing in the South Porch of Chartres Cathedral. He taught that leadership is a form of service and should be done in a spirit of humility.

The antidotes to the disease of arrogance in relation to leadership go back as far as Lao Tzu, a Chinese thinker in the fourth century BC, and supremely to Jesus. These antidotes may not have been very effective against the virus of pride in centuries past, but their value is beginning to be appreciated today. In the concept of leadership advanced by both Lao Tzu and Jesus there is a marked absence of assertiveness, a lack of vanity or presumption, and the feeling that a leader should see his or her part as something moderate or small in scale, especially in comparison to the contributions of others.

The Teaching of Lao Tzu

Lao Tzu was a native of Ch'u, a large state on the southern periphery of civilised China in ancient times. Almost nothing is known about him apart from what can be gleaned from the legends that surround his name. He probably served one of the ruling princes of China as a court sage and then he became a recluse in a hermitage. Even his book of sayings, entitled the *Tao Tê Ching*, has been much revised by later hands. So much so, in fact, that some scholars have doubted if Lao Tzu ever existed as an individual. In order to fill the gap of knowledge about Lao, events connected with various characters in Chinese mythology were ascribed to him at an early date.

In the early days, before it received its present name, Christianity was often called 'the Way'. That is also the literal meaning of *Tao* in Chinese. The 'way' that Lao has in mind is not easy to define. It is really Nature's way: the order, course or pattern of all things created.

For the school of Chinese philosophers who thought as Master Lao, every person and thing is only what it is in relation to others. Events fall into harmony if left alone. Someone who intuitively understands this energy in Nature, and works intelligently with the grain of natural phenomena, is a follower of the *Tao*.

'The *Tao* principle is what happens of itself', wrote Lao Tzu. The art of living, then, is more like steering a boat than struggling with an opponent. The image of water, flowing or still in cool, clear ponds, is never far from Lao's mind. Tzu jan, 'Nature', is that which is of itself. It is spontaneous. Everything grows and operates independently, on its own, but in harmony with all.

The principle of *wu wei*, of not forcing things, is a natural corollary to this vision of the world. Working with the grain, rolling with the punch, swimming with the tide, trimming sails to the wind, taking the tide at its flood: these are metaphors that reflect the spirit of *wu wei*.

If the follower of the *Tao* understands the principles, structures or trends of human nature, human society and the natural order, then he can expend least energy in dealing with them. When he does exert his power at the right moment, then his efforts will have a spontaneous, natural or effortless effort – with breathing. The same principle can be seen in *judo* today: because the opponent is off-balance or has over-extended himself, the least effort will topple him.

There is an even more superior from of *wu wei*, which does not seem to aim at anything in particular. Things are not done with an effect in mind; they are expressions of inner being. 'When good things are accomplished, it does not claim (or, name) them,' wrote Lao Tzu. He called it *te*, which is close in meaning to power or virtue. It is something within a person, and it is enhanced by following the *Tao*, or 'that from which nothing can deviate.'

Chuang Tzu, a later member of the Taoist school of thought, expressed it thus: 'In an age of perfect virtue, good men are not appreciated; ability is not conspicuous. Rulers are mere beacons, while the people are as free as the wild deer. They love one another without being conscious of charity. They are true without being conscious of loyalty.'

The Tao of Leadership

It is this quality of doing things spontaneously and in an unselfconscious way, without regard to their effects upon other people's perceptions of oneself, that links Lao Tzu with the teaching of Jesus. There is a freedom from acting for show, or indeed for outward things. It stems from this intuitive awareness of the inevitability of things as they follow their natural water courses into the sea, and the power that is naturally directed.

'The best leaders of soldiers in their chariots do not rush ahead,' wrote Lao. Socrates had appeared to say much the same thing when he suggested to a young cavalry commander that he had not sought that appointment in order to be first into battle – that honour belonged to the mounted skirmishers. But Lao is making a different point. The leader who follows the *Tao* does not need to dominate others or seize the glory first. Thus, in his behaviour, the sage (as Lao called the ruler who exemplifies these precepts) does no more than reflect the ultimate reality, the inner core of Nature itself. For 'the Tao loves and nourishes all things, but does not lord it over them.'

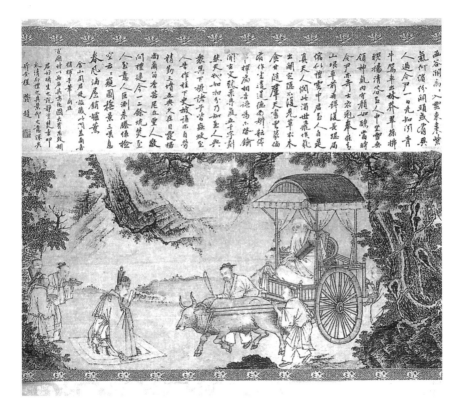

According to legend, when Lao Tzu retired in old age to western China, the Keeper of the Han Ku Pass would not let him through until he had written down all that he knew.

This refusal to dominate or lord it over others again parallels the teaching of Jesus. It is the attitude that man should adapt to all things – animals, birds and fish, mountains, lakes and sea – as well as to his fellow humans. It is because the sage has power or virtue, that he does not use force. It is close to the 'meekness' which Jesus advocated.

The natural badge of such inner humility towards all things is silence. 'Silence is of the gods', says a Chinese proverb. Again there is a paradox here, for the Greek and Roman traditions exalted the place of oratory in leadership. For Greek leaders, who had to persuade their fellow citizens by reason, it was speech that is golden, not silence. Yet listening is important, and it is difficult for a leader to listen if he or she is speaking or waiting to speak. 'No one can safely appear in public unless he himself feels that he would willingly remain in retirement,' wrote the medieval Christian writer Thomas à Kempis. 'No one can safely speak who would not rather be silent. No one can with safety command who has not learned to obey.'

Lao envisaged a leader who practises humility, being neither self-assertive nor talkative. In St Paul's famous words, he 'seeks not his own,' but spends himself without hope of any human reward. As Lao wrote:

> 'The sage is ever free from artifice and practises
> the precept of silence.
> He does things without desire for control.
> He lives without thought for private ownership.
> He gives without the wish for return.
> Because he does not claim credit for himself
> he is always given credit.
>
> Therefore the sage
> Puts himself in the background yet is always to the fore;
> Remains outside, but is always here.
> Is it not just because he does not strive for any personal end
> That all his personal ends are fulfilled?'

'Such a ruler benefits ten thousand people and yet is content in places which men disdain,' added Lao. The analogy of water as always is never far from his mind. 'The highest good is like that of water,' wrote Lao. 'The goodness of water is that it benefits ten thousand creatures, yet itself does not wrangle, but is content with the places that all men disdain. It is this that makes water so near to the Tao.' Water, then, is the symbol of the lowly, the yielding, the unassertive and the inconspicuous; it is content to find the lowest level in order to rest. Water also, streaming down the hillsides to the valleys, receives all kinds of defilements, but it cleanses itself and is never defiled. It reminds us vividly of Jesus baptising his followers or, taking a towel and a basin of water, kneeling to wash his disciples' feet. Lao wrote:

> 'How did the great rivers and seas get their kingship
> over the hundred lesser streams?
> Through the merit of being lower than they; that was
> how they got their kingship.
> Therefore the sage, in order to be above the people,
> Must speak as though he were lower than they,
> In order to guide them
> He must put himself behind them.
> Thus when he is above the people have no burden,
> When he is ahead they feel no hurt.
> Thus everything under heaven is glad to be directed by him
> And does not find his guidance irksome.
> The sage does not enter into competition
> And thus no one competes with him.'

It may well be that the thoughts of Lao Tzu would bear a different inter-pretation if they were placed in a historical context. Possibly in the China of the fifth century BC a ruler who appeared to do little or nothing would be the best preserver of traditional society. Lao made no suggestion, for instance, that a wise ruler should seek to educate his subjects. But thoughts of prophets and poets enjoy a life of their own; the golden grains of truth in them transcend whatever may have been their original social context. On leadership, for example, the following words of Lao Tzu have become justly famous:

> 'A leader is best,
> When people are hardly aware of his existence,
> Not so good when people praise his government,
> Less good when people stand in fear,
> Worst, when people are contemptuous.
> Fail to honour people, and they will fail to honour you.

But of a good leader, who speaks little,
When his task is accomplished, his work done!
The people say, "We did it ourselves."'

For Lao it is always some want within the inner life of the ruler that causes trouble among the people. If the leader lacks faith or trust, so will the people. The principle that 'there are no bad students but only band teachers' is very much in keeping with the spirit of Taoist thought. So too is the military maxim that 'there are no bad soldiers, only bad officers.' These sayings invite leaders to look in the mirror before they find fault with others.

Jesus and His Disciples

Jesus chose twelve disciples to be his Apostles. It was a symbolic number. Israel had originally been composed of twelve tribes, and the Israelites of Jesus's day traced their descent from them. Jesus apparently promised the disciples that when the kingdom of God came on earth they would sit on twelve thrones, as the judges or rulers of Israel. According to Matthew's Gospel, this reward for their share in his offerings was not enough for the mother of James and John, sons of Zebedee. She came up to Jesus with her sons and knelt before him in order to ask him for something. 'What do you want?' he asked her. She replied: 'Command that these two sons of mine may sit, one at your right hand and one at your left.' In Luke's version of the story, it is the two disciples themselves who make this self-seeking request. When the ten heard it, the story continues, they began to be indignant at James and John. Jesus called them to him and said to them, 'You know that the rulers of the Gentiles exercise lordship over them; and those in authority over them are called benefactors. But not so with you; rather let the greatest among you become as the youngest, and the leader as one who serves. For which is the greater, one who sits at table, or one who serves? Is it not the one who sits at table? But I am among you as one who serves.' The emphasis upon humility in leadership is unmistakable.

Incidentally, Jesus broke one fundamental rule of leadership: he did have favourites among the Twelve. However, it is arguable that the number of twelve is too large for a primary group and some subdivision was bound to occur. In John's Gospel, for example, we read three times about 'the disciple whom Jesus loved,' quite apart from Peter and the Sons of Zebedee who emerged as an 'inner ring' around Jesus. Any form of favouritism threatens the principle of justice – even-handed dealings with all – and by so doing it endangers the very cohesiveness of a group or community. Favouritism is the fount of jealousy and envy. If some bask in the leader's warm affection, others languish on the periphery with cold looks and crumbs of praise as their only reward. Implied rejection, often mainly in the mind, can breed bitterness and even hatred. Judas Iscariot may have experienced those feelings. He was the only non-Galilean among the Twelve. He was made treasurer, a chore that could not have done much to enhance his popularity. He was the lost sheep that no one bothered to find. If that was the case, it is no wonder that the disciples felt some personal responsibility for the crucifixion of Jesus after Judas had betrayed him to the authorities.

The teaching of Jesus on leadership stands out more sharply against a possible background of disciples strongly vying for his favour and perhaps ultimately for position in the new community they sensed would come about through Jesus. Selected from a largely self-chosen band of disciples, both men and women, who accompanied Jesus as he went about the country teaching and healing, the Twelve came to see themselves as the corps of leaders for the new movement. Jesus saw that they clearly needed instruction in that role, and especially in a style of leading other disciples or followers in 'the Way' that would not be divisive. Their quarrels over precedence gave him several opportunities to teach them about the true nature of leadership.

On one occasion, for example, as Jesus led his disciples on the road to Capernaum, he heard the noise of voices raised in argument behind him. When he was in the house he asked them, 'What were you discussing on the way?' But they were silent; for on the way they had been arguing with one another as to which of them was the greatest. Jesus sat down and called the Twelve; and he said to them, 'If any of you would be first, he must be last of all and servant of all'. And he took a child, and put him in the midst of them. Taking the small boy in his arms, he said, 'Truly, I say to you, unless you turn to become like children, you will never enter the Kingdom of Heaven. Whoever exalts himself will be humbled and he who humbles himself like this child will be exalted.'

Jesus washing the feet of the twelve apostles. By this act he set an example of the kind of leadership he expected them to exercise in turn.

According to John's Gospel, this distinctive teaching of Jesus on the need for a humble style of leadership reached a climax shortly before the end of his life on earth, in the most extraordinary scene in the whole history of leadership:

> *'Jesus… rose from supper, laid aside his garments, and girded himself with a towel. Then he poured water into a basin, and began to wash the disciples' feet and to wipe them with the towel with which he was girded. He came to Simon Peter; and Peter said to him, "Lord, do you wash my feet?" Jesus answered him, "What I am doing you do not know now, but afterwards you will understand…" When he had washed their feet, and taken his garments, and resumed his place, he said to them, "Do you know what I have done to you? You call me Teacher and Lord; and you are right, for so I am. If I then, your Lord and Teacher,*

have washed your feet, you also ought to wash one another's feet. For I have given you an example, that you also should do as I have done to you. Truly, truly, I say to you, a servant is not greater than his master, nor is he who is sent greater than he who sent him. If you know these things, blessed are you if you do them.'

Both in this action and the accompanying teaching there is an element of eastern hyperbole, but that is precisely what makes it so memorable. No leader should take it too literally. By becoming the group's slave a leader would cease to lead. Jesus would be unknown today if he had spent all his time meeting the physical needs of his disciples. What comes across to us, however, is the double message of Jesus: that a leader is one who meets needs and that his or her style should reflect that reality.

Servant Leadership in Perspective

Neither humility nor even modesty were virtues particularly admired by the Greeks, although arguably Socrates exemplified them both. In contrast to Xenophon, Aristotle and the Romans after him seem to have assumed that slaves were, by definition, mentally and spiritually inferior to free men, not unlike the views entertained about black people until recent times. The Romans learned the error of that opinion when the slaves rose in revolt under Spartacus and inflicted several defeats on the legions. The idea of self-effacing leadership ran contrary to the Greek desire for personal glory and distinction. Xenophon, for example, wrote his history of the Persian expedition primarily to ensure that his own exploits as a leader were not overshadowed. For other commanders wrote memoirs which had considerably played down his part in comparison to their own.

Indeed it could be argued that what Jesus taught about the status of a leader runs clean contrary to everything that we know about human nature. All societies have some form of hierarchy. More often than not they are stratified into social classes as well. Status, privileges and greater rewards tend to go to the dominant men in any society. The 'lords of the Gentiles' or their modern counterparts could therefore continue as before, secure in the knowledge that human nature supports their rule. The message of Jesus could be dismissed as unrealistic or utopian. The history of the

Christian Church itself shows how, in the course of time, the dominant ruler of the Gentiles came to eclipse the more modest style of leadership taught by Jesus. Yet to this day the Pope bears among his many titles a truly great one: 'Servant of the Servants of God.'

Water is a Taoist symbol for humility because it falls to the lowest level and is content to rest there.

The teachings of Lao Tzu and Jesus on humility in leadership should not, however, be lightly dismissed as unrealistic. Many people – not only Christians – would argue that Jesus was the greatest transformational leader in history: he came to change human nature or to restore it to God's original vision. It may be that we are becoming the kind of people who will value and respond to the kind of servant-leadership Jesus advocated. It does have strength and it does arouse admiration.

Jesus teaching the multitudes. The halo above the head of Jesus is this nineteenth century artist's way of suggesting the aura or charisma emanating from him.

There is evidence of a pragmatic kind from Greek and Roman times that, even in such a hierarchical society as an army, troops respond warmly to leaders who come down to their level, eating the same food and sharing the same hardships. These leaders are never more powerful than when they divest themselves, so to speak, of the artificial 'garments' of office and rely solely upon the authority of their knowledge and personality.

Wu Ch'i

'Regard your soldiers as your children, and they will follow you into the deepest valleys; look on them as your own beloved sons, and they will stand by you even unto death.'

Tu Mu drew an engaging picture of the famous general Wu Ch'i, 'He wore the same clothes and ate the same food as the meanest of his soldiers, refused to have either a horse to ride or a mat to sleep on, carried his own surplus rations wrapped in a parcel, and shared every hardship with his men. One of his soldiers was suffering from an abcess, and Wu Ch'i himself sucked out the virus. The soldier's mother, hearing this, began wailing and lamenting. Somebody asked her, saying: "Why do you cry? Your son is only a common soldier, and yet the commander-in-chief himself has sucked the poison from his sore." The woman replied: "Many years ago, Lord Wu performed a similar service for my husband, who never left him afterwards, and finally met his death at the hands of the enemy. And now that he has done the same for my son, he too will fall fighting I know not where".

"If, however, you are indulgent, but unable to make your authority felt; kind-hearted, but unable to enforce your commands; and incapable, moreover, of quelling disorder: then your soldiers must be likened to spoilt children, they are useless for any practical purpose.'

Hsun Tzu, *The Art of War*, c. 500 BC.

Jesus was advocating the same approach from the centre of his spiritual experience, which was complete dependence upon God as Father. Humility is essentially a God-centred or religious virtue: it is the reflection of oneself in the mirror of God. But humility colours all one's attitudes: to other people, to nature and to oneself. For, the believer sees God in all these guises.

In our own age these religious reflections may no longer speak to man. Can leaders who do not believe in God, let alone in trying in private to see themselves 'in the light of God's countenance,' still become humble? Yes, they can. For leadership at its most sublime touches the human spirit. That indefinable spirit includes the power we have to transcend ourselves for the common good, even to the point of laying down our lives. Experience deepens respect, trust and love. Such a leader will come to look upon leadership as a privilege in itself, not as a passport to privileges which would otherwise be denied to them.

Humility – a Test of Greatness

'I believe the first test of a truly great man is his humility. I do not mean by humility, doubt of his own power, or hesitation in speaking his opinions; but a right understanding of the relation between what *he* can do and say, and the rest of the world's sayings and doings. All great men not only know their business, but usually know that they know it, and are not only right in their main opinions, but they usually know that they are right in them; only, they do not think much of themselves on that account. Arnolfo knows he can build a good dome at Florence; Albrecht Dürer writes clearly to one who had found fault in his work. "It could not have been done better"; Sir Isaac Newton knows that he has worked out a problem or two that would have puzzled anybody else; – only they do not expect their fellow-men therefore to fall down and worship them; they have a curious under-sense of powerlessness, feeling that the greatness is not *in* them, but *through* them; that they could not do or be anything else than God made them. And they see something Divine and God-made in every other man they meet, and are endlessly, foolishly, incredibly merciful.'

John Ruskin, *Modern Painters* (1843).

The tradition of Lao Tzu lends support to this view. The leader senses the powers at work in groups of people and individuals: he works with these powers, like a carpenter working with the grain of the wood. He is humble before his materials, just as a good craftsman or artist might be. His humility also allows him to stand back in the hour of success. For he knows that it is the power of the group, which he has guided and served, which has achieved the result. 'When his task is accomplished, his work done, the people say "We did it ourselves."'

The difficulty, of course, is that leaders tend to be men and women with a higher-than-average level of self-assurance. They are often what are called strong personalities. These qualities do not mean that leaders are also necessarily self-centred or selfish: some are and some are not. But they do make it hard for many leaders to be self-effacing in the style taught by Lao Tzu and Jesus. Strong leaders can make for weak teams.

Take meekness, for example. Leaders are often meek in the sense of being unwilling to call attention to themselves. Meekness also suggests a tractable mildness or submissiveness, but not necessarily an avoidance of confrontation. Leaders are not often meek in that manner – perhaps they should be. In the Bible *meek* means gentle, kind, not easily provoked, ready to yield rather than cause trouble. 'Learn from me,' Jesus said, 'for I am gentle and lowly of hear.'

The world has been reluctant to learn that lesson. The English, for example, have always been more comfortable with the word *modest*, rather than *humble*, or *lowly* or *meek*. Modesty is a classically-based concept, which means essentially staying within one's limits. Whereas modest emphasises moderateness, *humble* and *lowly* distinctly suggest smallness. A modest person lacks vanity but does not have to be self-effacing to the degree taught by Lao Tzu and Jesus.

Sir Thomas Fairfax

'He never knew what envy was, nor hate. His soul was filled with worth and honesty, and another thing quite out of date called modesty'

This tribute was written by the Duke of Buckingham, son-in-law of General Fairfax, the first commander of the New Model Army, when Fairfax died in the reign of King Charles II.

In the English language humility has more and more acquired a patronising tone when used of other people and an air of sanctimonious piety when used of oneself. The villainous and cunning clerk, Uriah Heep in *David Copperfield*, who cloaked his misdeeds under a fawning humility, has become a byword for this particular form of hypocrisy in the English language. Of course, calling attention so blatantly to one's supposed lack of vanity by calling oneself humble would be far from being unpretentious or unassuming! When Lady Violet Bonham-Carter taxed Winston Churchill with his pride he replied: 'I accept that I am a worm, but I do believe that I am a glow-worm.'

The Japanese Contribution

Contact with Japanese society in various ways has served to remind us of the servant-nature of true leadership and the humility which accompanies it. Bernard Leach, for example, Britain's most distinguished potter, once studied under another famous potter called Hamada in Japan. Unlike Western potters, Hamada did not sign his pots for he did not wish to put an accent on his personality. It was not a signature that mattered but the integrity of the act. 'The work, the doing, the activity for its own sake is no longer the actual goal,' wrote Bernard Leach. 'Our salvation lies in preserving humility in a world of widening and changing demand.' Leach saw Hamada much later at Mashiko. The famous potter had been offered a variety of teaching positions in Europe and America, but he preferred to live in Japan and to hire himself out as a thrower. He did this lowly work partly to gain acceptance of himself as a human being and good workman, and partly to rid himself of all pretence and self. He used to call it 'getting rid of his tail.'

If not disciples of Taoism the Japanese still reflect something of that Eastern tradition in which he is the brightest star. 'One who excels in leading others,' wrote Lao Tzu, 'humbles himself before them.' For the Japanese practise a more self-effacing style of leadership than is customary in the West. In Japan the group is still valued more highly than the individual, and this induces a degree of what looks like humility in the leaders. Japanese managers tend to wear the same uniforms and eat in the same canteens as their work people. It is not unknown for Japanese managers to do such menial (or servant) tasks as sweeping the factory floor or cleaning out the lavatories. These are variations of a half-forgotten theme which lies within our own Western tradition of leadership.

This medieval ivory vividly depicts Jesus exerting his authority and power to heal the man possessed by devils.

The Servant-Leader

CHAPTER REVIEW

Summary

The Taoists believed that just as there was no real greatness or smallness of status in Nature, so there should be none in human society. The emphasis should be on mutual service. Most probably they looked back to a golden age long ago, before the advent of feudal lords, a time when spontaneous cooperation rather than directive force was the mainspring of a tribal society. Unlike feudal lords who use force to dominate people, a servant-leader works with the people, using their power like a carpenter works with the grain or a fisherman with the tides. Such leadership requires a deep understanding of human nature and why people behave as they do. As a later Taoist writer said, 'Whoever wishes to be a ruler of this world will fail if he does not consider the principles on which people move.' At its heart, this concept of leadership implies a self-effacing meeting of the needs of a people engaged in cooperative endeavours. It emphasises leadership as a function, not as position or rank. A leader should be able to place himself or herself on an equal footing with the others involved, relying upon his authority of knowledge and personality to gain respect. Such a stance does require considerable inner confidence; people will soon sense if it is there. They will soon sense, too, if a leader can show them the way forwards and lead them on their journey.

Key Concepts

- Leadership as service emphasises responsibility for the three areas of need – task, team and individual – as opposed to position, rank or privilege. A servant-leader is with or among people as well as being over them.

- The besetting temptation of leaders – the overgrown fruit of personal self-confidence – is arrogance; an overwelming attitude of superiority is often accompanied by an excessive sense of being right, an overbearing manner and dominance. The antidote and opposite of arrogance is humility.

- The teaching of Lao Tzu set leadership in the context of Nature's harmonious *Tao* or Way. Don't force things – let them take their natural course. Leadership is within you. Express it without self-consciousness or self-importance, without pride or show and with a refusal to dominate and lord it over others.

- Listening and silence, paradoxically, are often the badges of such a leader. 'No one can safely appear in public unless he himself feels that he would willingly remain in retirement,' wrote the mediaeval Christian writer Thomas à Kempis. 'No one can safely speak who would not rather be silent. No one can with safety command who has not learned to obey.'

- Again, paradoxically, the leader who puts himself or herself in to the background, so that the people say, 'We did it ourselves', will always be to the fore. 'But you made a difference,' the people may well add, when they have had time to think about it. Acceptance of proper recognition gracefully is a sign of humility, just as a false embarrassment at praise suggests its absence.

- As G. K. Chesterton said, 'It is always the secure who are humble.'

Further Reflection

- How does the idea of servant-leadership relate to today's hierarchical organisations and the barriers which so often exist with them? All organisations are hierarchical, for organisation is hierarchy: it is being organised into orders or ranks each subordinate to the one above it. The principal reason for it was originally communication rather than authority: the means by which a leader could communicate effectively with a large body of people. The real choice is between elaborate organisations with many layers or ranks and much more simple structures. For a variety of reasons, modern organisations have become flatter as unnecessary levels of management have been stripped out. We are moving towards just three broad and overlapping bands: strategic, operational and team leaders. However, this is still a hierarchy. Leadership is paradoxical in that it can and does work in a formal structure, fulfilling managerial roles and respecting order and system as the necessary means to an end. At the same time, however, leaders can seem anarchical. They persist in seeing others as free and equal partners. Such leaders put themselves on an equal footing with others without losing the respect that stems from their inner leadership. Even the unseen and entirely justifiable differentials in salary, they believe, should better reflect this essential equality of all the team members in the common enterprise.

- Qualities, knowledge, skills – all have been much emphasised in the context of leadership, but inner attitudes – the way you think and the way you are inside yourself – are as fully important, for, by a kind of extra-sensory perception, your people will always come to sense who you are. You cannot hide your inner self as a leader. As the Zulu proverb says: 'I cannot hear what you say, because what you are is shouting at me.' Leadership is just being you.

FOUR
The Ability to Give Direction

'Not the cry but the flight of the wild duck leads the flock to fly and to follow.'

CHINESE PROVERB

Daniel Boone, a famous American frontiersman, was once asked if he had ever been lost in the trackless forests of Kentucky. 'I can't say that I was ever lost,' he replied, 'but I was once sure bewildered for three days.' By definition, leaders are never lost, even though they are occasionally bewildered. Within their field they have a sense of direction.

This chapter focuses upon this core leadership ability of giving direction, which is especially necessary when an organisation is faced with the need for major change. In such situations sensing the way forwards, and giving a clear lead in that direction, is a leader's main contribution to achieving the common task. But on that journey of change leaders are also responsible for building or maintaining the team and for meeting individual needs. The Biblical image of the shepherd well illustrates that three-fold responsibility. It was exemplified by one of the great leaders of antiquity – Alexander the Great – on his journey through Asia. The word *leader* itself suggests the importance of guidance on a journey forwards in time.

What's in a Word?

The Anglo-Saxon root of the words *lead, leader* and *leadership* is '*laed*', which means a path or road. It comes in turn from the verb *laeden*, to travel or to go. The Anglo-Saxons extended it to mean the journey that people make upon such paths or roads. Being seafarers they used it also for the course of a ship at sea. A leader was the person who showed the way. On land he would do so normally by walking ahead, or taking the lead as we say. At sea he would be the navigator and steersman, for in those days the same man performed both functions.

Neither the original metaphor nor the word itself are unique to the English language. The metaphor of a journey, for example, is to be found in the Mashona language in Zimbabwe, as well as in Persian and Egyptian. The ancient Greek word for a leader, *hegemon*, probably rested on the same image of a road or journey, as did the Roman word for leader, *dux*. The image becomes crystal clear in the Latin *gubernator*, or governor, which meant literally the helmsman of a ship.

As for the English word, the Saxons brought it with them to Great Britain from North Europe. Other northern European nations have versions of it from the ancient languages. The Dutch *leider*, the Scandinavian *laedar* and the German *leiter*, are all instantly recognisable to an English-speaker. It comes as a mild cultural shock to discover that this particular word-concept – the path or journey image – is totally missing in other European languages. Even those near the troublesome neighbours of the Anglo-Saxons, the Scottish and Irish Celts, did not have it. Like the French who also lack the image, they used a word derived from a different image, namely the head of a man's body.

It need hardly be said that the two metaphors of the head and the journey have very different connotations. One is vertical and the other is horizontal. The head sits on top of the body and it is the most important member. The image lends itself naturally to a hierarchical understanding of tribes or societies. In a metaphorical language what is higher off the ground is usually thought to be more important or significant. That is why, incidentally, there has been persistent assumption in history that leaders should be tall men, accompanied by a perennial surprise when it is found that they are not always so. For this particular image the English borrowed the French word for a head, *chef*, which they rendered as *chief*.

By contrast, *leader* does not have hierarchical undertones. For leaders and followers are the same size and on the same level. Europeans whose languages do not have the etymological concept of leadership – notably French and Spanish – have recently had to borrow the word *leader* from the English language, just as the English language has borrowed other words, such as *morale* and *esprit de corps* from the French.

A reconstructed East Anglian tribal king's helmet from the pagan ship burial mound at Sutton Hoo in Suffolk, c. AD 625.

It is fascinating to look at the etymological cousins to that root word *laed*, a way or course. Our word *load* is a close relation. Load-stone, literally way-stone, was so named because the magnetic oxide of iron acted as a magnet in guiding mariners, just as the Load-Star (or North Star) was so called because it led them. *Lodeman* was in fact an old English word, now completely extinct, for leader. The syllable in *pilot* comes from the same root. In the course of time, the word *load* came to be reserved for the burden carried on a journey. Leaders metaphorically carry the load of responsibility – 'my care of all the churches,' as St Paul wrote in his second Letter to the Corinthians. Charles de Gaulle once said, that he had been called upon to shoulder 'the burden of France.'

As suggested by the German verb *begleiten*, to accompany or to go on the way with, the concept of leading always implies more than one person. The English word *conduct*, derived from the Latin words *con* (together with) and *ducere* (to lead), makes that plain. The most direct way of causing someone to go along with you is to take them by the hand and lead them. The Egyptian word for 'to lead' means literally 'to take by the hand'. That is the most simple way of ensuring that two or three people are not parted on a journey but stay close together. Even without the actual physical contact, it is vital that the leader and those whom he or she is conducting on the way remain 'in touch,' as we say, still using the same metaphor. Staying close or linked to those being conducted or led is therefore essential.

The Shepherd and His Flock

Learning about leadership comes mainly from widening one's span of analogy. People with a narrow span of analogy tend to rely – consciously or unconsciously – upon one or two metaphors for leadership, usually ones that are near to home. In the West, for example, we have made much use of military analogies. Today we overuse the metaphor of the industrial manager. Perhaps that preoccupation stems from the fact that business has now replaced military and ecclesiastical institutions as the dominant one of our times. The trouble with using only one analogy, however, is that we can so easily take them literally and forget their metaphorical nature. A head teacher, for example, may forget that the analogy of a manager applies to him or her in certain respects but not in others. The antidote is to develop a wider span of analogy: to see relevance in a variety of metaphors concerning leadership and draw lessons from them all. The further away they are from one's own field, country and time the better or richer will become one's knowledge of leadership. Knowing where a particular metaphor breaks down – they all do at some point – is part of coming to understand leadership in depth. A deeply influential metaphor of leadership, close to its core meaning in English, is the shepherd and his flock. Homer and Socrates both used it in order to point the lesson that a leader should meet the needs of his people. Outside the Bible, however, it was neither common nor was it ever developed. The Israelites, like the English of later times, thought in far more concrete or tangible terms than the Greeks, who had a gift for abstract thinking. For the Israelites, metaphors, such as the shepherd and his flock, were not ornaments to arguments but the very fibre of thought itself.

The shepherd provided direction, maintained the unity of the flock and met the individual needs of the sheep. Unfortunately these implicit messages have become obscure through the passage of time. It is hard for us in the West to understand the analogy. The shepherd in biblical lands gave direction to the flock by leading it from the front, sometimes for up to twenty miles a day, in search of the sparse grass that grows in the wilderness. Lambs naturally follow their mothers and fully-grown wild sheep follow their dominant ram. Early man in the Mediterranean basin observed this phenomenon and saw that sheep could be tamed and induced to follow a human leader instead of a ram. Until the middle of the last century, English shepherds also led their sheep from the front; now, of course, they train sheepdogs to drive them. Shepherds in the hill-country and in the wilderness of Judaea had dogs, but they were fierce mastiffs kept to protect their flocks of sheep and goats, not to round them up. In Europe, Spain is one of the few countries where shepherds can still be seen leading their flocks rather than driving them.

David – The Shepherd-King

The prophet Samuel chose David as a future king of Israel from among the sons of Jesse. As the youngest of them he was looking after the family's flock of sheep when summoned by this father to meet Samuel. Doubtless Samuel was impressed by the fact that this boy had the spirit to fight lions and bears to save the sheep entrusted to him. In a famous encounter he slew Goliath with his shepherd's sling. When eventually Saul fell in battle, 'all Israel' unanimously elected David as their king. First they reminded him: 'The Lord God said to you, "You shall be shepherd of my people Israel, and you shall be prince over my people Israel."' After making his covenant with the elders of the people, David was anointed as king. As the Psalmist wrote:

'He chose David his servant, and took him from the sheepfolds; from tending the ewes that had young he brought him to be the shepherd of Jacob his people and Israel his inheritance. With upright heart he tended them and guided them with skilful hand.'

During the guerrilla warfare before he became king, David's forces were led by thirty 'mighty men', his chosen captains. A hint of David's gift for leadership is given in the following story:

'And three of the thirty chief men went down, and came about harvest time to David at the cave of Adullam, when a band of Philistines was encamped in the valley of Rephaim. David was then in the stronghold; and the garrison of the Philistines was then at Bethlehem. And David said longingly, "Oh that someone would give me water to drink from the well of Bethlehem which is by the gate!" Then the three mighty men broke through the camp of the Philistines, and drew water out of the well of Bethlehem which was by the gate, and took and brought it to David. But he would not drink it; he poured it out to the Lord, and said, "Far be it from me, Oh Lord, that I should do this. Shall I drink the lifeblood of the men who went at the risk of their lives?" Therefore he would not drink it.

Keeping the flock close together was essential for their safety. No shepherd would go so far ahead as to lose sight or be out of earshot from his sheep. The natural instinct of predators, such as wolves and hyenas, was to scatter the flock and then kill their individual victims. Therefore the unity or cohesiveness of the flock was important to the shepherd. If he saw a sheep or goat wandering off, he called it back; should it still walk away, he hurled a stone from his sling, so as to fall just beyond it and send it scurrying back to the flock. If a sheep became lost in the hills and gullies of the Judaean wilderness, the shepherd had to decide whether or not to leave the flock in order to go in search of it. If several shepherds had charge of the flock it was easier for one to go off on his own, but even so his departure would weaken the collective strength of the shepherds. For the main threat to the flock came more from armed thieves rather than the leopards and lions, jackals and wolves, which lived in Judaea in Biblical days.

The shepherd, then, came to personify unity. Hence the proverbial saying in the Bible: 'I shall smite the shepherd and the sheep will be scattered.' In order to keep their flocks safe and together at night, a time of greater danger, shepherds often herded them into the limestone caves which abound in the Judaean hills, or they made sheepfolds with dry stone walls. In desert areas, where stones could not be found, they constructed their folds from thorn bushes. Wolves sometimes defied the dogs and leapt over these barriers, and so the shepherd might keep some of the lambs and young kids close to his tent for the night. 'O fairest among women', sings the author of the Song of Solomon, 'follow in the tracks of the flock, and pasture your kids besides the shepherd's tents.'

Flocks in Judaea are often composed of sheep and goats. Goats are especially fond of nibbling young leaves but will eat scrub, whereas sheep prefer the fresh short grass if they can find it. But sheep and goats in mixed flocks do not always co-exist happily and the shepherd must work to keep them together harmoniously. This characteristic made it often necessary to separate the goats from the sheep in the fold. In all human groups and organisations there are tendencies to such internal divisiveness.

The perpetual journeys of the shepherd and his flock brought danger and hardship for both of them. The shepherd shared these dangers on an equal footing with his sheep. The summer sun burnt both of them by day, both shivered in the winter snows and icy winds. It is not hard to believe that the shepherds became very fond of their charges; each could be recognised individually and be called by name.

A shepherd leading from the front his flock of sheep and goats in the wilderness of Judaea, which stretches from the Dead Sea to Jerusalem.

Like all analogies, the metaphor of the shepherd-and-sheep for leaders of people does break down eventually, because people and sheep differ in a considerable number of respects! But the core of leadership is there. For the good shepherd is skilled in his calling and gives his sheep a sense of direction. The Greek word for 'good' in Jesus's saying 'I am the good shepherd', is *kalos*, meaning skilful, as opposed to *agathos*, which means morally good. The shepherd has to respond to three kinds of implicit need present in the flock: they need to find food and so he leads them on the path to their desired destination; he holds them together in cohesive and harmonious unity; and, lastly, he meets their individual needs. He knows each sheep or goat by name. He makes sure that it finds the right food and enough water. He anoints an individual sheep's thorn-wounds with oil. He tends it when sick until the animal recovers its strength.

Interlude: The Three Circles

The shepherd-and-flock image illustrates a theme introduced in Chapter Two, namely that there are three kinds of need discernible in any human enterprise. Firstly, people need to know where they are going, literally or metaphorically, in terms of their common task. Secondly, they need to be held together as a team. Last but not least each individual, by virtue of being human and personal, also brings a set of needs that require satisfaction.

These three kinds of need should not be conceived as being separate entities: they overlap or interact in a rich variety of ways, sometimes with good and sometimes with ill effects. If, for example, an organisation fails completely to achieve its task, it will tend to disintegrate. Individual needs will then suffer, for our needs for money, security, recognition and personal or professional growth are to a large extent bound up with the common task. By drawing these areas of need – task, group and individual – as three overlapping circles, as below, it is much easier to visualise these inter-actions. For, as the Chinese proverb says, 'A picture is worth a thousand words.'

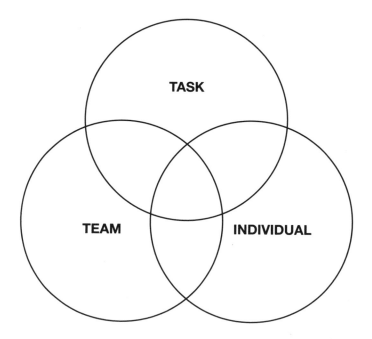

Leadership functions – such as identifying direction, planning, controlling, setting and maintaining standards, giving encouragement – are necessary if these three areas of need are to be met. But what a leader is, in terms of personality and character, will shape or colour the style in which he or she performs those functions. Qualities such as tenacity, firmness, fairness, enthusiasm and a sense of humour will inform the way in which the essential functions of leadership are performed.

The three-circles model does have the drawback of looking rather static. Leadership in reality, of course, is much more dynamic and ever-moving. It is an always-changing interaction between the needs and personalities of people and their leaders within an environment. Major changes in that environment invariably alter the relation of leader and followers, to the point of transforming them, as has been seen within the short span of this century.

Alexander the Great

In order to keep one's feet on the ground in studying leadership it is important not to stray too far from the basic journey image of the leader as one who shows the way ahead, holds people together as a group and encourages individuals – by example and word – to keep going despite the hardships and dangers of travel. These abilities are exemplified in Alexander the Great. He is one of the few unchallengeable geniuses when it comes to leadership. He certainly had his share of human failings and imperfections. But, despite these lapses, Alexander's contemporaries, especially his companions and followers, revered him as an exceptional leader. The following story helps to reveal why they did so.

Imagine a desolate desert of barren rocks and sand and scrub, scorched by the sun. It is midsummer, hence the furnace-like heat. Across the arid plain in Asia Minor, called the Gedrosian desert, marches Alexander's Greek army of some 30,000 foot soldiers with cavalry units in the rear. The best and most reliable historian of his conquests, Arrian – a Greek writer of the second century AD with the Latin name Flavius Arrianus, who saw himself as a second Xenophon – tells the story of what happened next:

'Alexander, like everyone else, was tormented by thirst, but he was none the less marching on foot at the head of his men. It was all he could do to keep going, but he did so, and the result (as always) was that the men were better able to endure their misery when they saw it as equally shared. As they toiled on, a party of light infantry which had gone off looking for water found some – just a wretched little trickle collected in a shallow gully. They scooped up with difficulty what they could and hurried back, with their priceless treasure, to Alexander; then, just before they reached him, they tipped the water into a helmet and gave it to him. Alexander, with a word of thanks for the gift, took the helmet and, in full view of his troops, poured the water on the ground. So extraordinary was the effect of this action that the water wasted was as good as a drink for every man in the army. I cannot praise this act too highly; it was a proof, if anything was, not only of his power of endurance, but also of his genius for leadership.'

The test of Alexander's leadership in the Gedrosian desert was not yet over. After taking the army first to the left and then to the right, the guides hired by the Greeks from the local natives eventually admitted that they no longer knew the way. The familiar landmarks, they declared, had been obliterated by the drifting yellow sands. There was nothing in that vast and featureless desert on which they could take their bearings – no trees and no hills.

With more than 30,000 thirsty men, their horses and pack animals under his command, Alexander suddenly found himself in a crisis. It was not unknown for an entire army to disappear in deserts, every man dying of thirst before the wind blew the sands and entombed them. Alexander gave no sign of panic. With commendable calmness he gave directions to the army.

Feeling by intuition that they should be heading more to the left he decided to reconnoitre ahead with a small party of mounted men. It was a calculated risk. When the horses began to succumb to the heat he left most of his party behind and rode on with only five men. At last they caught sight of the blue sea from a low rise in the dunes. Scraping away the shingle on the beach they came upon fresh water. The whole army soon followed, and for seven days marched along the coast getting its water from the beach. Finally the guides once more recognised their whereabouts, and a course was set for the interior again. Thus by his sure leadership Alexander saved the army from a potentially terrible disaster.

Alexander the Great.

Creating Unity and Teamwork

Alexander had inherited from his father, Philip of Macedon, the title 'Leader of the Greeks.' His courage and leadership in battle is renowned. But here we see him more as a shepherd leading a very large human flock rather than a general in action, resplendent in his shining armour. For in a sense his extended journey in the East was more like an explorer's expedition than a conqueror's campaign. Indeed Alexander was accompanied by those whom we should now call scientists. Before Alexander finally turned for home his soldiers had marched a staggering 11,500 miles. It was a journey that took them years, with many more days on the march than in battle.

The above incident in the Gedrosian desert, on the long weary way back to Greece from India, shows us a non-military example of Alexander's true leadership.

While Alexander is before our eyes it is worth remarking that he also met the other two areas of need we have identified. Less than half of his army came from Macedonia: the cities and states of mainland Greece supplied the rest. The Greeks were competitive by nature and not famous for co-operating well together. Homer captured their spirit in a phrase: 'Always to excel and to be superior to others.' Alexander succeeded in creating a spirit of unity in his army. In it, Greeks of diverse backgrounds and skills – cavalry and infantry, staff and engineers – had the unusual and rewarding experience of really working well together as a single unbeatable team.

This unity helped to produce teamwork on the battlefield between the different arms. They moved in unison like choristers singing at a competition, an analogy actually used by Herodotus in his description of one Greek army in battle. Even today choirs teach teamwork. Thus the cavalry did not look down upon the foot soldiers as their inferiors, nor did the pikemen despise the skirmishers or slingers. The Macedonian invention of staff officers, each entrusted with a special function, developed a sense of complementary skills interlocking like a jigsaw puzzle. Hephaestion, for example, was often charged with the matters of supply and transportation; Diades was the engineer; and Laomedon served as a provost marshal – a wise move because it took the potentially unpopular matter of policing the army out of Alexander's hands. Alexander even had a signals officer on his staff. Apart from a medical service he also developed a specialist unit with portable river-crossing equipment, together with catapult artillery to cover the crossing. A balanced force, lean and fit, Alexander's army proved to be invincible as long as it retained its cohesion.

The infusion of Persians into the army in ever-growing numbers did impose immense strains on its unity. Only the remarkable personality and presence of Alexander, his consistent leadership, could hold this flock of Greek rams and Persian he-goats together. After Alexander's death the unity of his army disintegrated, for it had all depended too much on him.

Alexander's generals who succeeded him were lost without him. Some years later, when they met to try to find that lost unity and peace, they chose to come together before his empty throne in his old tent. In death, as in life, Alexander was the only one who could hold them together.

Perhaps as they stood again in that familiar tent, Alexander's former generals – now his quarrelling successors – recalled their last sight of their young master as he lay on his deathbed under the tent's shade. The army had reached Babylon on its meandering way home, not 25 miles from the battlefield of Cunaxa where Xenophon had first encountered the Persian hosts. As word had spread among the Greeks in the now polyglot army that Alexander lay dying, the veterans crowded into the centre to see him, their hearts full of grief. They were bewildered, too, at the thought of what lay in store for them without Alexander as their leader. At last, on that sad Tuesday beside the waters of Babylon, they were allowed into the royal tent, filing past Alexander on his couch in their thousands. Lying speechless as the men passed, Alexander could be seen struggling to raise his head. In his eyes, once so famous for their intensity, there seemed to be a look of recognition for each individual as he passed. He was then thirty-two years and eight months old.

Caring for Individuals

Of course Alexander could not have known as individuals all the Macedonians, let alone all the Greeks in his army. But it was part of his genius as a leader that they felt he did. He met their individual needs. Arrian recorded plenty of examples of Alexander's humanity and care for his soldiers as individuals and persons. He never regarded them as mere spears or swords, but rather as companions and brothers-in-arms. After one battle Arrian writes: 'for the wounded he showed deep concern; he visited them all and examined their wounds, asking each man how and in what circumstances his wound was received, and allowing him to tell his story and exaggerate as much as he pleased.'

It was this care for individual needs, this deep sense of comradeship and humanity, which endeared Alexander to his troops. It appears again in his thoughtful concern for the young Macedonian pikemen who had hastily married on the eve of the expedition, perhaps on the grounds that they might not return from the wars. Feeling that some consideration was due to these men, Alexander dismissed them at the end of the first summer, sending them home to spend the winter with their wives. 'No act of Alexander's ever made him better beloved by his native troops,' commented Arrian.

The Greeks were individualists and they responded to a leader who related to them as individuals. Alexander understood that fact well. He understood that his commanders and soldiers would excel themselves if they knew his eye rested upon them and that their deeds and names were recorded in his mind. Of course he could not know the names of all the 30,000 or more Greek soldiers, but he did know the names of his officers. Xenophon, whom Alexander had almost certainly read on the subject, laid considerable stress on this importance of a leader learning the names of his people. It is a point that is as relevant today as it was in classical times, for human nature does not change. In the *Cyropaedia*, his presentation of Cyrus the Great as a role model for kings, Xenophon had written:

> *'Now Cyrus made a study of this; for he thought it passing strange that, while every mechanic knows the names of the tools of his trade and the physician knows the names of all the instruments he uses, the general should be so foolish as not to know the names of the officers under him.'*

Xenophon pointed out that those men who are conscious of being personally known to their general do more good and abstain more from evil than any others. Cicero, incidentally, who also read this passage in Xenophon, applied much the same principle in politics. He stocked his exceptional memory with the names of all the leading citizens of Rome. This knowledge, he found, greatly helped him when it came to gaining election and holding office in Rome.

Above all, Alexander possessed a great dream or vision of his destiny and the destiny of Greece as the civilising agent in the world. As 'Leader of the Greeks', he gave his compatriots a sense of purpose and that helped to give them unity. He inspired his officers and men with this energetic vision. Ovid's words could well apply to Alexander – 'He was a leader of leaders.'

The tomb of Cyrus the Great at Pasargardae built c. BC 530. This is an evocative relic of the great Persian leader whom Xenophon admired so much.

The Ability to Give Direction

CHAPTER REVIEW

Summary

People will look to their leader for direction in their common enterprise. How shall we achieve our purpose? Where should we be going? The leader may not know the way ahead too clearly, but he or she does need some vision, or at least a sense of direction. For, as the proverb says, 'In the country of the blind, the one-eyed man is king.' Yet, in times of doubt and anxiety, the good leader will not only direct people but also maintain the unity and morale of the team, and show concern for individuals. He or she does not forget about people in concentrating upon direction or task.

This core ability to give direction obviously meets the task circle in the three areas of overlapping need. At the lower levels of leadership, the task is usually fairly specific. It is often given to the working group in the form of an objective or target. At the higher levels, however, leaders may have to be able to cope with considerable uncertainty about where to go next: their skill here lies in clarifying purpose and aims or perhaps even in discerning a new goal for their organisation. Leadership and the management of change are inseparable. But to guide, steer or navigate an organisation or nation in this way, requires knowledge, experience and intellectual skill. For it's no good having a decisive and persuasive leader if he makes bad decisions or leads people in totally the wrong direction. These mental abilities, often neglected in discussions of leadership, are the subject of the next chapter.

Key Concepts

- Our word *leader* comes from a root meaning a path, road or course of a ship at sea. It is a journey word. If your organisation is not on a journey, don't bother about leadership – just settle for management.

- A leader is not always literally the person in front – in the military analogy that may be scouts, pioneers or an advance guard but a leader is expected to guide or give direction, keep the party together (staying in touch) and caring for individual needs on the journey.

- Journeys are sometimes hazardous, not least military ones that end in a crisis of violence. A leader shares the hardships and privations, risks and dangers, on an equal footing with others, as Alexander did in the Gedrosian Desert.

- An influential metaphor of leadership is the shepherd and his flock– the shepherd provides direction, maintains the unity of the flock and meets the individual needs of the sheep.

- The three circles illustrated the three kinds of need discernable in any human enterprise:
  - first people need to know where they are going in terms of their common TASK
  - secondly they need to be held together as a TEAM
  - thirdly each INDIVIDUAL has human and personal needs that require satisfaction.

- Alexander personified the cardinal military virtues, such as physical courage, as well as the mental qualities of a brilliant commander. He also had a genius for leadership which transcends time and place.

- A team is made up, like a jigsaw puzzle, of complementary parts fitting perfectly together. Under Alexander's compelling leadership, the Greek army worked as a high performance team. However desperate his circumstances, Alexander was able, with its aid, to defeat much bigger armies time after time. Teamwork was the key to his success.

- The Greeks, like us today, were very individualistic. Apart from caring for his men's individual needs – food and water, security, family – Alexander also ensured that the outstanding received personal recognition. He knew their names and praised them in public.

- Alexander had vision. He was not just out for himself or for Macedon. What mattered to him was spreading the humanistic values of Greece throughout the known world. What is your vision?

Further Reflection

- A chairman of a large company recently awarded himself and his fellow directors a 40 per cent pay rise, and new contracts with share options and very generous terms if they were terminated. At the same time, pleading the state of the economy, he asked the workforce to accept a 3.5 per cent pay rise and a cut in annual holidays. Profits were non-existent, he explained, and the company was in danger of being taken over. Those being compulsorily made redundant, he added, would receive only the legal minimum in redundancy payments. How do you think this chairman measures up as a business leader, compared to Alexander the Great in the Gedrosian Desert? If the purpose of business is simply profit and the main motive in it is personal greed for money, perhaps that chairman and his fellow directors acted rationally but these are not the actions of good leadership. What do you think? What is the true purpose of business enterprise? Does it call for leaders of Alexandrian greatness? Or is it only the battlefields of this world that evoke the best as well as the worst from human nature?

- On September 11, 2001 the Twin Towers of the World Trade Centre in New York were hit by two aircraft hi-jacked by terrorists. Rudolph Giuliani, the New York mayor as he then was, rushed to the scene immediately after the first plane struck. 'There was debris flying everywhere,' he recalled. 'My police officers kept telling me to look up so I didn't get hit, but when I saw the bodies coming down I couldn't bear it...' He watched while hundreds of police and firefighters and many of his best friends went in to evacuate the towers. 'They were my family. I shouted good luck to them...' He went into a nearby building to telephone the vice-president when suddenly the first tower collapsed in a nuclear cloud. 'I remember thinking it would be better to die on the street than trapped in a building.' Why do you think Mayor Giuliani's name went round the world as an example of great leadership?

FIVE
Making the Right Decisions

'Reason and calm judgement, the qualities especially belonging to a leader.'

TACITUS

In order to guide a group, organisation or nation in the right direction a leader needs the ability to think and decide. It could be called the intellectual dimension of leadership. Practical reason, intuition and imagination are all included under that heading. But it is not only a matter of the leader having some or all of these attributes. He or she has to be able to guide a problem-solving or decision-making body, such as a board of directors, whose members may have different mental abilities as well as different personalities. The case-study of Clement Attlee below shows how important it is to select the right team members and to lead decision-making meetings in an effective, businesslike way. Climate matters, too, when it comes to thinking together for results. A good leader will remain cool, calm and collected, and encourage others to do so. It things go wrong, he or she accepts full personal accountability.

Thinking to Some Purpose

The core activity is undoubtedly *thinking*. The Canadian entrepreneur Roy Thomson, who built up a vast publishing empire and owned *The Times*, insisted upon its importance. In *After I was Sixty* (1975), his autobiography, he wrote:

> *'Thinking is work. In the early stages of a man's career it is very hard work. When a difficult decision or problem arises, how easy it is, after looking at it superficially, to give up thinking about it. It is easy to put it from one's mind. It is easy to decide that it is insoluble, or that something will turn up to help us. Sloppy and inconclusive thinking becomes a habit. The more one does it the more one is unfitted to think a problem through to a proper conclusion.*

> *It I have any advice to pass on, as a successful man, it is this: if one wants to be successful, one must think; one must think until it hurts. One must worry a problem in one's mind until it seems there cannot be another aspect of it that hasn't been considered. Believe me, that is hard work and, from my close observation, I can say that there are few people indeed who are prepared to perform this arduous and tiring work.'*

The fact that Roy Thompson left school at fourteen warns us against equating this ability to think or reason with having attended a university. Reason in this context means the sum of a person's intellectual powers. Practical reason is a phrase that suggests intellectual powers disposed to action as opposed to speculation or abstraction.

The credit for first identifying in Europe the concept of practical reason belongs to the Greeks. Socrates personified it; his pupil at one remove, Aristotle, codified it. 'Now the origin of action (the efficient, not the final cause) is choice,' Aristotle wrote in Book Six of *Ethics*, 'and the origin of choice is apposite and purposive reasoning. Hence choice necessarily involves not only intellect and thought, but a certain moral state; for good conduct and its contrary necessarily involve thought and character. But no process is set going by mere thought – only by purposive and practical thought, for it is this that also originates productive thought.'

The Greeks called this practical common-sense, or practical wisdom when it is found to an uncommon degree, *phronesis*. The traditional English translation of it (by way of the Latin word for foresight), is 'prudence'. But in modern usage prudence has acquired nuances of thoughtful restraint; it is almost a synonym for caution. The Greek concept is much more positive. Aristotle instances Pericles and others like him as demonstrating the nature of *phronesis*, 'because they can envisage what is good for themselves and for people in general.' He added that this quality belonged to those who understand the management of estates, the forerunners of modern industry, as well as political states.

The British historian J. W. Fortescue gives us a synonymous phrase for *phronesis* in his biography of Wellington. The great Duke's real gift, he wrote, was 'transcendent common-sense, the rare power (shared also by Marlborough) of seeing things as they are which signifies genius.' Wellington's gift, of course, included translating perception into action. For common-sense means the natural capacity for seeing things as they are, without illusion or bias, combined with the ability to draw conclusions and *to take correct action*. Common-sense, experience, and moral goodness are the ingredients of such practical wisdom.

Pericles, the Athenian statesman who dominated Athenian politics from 461 BC as leader of the democratic party, possessed *phronesis* in a remarkable measure. Once firmly in the saddle, Plutarch wrote, Pericles' 'own conduct took on quite a different character. He was no longer so docile towards the people, nor so ready to give way to their caprices, which were as shifting and changeable as the winds. He abandoned the somewhat nerveless and indulgent leadership he had shown on occasion, which might be compared to a soft and flowery melody, and struck instead the firm, high note of an aristocratic, even regal statesmanship.'

Pericles created a confederation of cities under Athens' leadership, but the disasters of the Peloponnesian War some years later led to his overthrow. Although the Athenians quickly reinstated him he died soon afterwards. By common consent the age of Pericles marks the climax of Greek thought and culture. In a famous funeral oration delivered at the burial of the fallen in battle, Pericles celebrated the values and spirit which made Athens so powerful in its time and so influential throughout later ages. During the speech, Pericles praised the ability of the Athenians to base their decisions on *phronesis* or practical wisdom:

> *'We Athenians, in our own persons, take our decisions on policy or submit them to proper discussions: for we do not think that there is an incompatibility between words and deeds; the worst thing is to rush into action before the consequences have been properly debated. And this is another point where we differ from other people. We are capable at the same time of taking risks and of estimating them beforehand. Others are brave out of ignorance and, when they stop to think, they begin to fear.'*

As Athens was a democracy, Pericles assumed that all citizens would share in the work of solving the problem of what to do in a given situation: defining the aim or goal, identifying possible courses of action, selecting from them the feasible alternatives, debating the pros and cons of each in terms of foreseeable consequences, and, finally, making the best decision possible in light of the information available.

From the angle of leadership, the involvement of people in decision-making in this way has one enormous advantage. For the more that people share in decisions which affect their lives, the more they are motivated to carry them out. As leadership and motivation are so closely related, that factor must always loom large in any leader's mind. Especially when there are few if any other means of motivating people, or when the leader lacks the authority of position (as in voluntary organisations), engaging people in the decision of what to do or where to go is vitally important.

Power of Persuasion

'A trait always noticeable in a successful leader is his ability to persuade others. There are times, of course, when every leader must make a decision and see that it is carried out regardless of what others might think. But whenever men can be persuaded rather than ordered – when they can be made to feel that they have participated in developing the plan – they approach their task with understanding and enthusiasm.

'Churchill was a persuader. Indeed, his skill in the use of words and logic was so great that on several occasions when he and I disagreed on some important matter – even when I was convinced of my own view and when the responsibility was clearly mine – I had a very hard time withstanding his arguments. More than once he forced me to re-examine my own premises, to convince myself again that I was right – or accept his solution. Yet if the decision went against him, he accepted it with good grace, and did everything in his power to support it with proper action. Leadership by persuasion and the wholehearted acceptance of a contrary decision are both fundamentals of democracy.'

Eisenhower

As the ancient Greek proverb says, 'Two heads are better than one.' The quality of the decision will often be higher if more than one person has been involved in the prior process of practical reasoning. Our common experience of decisions in everyday life supports that conclusion.

Only an arrogant person will assume that he or she has all the information and all the wisdom necessary to make a decision. In order to guarantee that the best possible decision is taken, a wise leader will encourage as full a debate as possible among the members of the team and listen to it carefully. As Shakespeare wrote: 'Rightly to be great, is not to stir without great argument.'

But others involved in the argument do not necessarily have the same responsibility for action as the leader. It is the leader who is usually charged with ensuring that a decision is taken and that it is then implemented. Time, time that waits for no man, can now become a critical factor. 'Nine-tenths of wisdom,' said Theodore Roosevelt, 'is being wise in time.' Consensus or mutual consent among all upon what should be done, is always highly desirable, for no leader who wishes to be effective wants a minority of dissenters who will drag their heels because they are uncommitted to the course of action adopted. But that unanimity is not always attainable. Cromwell voiced the exasperation of many a leader when he declared in the House of Commons one day, 'I am as for consent as any man, but where shall it be found?'

Themistocles, the Athenian soldier and statesman who possessed many of the intellectual and moral qualities of leadership esteemed by the Greeks.

During the Peloponnesian War between Athens and Sparta, Thucydides recorded that the Athenian general Demosthenes showed inspiring leadership in opposing a landing by superior Spartan forces. First he had to quell the natural Athenian tendency to analyse the situation in detail. Having drawn up his pikemen in order to stop the enemy from landing, he spoke to them as follows:

> 'Soldiers, all of us together are in this, and I do not want any of you in our present awkward position to try to show off his intelligence by making a precise calculation of the dangers which surround us; instead we must simply make straight at the enemy, and not pause to discuss the matter, confident in our hearts that these dangers, too, can be surmounted. For when we are forced into a position like this one, calculations are beside the point: what we have to do is to stake everything on a quick decision. And in fact I consider that the odds are on our side, so long as we are determined to hold our ground and do not throw away our very real advantages through being frightened by the enemy's numbers.'

Where time is short for decision-making, as for instance in a crisis situation where life-and-death is involved, a leader will normally be expected to exercise his or her own practical common-sense and make a decision. Military leaders in particular need this ability to take a decision on their own, as do people in commercial fields. The general Clearchus (p.12) took upon himself that responsibility, although he had the benefit of listening first to a debate by his intelligent colleagues on their predicament, and what might be done.

Pericles himself showed that in times of crisis a democracy needs firm leadership from one person. When Athens' very existence was at stake at one period in the long Peloponnesian War, he curtailed debate and took all the major decisions himself. 'He would not summon the Assembly for fear that he might be forced to act against his better judgement,' wrote Plutarch. 'Instead, he behaved like the helmsman of a ship who, when a storm sweeps down upon it in the open sea, makes everything fast, takes in sail and relies on his own skill and takes no notice of the tears and entreaties of the sea-sick and terrified passengers.'

Leaders such as Pericles and Themistocles demonstrated their capacity to recognise the realities of situations and make the appropriate decision quickly. Later leaders of stature are marked by a similar character and ability.

Themistocles

The intellectual powers required in a leader are exemplified by this Athenian statesman and general who lived in the fourth century BC. Born of a father of no particular distinction and an alien mother, as a boy Themistocles showed unusual ability and application. Indeed his career proved a point made by Pericles, that in Athens 'what counts in not membership of a particular class, but the actual ability which the man possesses.' As Thucydides wrote, few surpassed Themistocles in practical reason:

'Themistocles was a man who showed an unmistakable natural genius; in this respect he was quite exceptional, and beyond all others deserves our admiration. Without studying a subject in advance or deliberating over it later, but using simply the intelligence that was his by nature, he had the power to reach the right conclusion in matters that have to be settled on the spur of the moment and do not admit of long discussions, and in estimating what was likely to happen, his forecasts of the future were always more reliable than those of others. He could perfectly well explain any subject with which he was familiar, and even outside his own department he was still capable of giving an excellent opinion. He was particularly remarkable at looking into the future and seeing there the hidden possibilities for good or evil. To sum him up in a few words, it may be said that through force of genius and by rapidity of action this man was supreme at doing precisely the right thing at precisely the right moment.'

From Ideas to Responsible and Decisive Action

A leader, then, accepts the responsibility for seeing that decisions are taken and that the correct action ensues. In both respects, he or she must be a progress-chaser. 'I am certainly not one of those who need to be prodded,' Churchill said, with a characteristic twinkle in his eye. 'In fact, if anything, I am the prod.'

Sir Winston Churchill. Probably the most eminent British national leader of the twentieth century, Churchill personified his compatriots' qualities of courage and resolution in adversity.

The invention and production of what came to be known as Mulberry harbours illustrated well Churchill's foresight and prodding insistence on action at work. Without harbour facilities the allied invasion of Normandy in 1944 could not have taken place. As the enemy held all the French harbours, the allies would have to invent a new harbour facility and take it with them. In 1941, three years before the event, Churchill wrote a memo to Admiral Mountbatten, then in charge of combined operations:

> 'We must devise pierheads for the major unloading of thousands of tons. The piers must float up and down with the tide. The anchor problem must be solved. Don't argue the matter, the difficulties will argue for themselves.'

A good leader will also accept complete personal responsibility if the decision he has made leads to failure. He will not 'pass the buck' to his colleagues or subordinates. After the failure of his first attack on Quebec, General Wolfe wrote:

> 'The blame I take entirely upon my shoulders and I expect to suffer for it. Accidents cannot be helped. As much of the plan as was defective falls justly on me.'

Eisenhower also shouldered the responsibility of failure. The weather conditions in the first few days of June 1944 caused his air commander to argue for further postponement of the invasion of Europe. After consultation with his generals and specialist advisers, Eisenhower himself took the momentous decision to take the risk and go ahead on 6 June 1944. Before the invasion fleet set out he wrote this press release, to be used if necessary:

> 'Our landings have failed and I have withdrawn the troops. My decision to attack at this time and place was based upon the best information available. The troops, the air and the Navy did all that bravery and devotion to duty could do. If any blame or fault is attached to the attempt it is mine alone.'

Hitler exemplified the opposite side of the coin – irresponsibility. He persistently blamed the failure of his military plans upon the incompetence of his subordinates or their lack of will-power, while taking for himself the credit of the early successes. When the roof fell in, Hitler castigated the German people for letting him down. He could neither see nor face his ultimate responsibility as leader.

Dwight D. Eisenhower. Supreme Commander of all the Allied armies in the West in the Second World War and later President of the United States.

The emphasis upon decisiveness in leadership is important because of the danger that those in posts of leadership will never stop taking evidence, and accumulating and weighing facts. As the future is, by definition, not entirely predictable, it is impossible to have all the facts and information before you make a decision. In this respect, decision-making differs from the kind of problem-solving where all the information is there but has to be sorted out into a solution, like a jigsaw puzzle. In life, bits of the jigsaw are often missing. A leader must often decide – or press a group to decide – whether to trade more time and money for more information, or to act upon the best information available. That is a choice which in itself calls for judgement. The desire to look at all sides of the question and to collect more information is a tendency among those professionally given to study and reflection. That is why they seldom make good leaders.

In his book *The Art of Leadership* (1929), Ordway Tead summarised this key importance of decisiveness. 'Ultimately the leader has to get results,' he wrote. 'There must be action and accomplishment. The group objective must be measurably realised. This is vital. To cut across indecision with decision, to galvanise indifference into enthusiastic performance, to translate doubt of possibilities into the swing of going actuality – to effect these transitions is the leader's peculiar prerogative and duty. "He did the job" is the tribute from which leadership cannot escape. How he did it, what motives he summoned and what residuum of achieved satisfaction he has left with his followers – these too are intrinsic aspects of his success. But leadership is at a premium because so many people are loath to make irrevocable decisions, are tepid in their enthusiasms, timid in their faith in themselves and others, afraid of the burden of responsibility and undecided about their direction.'

Case-study: Chairing the Cabinet

Clement Attlee served as Prime Minister of Great Britain from 1945 to 1951. 'In the Driver's Seat,' and article which appeared in *The Observer* on 18 October 1964, contains his thoughts on leading a team which was itself composed of leaders (some of them – such as Aneurin Bevan, Herbert Morrison and Ernest Bevin – with a tendency to be prima donnas). It is written in his characteristically succinct, even terse, style of talking. Attlee began with some reflections on selecting the right people for the Cabinet:

'In a way it [forming a Cabinet] is more difficult than winning the election, because in choosing his Cabinet the Prime Minister is on his own, and carries the can for his mistakes. Once the appointments have been made, he is going to be stuck with them for a considerable period. If some of the choices soon look unsatisfactory, he cannot start sacking them right away. However, he must give each man a chance, and stand the racket while he improves, grows to the job. If the Prime Minister starts pushing his departmental heads, the morale of the Cabinet as a whole will suffer.

'The qualities of the ideal Cabinet Minister are: judgement, strength of character, experience of affairs, and an understanding of ordinary people.

'Judgement is necessary because the Cabinet is the instrument by which decisions are reached with a view to action, and decisions stem from judgement. A Cabinet is not a place for eloquence – one reason why good politicians are not always good Cabinet Ministers. It is judgement which is needed to make important decisions on imperfect knowledge in a limited time. Men either have it, or they haven't. They can develop it, if they have it, but cannot acquire it if they haven't.

'Strength of character is required to stand up to criticism from other Cabinet members, pressure from outside groups, and the advice of civil servants.

'It is also necessary when policies, on which the Cabinet has agreed, are going through the doldrums, or are beginning to fail. A man of character will neither be, nor seem to be, bowed down by this. Nor will he be blown about by "every wind of vain doctrine".'

Clement Attlee, sitting in the Cabinet Room at 10 Downing Street where he presided over meetings in the manner he so graphically describes here.

Attlee then discussed the value of a wide general experience in senior members of the government.

> 'It is more important that the Cabinet discussion should take place, so to speak, at a higher level than the information and opinions provided by the various departmental briefs. A collection of departmental Ministers does not make a Cabinet. A Cabinet consists only of responsible human beings. And it is their thinking and judgement in broad terms that make a Government tick, not arguments about the recommendations of civil servants. It is interesting to note that quite soon a Cabinet begins to develop a group personality. The role of the Prime Minister is to cultivate this, if it is efficient and right-minded; to do his best to modify it, if it is not.

'While a collection of departmental heads mouthing their top civil servants' briefs is unsatisfactory, a collection of Ministers who are out of touch with administration tends to be unrealistic. And a Minister who has an itch to run everybody else's department as well as, or in preference to, his own, is just a nuisance. Some men will be ready to express a view about everything. They should be discouraged. If necessary, I would shut them up. Once is enough. Ernie Bevin held forth on a variety of subjects, but Ernie had an extraordinary variety of practical knowledge.

'It is a curious thing that nearly every Cabinet throws up at least one man, whether he is a departmental Minister or not, of whom a newcomer might ask, "What is he doing here?" he is there because he is wise. You will hear a junior Cabinet Minister being told by the Prime Minister, perhaps, "If you are going to do that, you would be well advised to have a talk with X."

'The ability to talk attractively in Cabinet is not essential. Being able to put a case clearly and succinctly and simply is what counts. The Cabinet is certainly not the place for rhetoric. Though an excellent head of department and a conciliator of genius, Nye Bevan used to talk a bit too much occasionally. Usually he was extremely good, often wise, and sometimes extremely wise. "75 per cent of political wisdom is a sense of priorities." I remember him saying once – an admirable remark, and good advice for Cabinet Ministers.

'The occasions when he talked to much were when he got excited because he felt that our policies were falling short of the pure milk of the word. This goes for most such interruptions, and a Prime Minister should try to avoid these time-consuming expressions of guilt – or electoral fear – by trying to reassure from time to time the pure in heart who feel the Government is backsliding.

'However, you cannot choose people according to what makes an ideal Cabinet Minister. In the first place, you must choose people with regard to keeping balance within the party. This need not be overdone. It is a matter of democratic common-sense, not a craven below-the-scenes manipulation. It would not do to have all trade unionists in a Labour Cabinet, or all constituency members, or all middle-class intellectuals, or all ornaments of the Co-operative Party. Some working-class trade unionists are in fact honorary members of the intelligentsia – Nye again – while I have known upper-class intellectuals try desperately to behave like heavy-handed sons of toil...'

A Prime Minister must have his own view of a man's capacity to serve in the Cabinet. Nor can selected members always have the job they want. High qualifications are required for the most important posts in the Cabinet.

'The Cabinet usually meets once a week. That should be enough for regular meetings, and should be if they grasp from the start what they are there for. They should be back at their work as soon as possible, and a Prime Minister should put as little as possible in their way. We started sharp at 11, and rose in time for lunch. Even in a crisis, another couple of meetings should be enough in the same week: if there is a crisis, the less talk the better.

'The Prime Minister shouldn't speak too much himself in Cabinet. He should start the show or ask somebody else to do so, and then intervene only to bring out the more modest chaps who, despite their seniority, might say nothing if not asked. And the Prime Minister must sum up. Experienced Labour leaders should be pretty good at this; they have spent years attending debates at meetings of the Parliamentary Party and the National Executive, and have to sum those up. That takes some doing – good training for the Cabinet.

'Particularly when a non-Cabinet Minister is asked to attend, especially if it is his first time, the Prime Minister may have to be cruel. The visitor may want to show how good he is, and go on too long. A good thing is to take no chance and ask him to send the Cabinet a paper in advance. The Prime Minister can then say, "A very clear statement, Minister of...Do you need to add anything?" in a firm tone of voice obviously expecting the answer, no. If somebody else looks like making a speech, it is sound to nip in with "Has anybody any objection?" If somebody starts to ramble, a quick, "Are you objecting? You're not? Right. Next business," and the Cabinet can move on.

'It is essential for the Cabinet to move on, leaving in its wake a trail of clear, crisp, uncompromising decisions. That is what government is about. And the challenge is how to get it done quickly.'

Intuition and Imagination

The practical wisdom of a leader consists of more than the mental skill of analysing people or things. As we have seen, paralysis by analysis is a common failing in leaders who have not learned to be decisive. Analytical or logical thinking is a valuable asset in a leader at any level, and an education which develops that ability is to be prized. A leader who does not have a mind schooled in some discipline which has taught him to think clearly and systematically would be wise to include among his counsellors those who are so trained. One of Hitler's many mistakes as a leader was to despise the German General Staff, disciplined experts in logical thinking within the confines of war.

Hitler certainly possessed intuition. This attribute is often present in the intellectual powers of a leader above a certain level. 'Intuition comes very close to clairvoyance,' writes Alexis Carrel in his *Reflections Upon Life*. 'It appears to be the extrasensory perception of reality. All great men are gifted with intuition. They know without reasoning or analysis what they need to know.'

Leaders are often deterred from recognising and using their own intuitive powers because they feel that, somehow, intuition is not intellectually respectable. It is certainly, they believe, not scientific enough. The cult of the rational manager has an iron grip on such minds. But this is nonsense. Some of the most celebrated scientists have been intuitive in their work. Some words by Einstein prove that point:

> 'There is no logical way to the discovery of these elemental laws. There is only the way of intuition, which is helped by a feeling for the order lying behind the appearance.'

Intuition, then, is the power or faculty of immediately apprehending that something is the case. Apparently it is done without intervention of any reasoning process. There seems to be no deductive or inductive step-by-step reasoning, no conscious analysis of the situation, no employment of the imagination – just a quick and ready insight – 'I just know.' It is important however, that intuition is soundly based upon experience and a history of sound reasoning.

A person who consistently deploys an instinctive power of discernment in a certain field is said to have flair. He or she can 'smell' a good prospect or in what direction the truth might lie, rather than reasoning towards a goal in a step-by-step manner. Indeed flair comes from the French verb *flairer* meaning to smell. J. Paul Getty gave this example:

> 'When I first started drilling in the Oklahoma oil fields the consensus of expert judgement held that there could be no oil in the so-called Red Beds region. But like so many oilmen, I chose to temper all "analytical" thinking with a healthy dose of non-logical subjectivity. To me, the area looked as if it might hide oil. Largely on the basis of a hunch, I decided to see for myself. I began drilling in the Red Beds, and struck oil and brought in a vast new producing field. I rather suspect that by relying upon such nontextbook thought – processes and taking attendant risks, the biggest fortunes have been made – in oil and other endeavours.'

Business flair is a consistent theme in the lives of great industrial leaders. They can intuitively spot an opportunity for making money. They can smell a potential profit where others can see nothing but present losses. It is an instinct apart from the dictates of reason or logic which guide more plodding minds. When it is not followed, such businessmen frequently find out later their mistake, just as Golda Meir did. For, as the Arab proverb says, 'Dawn does not come twice to awaken a man.'

The Computer of Practical Reason

'I must now ask myself: what was it that gave me this self-confidence, this determination and adventurous spirit in business...at 67?

'It was at least partly due to my discovery over a fairly long period, but more than ever during these latter years in Edinburgh and London, that experience was a very important element in the management side of business and it was, of course, the one thing that I had plenty of. I could go further and say that for management to be good it generally must be experienced. To be good at anything at all requires a lot of practice, and to be really good at taking decisions you have to have plenty of practice at taking decisions. The more one is exposed to the necessity of making decisions, the better one's decision-making becomes.

'At various times during my business life I have had to take some important decisions, and, particularly in the early days, I often got these wrong. But I found later that the early mistakes and, for that matter, the early correct decisions stood me in good stead. Most of the problems that I was confronted with in London were in one way or another related to those earlier ones. It was often a matter of just adding some zeros to figures and the sums were the same. In a great many instances I knew the answer immediately.

continued...

'I cannot explain this scientifically, but I was entirely convinced that, through the years, in my brain as a computer, I had stored details of the problems themselves, the decisions reached and the results obtained; everything was neatly filed away there for future use. Then, later, when a new problem arose, I would think it over and, if the answer was not immediately apparent, I would let it go for a while, and it was as if it went the rounds of the brain cells looking for guidance that could be retrieved, for by the next morning, when I examined the problem again, more often than not the solution came up right away. That judgement seemed to be come to almost unconsciously, and my conviction is that during the time I was not consciously considering the problem, my subconscious had been turning it over and relating it to my memory; it had been held up to the light of the experiences I had had in past years, and the way through the difficulties became obvious...It is only the rare and most complex problems that require the hard toil of protracted mental effort.'

Roy Thomson, *After I was Sixty* (1975)

As a general rule, the sooner an intuition comes to a leader, the more time he or she should take to verify it as far as that is possible. By contrast, intuition that is born out of a longer period of thought, study and experience, is more likely to be true. Consequently intuition later in life can perhaps be trusted more than earlier on, because of experience and practice in reasoning.

In this context, imagination and intuition are closely related. A leader needs imagination in many situations – where the next move is not blueprinted. It is true that as a leader you do not have total freedom. You do not have the relative freedom of someone writing a television script or the composer of a poem. You are more like a person crossing an unmapped plateau with others. You have to think things out for yourself and then suspiciously try out possible ways of getting where you want to be – and the solutions to these problems are not in books, nor can they be recalled from your memory bank. For you have never been here before. You have to originate or innovate, and you cannot innovate by following established precedents or by applying common recipes. John Sainsbury, chairman of the highly successful chain of grocery supermarkets which bears his name, stated:

> 'The characteristic in a good manager which I appreciate almost above all else is that of imagination. The good manager has to be imaginative in order to be a successful innovator. Success in that respect brings not only a valuable contribution to any enterprise, but also the considerable personal satisfaction of creative achievement. It is imagination which is needed to anticipate events and to respond to change. It is only those with a lively imagination who can really develop sensitive understanding of others, be they customers, colleagues or shop floor workers. To be able to do that is a vital ingredient of success in commerce or industry.'

Lord Thomson of Fleet. A warm, approachable man and a good listener, who wrote a marvellously clear description of how he made decisions in business.

Imagination should not be promoted to top place in the hierarchy of thinking abilities. It should be a team player, not the captain. The specific role of imagination is to lead us into innovating, inventing, creating, exploring, risk-taking and adventuring. It is the vanguard or the advanced scouting party of thinking.

The leader who knowingly ventures off or beyond the beaten track, the path of well-trodden expectations, is showing some degree of imagination. His or her ventures may turn out to be fruitless, random or crazy. For leaders who dream dreams may be pathfinders, but they may also lead themselves and others into the bankruptcy courts. Of those who depart from well-established ways only a few are explorers. 'Imaginative,' 'inventive' and 'adventurous' are terms of praise but, equally, 'fanciful,' 'reckless' and 'crazy' describe those who are failed imaginative thinkers. We should therefore be on guard against any tendency to glorify the notion of imagination as an end itself. People sometimes forget that a lively imagination can also be a silly one. Scope for originality is also freedom to be a crackpot. Both the genius and the crank are imaginative thinkers – some are both at the same time.

Yet imagination covers some crucial qualities in the leader. There are plenty of situations in leadership that call for powers of originating, inventing, improvising, discovering, innovating, exploring, experimenting, and of knowingly leaving the beaten track. 'As a rule', wrote Kenneth Grahame, author of *The Wind in the Willows*, 'grown-up people are fairly correct on matter of fact; it is the higher gift of imagination that they so sadly lack.'

Calmness Under Pressure

Tacitus, in the words quoted at the head of this chapter, included calmness in the qualities that belong especially to a leader. The process of deciding the cut-off point between thought and action can be fraught with anxiety in various shapes and sizes. One is the anxiety of holding the decision until as much information as possible has been gathered. The other is the anxiety of making the decision when there really isn't enough information – which, on critical decisions, is usually the case. All of this is complicated by pressures building up from those who 'want an answer'. Again, trust is at the root of it. Has the leader a really good information base (both hard data and sensitivity to feelings and needs of people) and a reputation for consistently good decisions that people respect? Can the leader defuse the anxiety of other people who want more certainty than exists in the situation?

Communication plays an important part in dispelling anxiety. But the inner calmness of the leader also has influence. Anxious people look at the faces of their leaders. An absence of visible tension or excitement when such reactions might well be expected in the circumstances has a calming effect on them. It is not that a leader lacks such emotions. Courage is not being devoid of fear; it is the will or ability to control fear and to draw from it energy and resolution. It is vital to maintain self-control if one hopes to be able to control others.

Coolness in Action

General Robert E. Lee was perhaps the finest military leader in the American Civil War. At the outset both sides sought him as their commander-in-chief, but Lee's loyalty to his native state of Virginia drew him into the camp of the Confederacy. By skilful generalship and good leadership he waged a remarkably successful war against the North. But at the three-day battle of Gettysburg any hope of victory for the South virtually disappeared. The decisive point in the battle came when an attack led by one of Lee's subordinates, General Pickett, failed. An eyewitness was present when news of this disaster reached Lee:

'His face did not show the slightest disappointment, care or annoyance, and he addressed every soldier he met with a few words of encouragement – "All will come right in the end, we'll talk it over afterwards". And to a Brigade Commander speaking angrily of the heavily losses of his men: "Never mind, General, all this has been my fault. It is I who have lost this fight, and you must help me out of it the best way you can."'

General Robert E. Lee. Perhaps the finest strategist of the American Civil War and one of its best leaders.

A coolness which resists excitability and a composure which gives that dignified demeanour and conduct in the midst of confusion is valuable to other people as well as to generals. Field Marshal Lord Alanbrooke, Britain's Chief of General Staff during the Second World War, recorded in his diary how people in the War Office – officers, civilians and typists – used to watch his face in the dark days of 1941 and 1942 as he walked through the corridors of the building to his room. They were scrutinising it for signs of how the war was going. It was a struggle at times, admitted this humane and sensitive man, to prevent his face from sending out signals of alarm and despondency.

Cool, calm and collected: these words are often bracketed together. They suggest that a leader's mental resources are completely intact in the face of difficulty. 'Calm' stresses a quiet approach to a problem, devoid of hysterical actions or utterances, while 'collected' emphasises the application of practical reason to the solution of the problem. To be free from agitation of any sort in the face of danger or provocation, to be able to concentrate the mind, eliminating distractions, especially in moments of crisis: these are indeed qualities essential in any leader of stature. As Voltaire said of John Churchill, first Duke of Marlborough, he possessed 'that calm courage in the midst of tumult, that serenity of soul in danger, which the English call a cool head.'

Anthony Eden, British Prime Minister during the Suez Crisis of 1956, showed in its duration how he lacked these particular qualities of leadership. He flapped his wings in effectively. Eden's natural irritability erupted in fits of temper. Nor could he delegate properly. His Cabinet colleagues were constantly interrupted by him as he telephoned them in a state of excitement or worry. Rather than letting ministers get on with what needed to be done, Eden kept nagging and fussing. He showed an acute lack of self confidence. He was very nervous and could not make up his mind. In the Suez Crisis he commanded every platoon. Clearly Eden was no leader. By contrast, Harold Macmillan's 'unflappability' was a byword. In the Cabinet Room he had framed the reminder: 'Quiet, calm deliberation disentangles every knot.' That is a good practical guideline for a leader to act upon.

The Value of Humour

One of Churchill's endearing characteristics was his sense of humour. His biographer, Martin Gilbert, who spent a quarter of a century on his monumental work, came to know him in a unique way. 'What of Winston Churchill himself?', he wrote, reflecting upon his experience. 'I doubt if anyone could have enjoyed delving into his life for 25 years if he had been an ogre. How right his daughter Mary was when she wrote to him, in 1951:

> *"It is hardly in the nature of things that your descendants should inherit your genius – but I earnestly hope that they may share in some way the qualities of your heart."'*

Gilbert added that as the years of research and writing advanced, Churchill's sense of fun was a constant companion. 'In almost every file there was something to make me laugh. Puzzled in 1941 by the silence of General Wolfe Murray at a war conference, Churchill at once renamed him General "Sheep" Murray. In 1940, wanting to speak to his principal private secretary, Eric Seal, he asked a secretary: "Fetch Seal from his ice floe."'

Apart from making conversation much lighter, humour also has a functional value: it helps to defuse tension. Anxiety can be like electricity: if it strikes the pole of humour it can be conducted safely into the ground. Because of the situational pressure inclining people to laugh in order to relieve their tension, the joke made by a leader – or anyone else in the team – doesn't have to be a particularly good one.

Remaining cool, calm and collected is essential for a leader. If, like an acrobat balancing on the high wire of risk and difficulty, a leader can smile as well – and cause others to smile – it can have a magic effect on morale. For people tend to take a cue from their leaders.

Hannibal at Cannae

'Varro insisted on observing the practice whereby each consul took command of the army on alternate days. He then pitched his camp opposite Hannibal's on the banks of the river Aufidus near the town named Cannae, and at daybreak hoisted the signal for battle, a scarlet tunic hung out over the general's tent. At first even the Carthaginians were dismayed, not only by the Roman commander's apparent boldness, but also by the strength of his army, which was more than double their own. Hannibal ordered his troops to prepare for action, while he himself with a few companions rode to the crest of a gently rising slope, from which he could look down on the enemy as they formed their order of battle.

'When one of his companions, an officer of high rank, remarked that the numbers of the enemy seemed amazingly large, Hannibal looked grave for a moment, and said: "There is another thing you have not noticed, Gisco, which is even more amazing." When Gisco asked what this was, he replied, "The fact that in all this enormous host opposite there isn't a single man called Gisco." The joke caught the whole party off guard and they all began to laugh: then as they rode down from the high ground they repeated it to everyone they met, so that their high spirits quickly spread among the troops and the officers of Hannibal's staff were completely over-come with laughter.

'The Carthaginians took heart when they saw this, for they thought that their general must have a great contempt for the Romans if he could laugh and joke like this in the face of danger.'

Plutarch

Making the Right Decisions

CHAPTER REVIEW

Summary

This chapter has explored the intellect necessary in a leader. No good leader relies upon chance or luck. 'Chance fights on the side of those who use their practical reason,' wrote Cicero. Practical reason is the foremost intellectual quality required in a leader. Part of the art of leadership, it must be added, is getting others to use their practical reason to the full. For the more that people share in the thinking and discussion that should precede decisions, the more committed they will tend to be when those decisions are implemented.

Practical reason is often supplemented by intuition which, if managed carefully, does have a role to play in decision-making. Imagination is also necessary, for new circumstances call for new ideas. Again, a leader does not have to be particularly imaginative personally, but should be able to stimulate and respond to imaginative thinking in the organisation. The ability to make things happen is essential. It helps immeasurably if a leader creates a climate of energetic purpose, in which people do what has to be done in a calm and collected way. Humour defuses tension in times of crisis and adds an element of enjoyment. Yet, making the right decisions is not the whole of leadership: it includes the art of inspiring willing work by informing or communicating.

Key Concepts

- Leadership is about giving direction, but it has to be the right direction. That calls for a practical intellectual ability, both natural and educated, which issues in clear thinking and correct decisions. The Greeks called it *phronesis*, which we might translate as practical judgement or transcendent common sense.

- Such thinking, as Roy Thomson says, is arduous and tiring work, but it is the chief key to success as a leader. 'If one wants to be successful, one must think,' he wrote, 'one must think until it hurts.'

- Thought and reflection on your own must be interwoven with hearing the issues discussed by your group. Feasible courses of action have to be identified, and their pros and cons debated hard. Out of such discussion arises intelligent and committed action. It produces the optimum course or way forward, not necessarily the perfect one.

- Thought precedes decision; decision leads to action. Depending on the circumstances, and especially upon the degree of crisis, as a leader you need to know when to cut off the debate and to initiate the action phase.

- Intuition is sensing situations as they really are when the evidence is incomplete. It can be distorted by anxiety or fear, and it should always be tested by reason or experiment before being accepted. 'In the country of the blind, the one-eyed man is king,' but even a leader with partial vision may sometimes rely upon the blind man's guide dog – intuition.

- Imagination is also necessary, for new circumstances call for new ideas. Again, a leader does not have to be particularly imaginative personally, but should be able to stimulate and respond to imaginative thinking in the organisation.

- The ability to make things happen is essential. It helps immeasurably if a leader creates a climate of energetic purpose, in which people do what has to be done in a calm and collected way. Humour defuses tension in times of crisis and adds an element of enjoyment. Where possible, good leaders make work more fun than fun.

Further Reflection

- In order to understand a concept such as *leadership* you have to understand also its immediate neighbours, such as *decision-making* and *communication* (the subject of the next chapter). The foundations of effective decision-making are clear thinking, intuition and imagination. Such are the complexities of change today that we need what T. E. Lawrence called 'brainy leadership'. Do you agree that the intellectual cost of living has gone up for all leaders these days?

- 'The fine art of executive decisions,' wrote Chester Barnard, 'consists in not making decisions that cannot be made effective and in not making decisions that others should make.' Do you agree?

- 'Nothing is more difficult, and therefore more precious, than to be able to decide,' wrote Napoleon. A leader's task is to help a group or organisation to overcome the difficulty of decision. Decision should be a step in the right direction, even if the end of the journey is not always clear.

- It is often said that leaders need vision and certainly great leaders show it. Vision means literally to see ahead: it is far-sightedness. Vision can also be the art or power of forming a mental image of something not actually present to the senses or never before wholly perceived or experienced in reality. It can be an imaginative and exciting concept of how things might be tomorrow. Leaders deal in visions; their stock in trade is hope. Some visions turn out to be illusions, but others are the stuff of progress. Learn to know the difference! As a leader, then, you need imagination as well as foresight if you are going to bring the gift of vision.

SIX
The Art of Inspiring While Informing

'Not geniuses, but average men require profound stimulation, incentive towards creative effort, and the nurture of great hopes.'

JOHN COLLIER

Communication is a dimension or facet of almost all that a leader does. A leader communicates in order to achieve the common task, to build the team and to meet individual needs. Leaders and the others involved must communicate with each other. It is practically impossible for a leader, short of doing everything himself or herself, to make things happen without communicating. And effective leadership implies making the right things happen at the right time.

The simple truth that things do not happen without communication highlights the importance of *how* a leader communicates. To lead at all requires communication; to lead well requires that a leader communicate effectively. In this chapter we shall look at some examples of leaders who did communicate supremely well.

The Effective Communicator

In the context of leadership, to communicate means to share with or impart to others one's thoughts and information in order to obtain a desired response. 'You make an audience say "How well he speaks!"' said Demosthenes, the greatest orator in Athenian history, to a political rival. 'I make them say, "Let us march against Philip of Macedon!"'

The primary responsibility for good communication lies with the leader. In *The Art of War*, written in China by Hsun Tzu in about 500 BC and therefore the world's oldest book on the subject, the Chinese sage emphasised the importance of clarity in giving orders. 'If the words of command are not clear and distinct, if orders are not thoroughly understood, the general is to blame.'

It is not too difficult to define effective communicators. First, they know what the aim is. What are the effects or actions that should result from this communication? Secondly, they understand the feelings and information already present in the minds of their hearers or readers. Thirdly, they put over what they have to say clearly, simply and vividly, using the most appropriate method of communication – personal conversation, telephone, presentation, report or letter.

In the context of human enterprise, leaders must both impart and receive a great deal of information daily. They need to be skilled both in putting across information with the necessary clarity and conciseness, and in listening to what others have to report. People need information from their leader or leaders on where the enterprise is going. How is the common task to be achieved? What is the plan? What information is there about the opposing forces, such as competitors, who lie in wait along the way to prevent us from achieving our goal?

However, if information flows out from the centre to the periphery in organisations, so information constantly comes back from the periphery to the centre. The work of interpreting and digesting this data is partly an intellectual one, but it is also partly a matter of communication. Does the leader actually listen to those who know what is happening operationally?

'I hear what you say,' is listening on a low level. A good listener is not necessarily the one who makes the most feedback-type physical response, such as head-nodding or grunts of comprehension. A leader who is a good listener asks questions to clarify the information and to test its validity. Above all, such a leader is genuinely open to the possibility of a change of view or adding to his or her store of information as a result of the act of listening.

The Art of Inspiring Others

Having a worthwhile vision which one wishes to impart is one important dimension in the art of inspiring others. What is vision? The word suggests the power of seeing, and by implication the ability to see further ahead and to see a wider field than others. It is, essentially, foresight together with an unusual discernment of the right way forwards. More often than not, a leader will take elements of his or her vision from others, but they still have to be internalised and synthesised. In religious contexts, a vision may be credited to supernatural sources. It may be seen in a dream, trance or ecstasy; it can be a supernatural appearance conveying a revelation. Few industrial or commercial leaders would claim divine authority for their ideas, but creative imagination does enter into the everyday visions which guide our steps forward. A visionary – one whose ideas or projects are impractical – will not last long in a leadership position. But a vision-less leader – lacking in vision or inspiration – is almost a contradiction in terms. In order to inspire others a leader first needs to be inspired. A cynic might suggest that it is the prospect of personal fame or glory, or relish in exercising power over others, which invariably motivates leaders. Neither common sense nor history entirely supports this view, although there are undoubtedly elements of truth in it. Usually it is some higher purpose or exalted cause which inspires the leader. But there is more to inspiration than communicating a vision, however exalted. An effective leader seems to impart emotion, feeling and energy as well.

It is this ability to inspire energy, to enthuse others, that history records so clearly in the lives of great leaders. Some military and political leaders in history, such as Alexander the Great, Napoleon and Hitler, saw themselves as the powerhouses of their armies and nations, constantly energising them to greater effort. That self-perception has two main disad-vantages. First, a severe physical and mental toll has to be paid by the leader. Secondly, it breeds dependence. A better approach would be to see the power or energy as already there within the people. The leader has to locate the hidden reserves of energy, to release them and to channel them into purposeful action. His or her words and example are more like triggers than dynamos.

Therefore a leader has to be concerned with emotion and motive. Those two words come from the same Latin verb 'to move'. The extent to which he has to try to stir up emotion and motive force does depend upon the situations and the followers. Where people are essentially self-motivating and fully committed, attempts to make them more so can actually be counter-productive. Armies in defeat or industrial organisations in trouble are instances where the leader must give special attention to morale, which means essentially the attitude of people to their common task. Where there is low morale, people are 'switched off' in terms of the energy devoted towards the task that has to be done. Their attitude is one of indifference or defeatism. In such situations the leader must impart a positive attitude, stir up the energies of the group and redirect them into a path that is likely to lead to results.

The Art of Rhetoric

Pericles came to hold what the Romans would later call dictatorial powers in Athens during its long struggle with Sparta. Plutarch wrote:

'Since he used his authority honestly and unswervingly in the interests of the city, he was usually able to carry the people with him by rational argument and persuasion. Still there were times when they bitterly resented his policy, and then he tightened the reins and forced them to do what was to their advantage, much as a wise physician treats a prolonged and complicated disease, allowing the patient at some moments pleasures which can do him no harm, and at others giving him caustics and bitter drugs which cure him. There were, as might be expected, all kinds of disorders to be found among a mass of citizens who possessed an empire as great as that of Athens, and Pericles was the only man capable of keeping each of these under control. He achieved this most often by using the people's hopes and fears as if they were rudders, curbing them when they were arrogant and raising their hopes or comforting them when they were disheartened. In this way he proved that rhetoric, in Plato's phrase, is the art of working upon the souls of men by means of words, and that its chief business is the knowledge of men's characters and passions which are, so to speak, the strings and stops of the soul and require a most skilful and delicate touch. The secret of Pericles' power depended, so Thucydides tells us, not merely upon his oratory, but upon the reputation which his whole course of life had earned him and upon the confidence he enjoyed as a man who had proved himself completely indifferent to bribes. Great as Athens had been when he became her leader, he made her the greatest and richest of all cities.'

Pericles. He created a confederation of cities under the leadership of Athens.
His period of rule coincided with the climax of Athenian culture and achievement.

A leader, then, is usually communicating on several levels at the same time.
While he or she is imparting information (or listening to it) he or she is
also communicating ideas and values, feelings and emotional energy. He
or she is looking for a response on this level: a change in morale which
will lead to the more energetic pursuit of an attainable success.

The Relevance of the Second World War

Both the case-studies that follow are from the military field, and in particular from British armies in the Second World War. But leadership is neither
a British nor a military phenomenon. Why, then, choose two examples of
the art of inspiring while informing from the military field?

There are three reasons. First, armies throw light on how leadership can
be given in big organisations. The chief barriers to leadership and good
communication are size and geographical distance. How do you lead and
inspire an organisation made up of many thousands of men and women
spread in units over a country or even several continents? That problem,
common to strategic leaders of large public or private corporations, appears
first in history in the context of armies. The word 'strategic,' incidentally,
comes from two Greek words for an 'army' or a large body and a 'leader':
the *strategikos* was the leader of the army.

Secondly, the Second World War brought about changes which led eventually to better leadership in industry, because thousands of officers and
men in the citizen armies of Britain experienced there for the first time
good leadership and communication. Just as the war proved to be the
seedbed of technological change – radar, computers and jet engines – so
it stimulated a change of attitude towards leadership. Slim and Montgomery
in particular were models of leadership perceived to be appropriate in a
democratic army. Their philosophy and methods had a growing influence
on British industry after the war, not least because many of the officers
and men who served under them subsequently became managerial leaders
and 'captains of industry.'

Thirdly, in every field of study there are classic examples which will always
endure. They transcend their context. No military commander, not even
among those of genius, nor any other leader in a non-military field, has
left such a clear and vivid explanation of how he thought through the
problem of leadership as Slim has done in *Defeat Into Victory* (1956). It is
still one of the best examples of a leader thinking out aloud that history
can provide. The same is true in a more limited sense of Montgomery's
speech to his staff in 1942, delivered shortly after he took command of
the Eighth Army. Down the ages generals have always been expected to
talk to their senior officers, if not to their troops, on the eve of battle. They

explain their plans. If they are leaders they will arouse emotions to a fever pitch, which is not hard to do when uncertainty, anxiety and fear are already in the air. Hatred of the enemy, justness of the cause, proffered fruits or rewards of victory, hopes of enduring fame and glory: these are some of the staple emotions or motives which must be appealed to. By their nature, such inspirational speeches are seldom recorded. By hindsight, when writing their memoirs, leaders sometimes compose the speech that they should have made! Historians are also guilty of such fictions, possibly basing their efforts on scraps of information gleaned from eye-witness accounts. Shakespeare's famous speech in *King Henry V* – 'Once more unto the breach, dear friends....' uttered before the English assault on Harfleur – is a good example of how a poet of genius can improve vastly on nature. Montgomery's speech, however, was taken down in shorthand, and so we know that we are getting the genuine article.

Case-Study: The Forgotten Army

In 1943 Slim had taken command of the Fourteenth Army. The all-conquering Japanese had driven it out of Burma, and it now sat in India, licking its wounds. Slim identified his main problem: to restore the Fourteenth Army's morale. But how was it to be done? In *Defeat Into Victory* he recollected how he thought through the problem:

> *'So when I took command, I sat quietly down to work out this business of morale. I came to certain conclusions, based not on any theory that I had studied, but on some experience and a good deal of hard thinking. It was on these conclusions that I set out consciously to raise the fighting spirit of my army.*

> *'Morale is a state of mind. It is that intangible force which will move a whole group of men to give their last ounce to achieve something, without counting the cost to themselves; that makes them feel they are part of something greater than themselves. If they are to feel that, their morale must, if it is to endure – and the essence of morale is that it should endure – have certain foundations. These foundations are spiritual, intellectual, and material, and that is the order of their importance. Spiritual first, because only spiritual foundations can stand real*

strain. Next intellectual, because men are swayed by reason as well as feeling. Material last – important, but last – because the highest kinds of morale are often met when material conditions are lowest.

'I remember sitting in my office and tabulating these foundations of morale something like this:

1 Spiritual

- There must be a great and noble object.

- Its achievement must be vital.

- The method of achievement must be active, aggressive.

- The man must feel that what he is and what he does matters directly towards the attainment of the object.

  'At any rate, our spiritual foundation was a firm one. I use the word spiritual, not in its strictly religious meaning, but as belief in a cause…

2 Intellectual

- He must be convinced that the object can be obtained; that it is not out of reach.

- He must see, too, that the organisation to which he belongs and which is striving to attain the object is an efficient one.

- He must have confidence in his leaders and know that whatever dangers and hardships he is called upon to suffer, his life will not lightly be flung away.

3 Material

- The man must feel that he will get a fair deal from his commanders and from the army generally.

- He must, as far as humanly possible, be given the best weapons and equipment for the task.

- His living and working conditions must be made as good as they can be.

General William Slim. Known affectionately to his officers and men as 'Uncle Bill', Slim was one of the outstanding leaders of the Second World War.

'It was one thing thus neatly to marshal my principles but quite another to develop them, apply them, and get them recognised by the whole army.

'We had this; and we had the advantage over our enemies that ours was based on real, not false, spiritual values. If ever an army fought in a just cause we did. We coveted no man's country; we wished to impose no form of government on any nation. We fought for the clean, the decent, the free things of life, for the right to live our lives in our own way as others could live theirs, to worship God in what faith we chose, to be free in body and mind, and for our children to be free.

We fought only because the powers of evil had attacked these things. No matter what the religion or race of any man in the Fourteenth Army, he must feel this, feel that he had indeed a worthy cause, and that if he did not defend it life would not be worth living for him or for his children. Nor was it enough to have a worthy cause. It must be positive, aggressive, not a mere passive, defensive, anti-something feeling. So our object became not to defend India, to stop the Japanese advance, or even to occupy Burma, but to destroy the Japanese Army, to smash it as an evil thing.

'The fighting soldier facing the enemy can see that what he does, whether he is brave or craven, matters to his comrades and directly influences the result of the battle. It is harder for the man working on the road far behind, the clerk checking stores in a dump, the headquarter's telephone operator monotonously plugging through his calls, the sweeper carrying out his menial tasks, the quartermaster's orderly issuing bootlaces in a reinforcement camp – it is hard for these and a thousand others to see that they too matter. Yet every one of the half-million in the army – and it was many more later – had to be made to see where his task fitted into the whole, to realise what depended on it, and to feel pride and satisfaction in doing it well.

'Now these things, while the very basis of morale, because they were purely matters of feeling and emotion, were the most difficult to put over, especially to the British portion of the army. The problem was how to instil or revive their beliefs in the men of many races who made up the Fourteenth Army. I felt there was only one way to do it, by a direct approach to the individual men themselves. There was nothing new in this; my corps and divisional commanders and others right down the scale were already doing it. It was the way we had held the troops together in the worst days of the 1942 retreat; we remained an army then only because the men saw and knew their commanders. All I did now was to encourage my commanders to increase these activities, unite them in a common approach to the problem, in the points that they would stress, and in the action they would take to see that principles became action, not merely words.

'Yet they began, as most things do, as words. We, my commanders and I, talked to units, to collections of officers, to headquarters, to little groups of men, to individual soldiers casually met as we moved around...'

No Bad Soldiers – Only Bad Officers

'The real test of leadership is not if your men will follow you in success but if they will stick by you in defeat and hardship. They won't do that unless they believe you to be honest and to have care for them.

'I once had under me a battalion that had not done well in a fight. I went to see why. I found the men in the jungle, tired and hungry, dirty, jumpy, some of them wounded, sitting miserably about doing nothing. I looked for the commanding officer, for any officer; none could be seen. Then as I rounded a bush, I realised why that battalion had failed. Collected under a tree were the officers, having a meal while the men went hungry. Those officers had forgotten the tradition of the Service that they look after their men's wants before their own. I was compelled to remind them.

'I hope they never again forgot the integrity and unselfishness that always permeate good leadership. I have never known men fail to respond to them.'

Slim, speaking to British managers (1957)

Slim then described the reactions of different nationalities to these addresses.

'I learnt too, that one did not need to be an orator to be effective. Two things were necessary: first to know what you were talking about, and, second and most important, to believe it yourself. I found that if one kept the bulk of one's talk to the material things that men were interested in, food, pay, leave, beer, mails, and the progress of operations, it was safe to end on a higher note – the spiritual foundations – and I always did.

'To convince the men in the less spectacular or less obviously important jobs that they were very much part of the army, my commanders and I made it our business to visit these units, to show an interest in them, and to tell them how we and the rest of the army depended upon them. There are in the army, and for that matter any big organisation, very large numbers of people whose existence is only remembered when something for which they are responsible goes wrong. Who thinks of the telephone operator until he fails to get his connection, of the cipher

officer until he makes a mistake in his decoding, of the orderlies who carry papers about a big headquarters until they take them to the wrong people, of the cook until he makes a particularly foul mess of the interminable bully? Yet they are important. It was harder to get this over to the Indian subordinates. They were often drawn from the lower castes, quite illiterate and used to being looked down upon by their higher-caste fellow-townsmen or villagers. With them I found I had great success by using the simile of a clock. "A clock is like an army." I used to tell them. "There's a main spring, that's the Army commander, who makes it all go; then there are other springs, driving the wheels round, those are his generals. The wheels are the officers and men. Some are big wheels, very important, they are the chief staff officers and the colonel sahibs. Other wheels are the little ones, that do not look at all important. They are like you. Yet stop one of those little wheels and see what happens to the rest of the clock! They are important!"

'We played on this very human desire of every man to feel himself and his work important, until one of the most striking things about our army was the way the administrative, labour and non-combatant units acquired a morale which rivalled that of the fighting formations. They felt they shared directly in the triumphs of the Fourteenth Army and that its success and its honour were in their hands as much as anybody's. Another way in which we made every man feel he was part of the show was by keeping him, whatever his rank, as far as was practicable in the picture concerning what was going on around him. This, of course, was easy with staff officers and similar people by means of conferences held daily or weekly when each branch or department could explain what it had been doing and what it hoped to do. At these conferences they not only discussed things as a team, but what was equally important, actually saw themselves as a team. For the men, talks by their officers and visits to the information centres which were established in every unit took the place of those conferences.

'It was in these ways we laid the spiritual foundations, but that was not enough; they would have crumbled without the others, the intellectual and the material. Here we had first to convince the doubters that our object, the destruction of the Japanese army in battle, was practicable. We had to a great extent frightened ourselves by our stories of the *superman. Defeated soldiers in their own defence have to protest that their adversary was out of the ordinary, that he had all the advantages of preparation, equipment, and terrain, and that they themselves suffered from every corresponding handicap. The harder they have run away, the more they must exaggerate the unfair superiority of the enemy. Thus many of those who had scrambled out of Burma without waiting to get to grips with the invader, or who had been in the rear areas in 1943, had the most hair-raising stories of Japanese super-efficiency. Those of us who had really fought him, believed that man for man our soldiers could beat him at his own jungle game, and that, in intelligence and skill, we could excel and outwit him.*

'We were helped, too, by a very cheering piece of news that now reached us, and of which, as a morale raiser, I made great use In August and September 1942, Australian troops had, at Milne Bay in New Guinea, inflicted on the Japanese their first undoubted defeat on land...'

Slim also ordered aggressive patrolling in the forward areas, and larger scale actions designed to build up unit and formation self-confidence.

'We had laid the first of our intellectual foundations of morale; everyone knew we could defeat the Japanese; our object was attainable.

'The next foundations, that the men should feel that they had belonged to an efficient organisation, that the Fourteenth Army was well run and would get somewhere, followed partly from these minor successes...Rations did improve, though still far below what they should be; mail began to arrive more regularly; there were signs of a welfare service...'

Other steps towards higher morale included the improvement of rest and training facilities, the reinforcement of disciplinary standards such as saluting, and the institution of a newspaper. When Admiral Mountbatten arrived to take command of the newly-formed South-East Asia Command, his presence and personal talks to the troops proved to be a 'final tonic' to morale. Meanwhile supplies of material gradually improved, but due to the priority of the war in Europe they remained small compared to the needs of the Fourteenth Army, a reason which Slim was careful to explain to the soldiers.

'These things were frankly put to the men by their commanders at all levels and, whatever their race, they responded. In my experience it is not so much asking men to fight or work with inadequate or obsolete equipment that lowers morale but the belief that those responsible are accepting such a state of affairs. If men realise that everyone above them and behind them is flat out to get the things required from them, they will do wonders, as my men did, with the meagre resources they have instead of sitting down moaning for better.

'I do not say that the men of the Fourteenth Army welcomed difficulties, but they grew to take a fierce pride in overcoming them by determination and ingenuity. From start to finish they had only two items of equipment that were never in short supply: their brains and their courage. They lived up to the unofficial motto I gave them, "God helps those who help themselves." Anybody could do an easy job, we told them. It would take real men to overcome the shortages and difficulties we should be up against – the tough chap for the tough job! We had no corps d'élite which got preferential treatment; the only units who got that were the one in front. Often, of course, they went short owing to the difficulties of transportation, but, if we had the stuff and could by hook or crook get it to them they had it in preference to those farther back. One of the most convincing evidences of morale was how those behind – staffs and units – accepted this, and deprived themselves to ensure it. I indulged in a little bit of theatricality in this myself. When any of the forward formations had to go on half rations, as throughout the campaign they often did, I used to put my headquarters on half rations too. It had little practical effect, but as a gesture it was rather valuable, and it did remind the young staff officers with healthy appetites that it was urgent to get the forward formations back to full rations as soon as possible...

'The individual, we took pains to ensure, too, was judged on his merits without undue prejudice in favour of race, caste, or class...In an army of hundreds of thousands, many injustices to individuals were bound to occur but, thanks mainly to officers commanding units, most of the Fourteenth Army would, I believe, say that on the whole they had, as individuals, a reasonably fair deal. At any rate we did our best to give it to them.

'In these and in many other ways we translated my rough notes on the foundations of moral, spiritual, intellectual, and material, into a fighting spirit for our men and a confidence in themselves and their leaders that was to impress our friends and surprise our enemies.'

Slim talking to a soldier in 1945, shortly after days of grim fighting for the last Japanese stronghold in central Burma had ended with the enemy's withdrawal.

From this passage it is clear that 'Uncle Bill', as he became affectionately known to his troops, had the power of communicating energy while imparting information. Slim's instinctive honesty of mind and deed, natural authority and humanity came across to all who met him and won him affection. Everyone found him thoughtful, dignified, courteous and considerate. Ronald Lewin, his biographer, judged him to be a genuinely humble person, in the sense of being devoid of vanity, self-complacency or *folie de grandeur*. Not that Slim lacked personal drive or worldly wisdom, but his humility disinfected his natural ambition – 'the soldier's virtue', as Shakespeare called it. His desire to get on neither tarnished his reputation nor made him pitch his hopes too high. Instead, throughout his career Slim showed an inability to set the same high valuation upon himself as others did. Self-assurance in him was balanced by a proper measure of self-questioning. 'Life seems to glide past some people without leaving an impression; others absorb and digest,' wrote Lewin. 'Slim was a pondering man, chewing the cud of experience, and it is striking how often during his time of high command he would draw on what he had deduced from episodes, often apparently trivial, which had occurred many years ago. He was always a pupil-learner in the classroom of the world.' Slim was also a teacher – one of the few exceptional leaders to be also an outstanding teacher of the British tradition of leadership.

Case-study: Montgomery

On 13th August 1942 Montgomery arrived to take command of the Eighth Army, two months before the battle of Alamein. 'The atmosphere was dismal and dreary,' he wrote in his diary. That evening he addressed the entire staff of Eighth Army Headquarters, between fifty and sixty officers. As he was their fourth Army Commander within a year, he faced a sceptical audience. The seasoned commanders and staff officers plainly doubted that this new general from Britain was the man to reverse their recent defeats and failures. Montgomery knew that he had to win their minds and hearts that evening if the morale of the broken army was to be restored to full pitch

Montgomery visited the front to get the 'feel' of the battle.

Montgomery stood on the steps of his predecessor's caravan and bade the gathering sit on the sand. He spoke without notes, looking straight at his audience. Here is what he said:

'I want first of all to introduce myself to you. You do not know me. I do not know you. But we have got to work together; therefore we must understand each other and we must have confidence in one another. I have only been here a few hours. But from what I have seen and heard since I arrived I am prepared to say, here and now, that I have confidence in you. We will then work together as a team; and together we will gain the confidence of this great army and go forward to final victory in Africa.

'I believe that one of the first duties of a commander is to create what I call "atmosphere"; and in that atmosphere, his staff, subordinate commanders and troops will live and work and fight.

'I do not like the general atmosphere I find here. It is an atmosphere of doubt, of looking back to select the next place to which to withdraw, of loss of confidence in our ability to defeat Rommel, of desperate defence measures by reserves in preparing positions in Cairo and the Delta. All that must cease. Let us have a new atmosphere... We will stand and fight here. If we can't stay here alive, then let us stay here dead.

'I want to impress on everyone that the bad times are over. Fresh divisions from the UK are now arriving in Egypt, together with ample reinforcements for our present divisions. We have 300 to 400 new Sherman tanks coming and these are actually being unloaded at Suez now. Our mandate from the Prime Minister is to destroy the Axis forces in North Africa; I have seen it written on half a sheet of notepaper. And it will be done. If anyone here thinks it can't be done, let him go at once; I don't want any doubters in this party. It can done, and it will be done; beyond any possibility of doubt...

'What I have done is to get over to you the atmosphere in which we will now work and fight; you must see that that atmosphere permeates right down through the Eighth Army to the most junior private soldier. All the soldiers must know what is wanted; when they see it coming to pass there will be a surge of confidence throughout the army.

'I ask you to give me your confidence and to have faith that what I have said will come to pass.

'There is much work to be done. The orders I have given about no further withdrawal will mean a complete change in the layout of our dispositions; also that we must begin to prepare for our great offensive...'

'The great point to remember,' Montgomery concluded at the famous initial briefing, 'is that we are going to finish with this chap Rommel once and for all. It will be quite easy. There is no doubt about it. He is definitely a nuisance. Therefore we will hit him a crack and finish with him.'

Montgomery talks to British and New Zealand troops in the Western Desert after their successful outflanking armoured thrust had compelled the enemy to abandon a defensive line shortly after the Battle of Alamein.

As Montgomery stepped down the officers rose and stood to attention. 'One could have heard a pin drop if such a thing were possible in the sand of the desert,' recollected Montgomery. 'But is certainly had a profound effect, and a spirit of hope, anyway of clarity, was born that evening.' His Chief-of-Staff, General de Guingand, agreed: 'It was one of his greatest efforts,' he wrote. 'The effect of the address was electric – it was terrific! And we all went to bed that night with new hope in our hearts, and a great confidence in the future of our Army. I wish someone had taken it down in shorthand, for it would have become a classic of its kind.' Fortunately, it was taken down in shorthand and filed away for many years before appearing in print for the first time in 1981.

Whatever Montgomery's personal faults, and however much military historians may argue about the wisdom of some of his decisions, few deny the extraordinary loyalty and trust he won from the troops he commanded. His positive approach is striking: it is a model for all leaders. Montgomery's secret was simple but painstaking. He was meticulous in explaining in detail, in advance of a battle or training exercise, precisely what his plans were and why he had arrived at them. He took immense care to explain himself personally to large numbers of those in his units, and was adamant that this sharing should be conveyed to every single soldier in his command. Montgomery could not of course know every soldier, but in a real way every soldier knew him, and they gave him their trust in a fashion unsurpassed by any other army this century.

Like the great leaders of earlier times, Slim and Montgomery wrote their own speeches. Today political leaders in particular hire speech-writers, professionals who help them to communicate more effectively. It must be difficult, however, to appear sincere when one is using borrowed words in order to inspire others. Indeed, it may be a contradiction in terms to suppose that such speeches could ever be inspiring. Matters are made worse by the advent of radio and television. Although in some ways these media have been boons to leaders of nations or large organisations, they have also renewed an old temptation for leaders: to believe that they can create and sustain an 'image' of leadership, rather than having to develop within themselves the real qualities and abilities of a leader.

The Effects of Telecommunications

The Greek word for 'far off' supplies the *tele* in telephone, telegraph and television. They are all forms of telecommunication: communicating at a distance. Until comparatively recent times a leader was limited by the range of the human voice. With a trained voice a speaker could be heard by some thousands of people if they sat on a hillside or, better still, in an amphitheatre. The invention of the microphone and loudspeaker increased that range, but radio brought a new dimension. Film, first in the form of cinema newsreel and then as television and video, added another dimension. How does the advent of telecommunication affect leadership?

The most immediate effect has been on leaders in the political field. In order to get over their message before the advent of modern telecommunications, political leaders had to rely upon oratory at public meetings or political assemblies, and their ability to write speeches, pamphlets or books for publication. Now oratory does not come across well on the radio: a more conversational style is much more effective. Franklin D. Roosevelt mastered the technique in his famous 'fireside chats' to the American people. He received some 460,000 letters of appreciation after the first one.

As Prime Minister from 1940, by means of radio broadcasts Winston Churchill roused the nation to withstand privation and air raids, and to face the prospect of a Nazi invasion. By the end of the war, however, his rhetoric was wearing thin.

Churchill subjected himself to a television test but wisely decided that it was not the medium for him. Television does enable us to see political leaders close up: they appear to look at us and talk to us as individuals in our own homes. The rise of the medium has coincided with the rise in importance of leadership among those who govern. As electors we scrutinise our would-be governors for signs of leadership. Television is a cruel medium to those who do not look the part.

This emphasis upon the supposed or actual leadership competence of candidates for high political office must be set against a background of growing political consensus. For, in politics, all nations are moving down the road of what has been called Social Capitalism. This is essentially a value-system. In it, moral value is given in varying degrees to money, (euphemistically called wealth creation), society, the individual and the environment. The relative emphasis placed upon these four values differs partly according to the situation and partly according to the particular tradition of each nation or each major political party within it. Within the growing consensus of Social Capitalism, there is little room for real policy differences. Therefore the consumer in the shape of the elector has to be offered the 'extra' factor – the ingredient of leadership.

Churchill broadcasts to the people during the Second World War. These radio addresses did much to maintain the nation's morale and to build its sense of common purpose.

Some politicians seem to believe that it is the image of leadership that wins votes, not necessarily the substance of it. Without experience in the office of President or Prime Minister, it is difficult for a candidate to present that image. Senator Robert Dole, an unsuccessful candidate for the Republican nomination in 1988, was reduced to telling the electors on television that he was a leader. That is a mistake. No one should call himself or herself a leader: that is a tribute that other people may or may not pay to one.

Most aspirants to high political office get specialist help to enable them to put over the image of relaxed, friendly but confident leadership on television. President Ronald Reagan had the advantage of a previous career as a professional actor. His former Chief-of-Staff at the White House, Donald T. Regan, wrote about the theatrical nature of his presidency. He described him as a star who walked to chalk marks like an actor and was at his happiest watching old movies or discussing early days in Hollywood. 'The President's daily schedule,' he wrote, 'was something like a shooting script, scenes were rehearsed and acted out... not always in sequence; the staff was like the crew, invisible behind the lights, watching the performance.'

A certain theatricality, it must be said, has always gone hand-in-hand with leadership. All leaders have to act the part on their off-days. Some, like Alexander and Nelson, Napoleon and Montgomery, also had a well-developed sense of drama. Television is more revealing than the theatre.

True, interviews can be stage-managed and partly packaged like commercials, but there are limits to what the public relations specialists can do for a politician. The public is much more discerning and knowledgeable about leadership. Electors have learnt, from experience, that there is a difference between the rhetoric of leadership and its reality. In the future politicians are going to have to find better ways of developing their potential as leaders, ways which may include periods of study and reflection about the nature and practice of leadership in a democratic society. It will not be enough for them to master the methods of merely presenting themselves as leaders.

The Art of Inspiring While Informing

CHAPTER REVIEW

Summary

Communication is the sister of leadership. Essentially, in this context, it means the ability to impart information to others in order to secure a desired and real effect. Good leaders, however, are not impersonal transmitters of information. They also communicate their inner thoughts, emotions and spirit. In particular, they impart energy. They have the ability to inspire while they inform. As Lord Rosebery said of William Pitt the Elder: 'It is not merely the thing that is said, but the man who says it that counts, the character which breathes through the sentences.'

An effective communicator needs also to be a good listener. Today we need listening leaders at all levels – leaders who are genuinely open to new ideas or ways of doing things. For no single person knows all the answers. A good leader tends to show empathy – the capacity for participating in another's feelings and ideas.

Large organisations such as armies or industrial corporations, by virtue of their size and geographical spread, create major communication problems for leaders. Although systems and methods of communication, including telecommunications, have a part to play, a wise leader will seize or make opportunities to impart his energetic vision – in his own words – to key groups in the organisation. He or she makes the 'little wheels' feel important, not just the next level down. For a leader who is invisible and inaudible to all but a select few is seldom effective and certainly not great.

Key Concepts

- Two-way communication is inseparable from leadership. It involves the basic skills of speaking and listening, reading and writing. A good communicator is well prepared, clear, simple and concise. Listening leaders are still comparatively rare. To listen well you must listen not only by giving thoughtful, attention but by opening your third inner ear to the leanings and feelings that lie like music behind the words. Listen with your eyes, too, for so much communication is still non-verbal.

- Communicating at the leadership level is not just about imparting information or ideas; it is a stirring up of energy and enthusiasm for the work in hand. It is not a matter of the leader imparting his or her own energy, but releasing the greatness that is there already.

- 'Anyone can hold the helm when the seas are calm.' The test of your powers of communication come when the seas are rough with change, and people feel disorientated and out of touch. Can you communicate hope when all about you are doubting the promise of the future?

- Both Slim and Montgomery served as strategic leaders of very large multinational organisations. Both had a passion for good communication. Although neither could be described as naturally charismatic, they mastered the art of inspiring while informing. They kept to the basics of the three circles, and added the descant of inspiration.

- The effect or result of good communication in organisations – downwards, upwards and sideways – is that everyone feels that they are partners in the common enterprise.

Further Reflection

- Good leaders are not impersonal transmitters of information. They also communicate their inner thoughts, emotions and spirit. In particular, they impart energy. They have the ability to inspire while they inform. As Lord Roseby said of William Pitt the Elder: 'It is not merely the thing that is said, but the man who says it that counts, the character which breathes through the sentences.'

- Trust and good communication go hand-in-hand. Where there is trust even seemingly bad news can be communicated. The more you communicate the plain truth or the realities of the situation, the more people will trust and support you. ('The bird carries the wings, but the wings carry the bird.') Techniques have a place, but truth is the great communicator.

- Large organisations such as armies or industrial corporations, by virtue of their size and geographical spread, create major communication problems for leaders. Although systems and methods of communication, including telecommunication, have a part to play, a wise leader will seize or make opportunities to impart his or her own energetic vision – in their own words – to key groups in the organisation. He or she makes the 'little wheels' feel important, not just the next level down. A leader who is invisible and inaudible to all but a select few is seldom effective and certainly not great. What is going to be your policy when you become an operational or strategic leader?

PART 2

SEVEN
The Roots of British Tradition

*'He that would have
pure water must go to
the fountain-head.'*

ITALIAN PROVERB

This chapter identifies the three strands of tradition which intermingled and gave shape to a new concept of leadership in Britain and colonial America. The first of these strands is already familiar: it is the tradition that stems from the Athens of Socrates and Xenophon. The second strand, also mentioned already, came to Britain from Judaea embedded in the Old and New Testaments of the Christian Bible. The third root, by far the strongest, was native to the British Isles: the immemorial custom of the tribes who inhabited the islands before the coming of the Romans. The slow fusion of these traditions over centuries, among a people who, like the Greeks, loved personal freedom passionately and hated to be dominated by their rulers, produced a concept of leadership that was distinctively British. The emergence of the United States of America as an English-speaking nation, and the rise of the British Empire, helped to spread that concept far beyond the shores of the British Isles.

Eagles of Rome

When Julius Caesar first invaded Britain, with two Roman legions, the Britons opposed his landing on the beaches, hurling their javelins and galloping their horses into the shallows. Caesar admitted that the legionaries, used to fighting on dry land and terrified by these unfamiliar tactics, lacked their usual dash and drive.

'As this critical moment,' he recalled, 'the standard-bearer of the Tenth Legion, after calling on the gods to bless the legion through his act, shouted: "Come on, men! Jump, unless you want to betray your standard to the enemy! I, at any rate, shall do my duty to my country and my commander." He leapt down from the transport ship into the sea and waded forward with the eagle. The rest of his cohort were not going to disgrace themselves. Cheering loudly they followed him into the white-foamed green sea, and when the men in the other ships saw them they quickly followed their example.'

The conquest of most of Great Britain – the largest of the British Isles beyond the western coast of Europe – brought to Rome its most westerly province. Rome had already conquered much of Western Europe. Italy, Greece, Spain and a large part of modern France already experienced the benefits of Roman rule.

> 'Let it be your task, Roman, to control the nations with your power (these shall be your arts) and to impose the way of peace; to spare the vanquished and subdue the proud!'

As the words of Virgil in the *Aeneid* suggest, Rome saw itself as more than a conqueror. By its military might Rome brought peace to a warring world. Law and order, together with the more material benefits of cities and towns, roads and aquaducts, followed in the wake of the victorious legions. What might the tribes of Western Europe have learned from the Romans about leadership, a quality which Rome prizes so highly?

In the course of time British tribesmen enlisted in auxiliary units of the Roman Army and served in all parts of the Empire. Some rose to be standard-bearers and centurions. Around campfires they may have heard their Roman companions tell stories of Julius Caesar, one of the great leaders that Rome produced. Before invading Britain, Caesar had campaigned in Gaul for eight years. There, according to Plutarch, 'he proved himself to be as good a soldier and a commander as any of those who have been most admired for their leadership and shown themselves to be the greatest generals. His ability to secure the affection of his men and to get the best out of them was remarkable.'

The Roman Army worked reasonably well operationally without inspiring leadership. It was military machine held together by the ropes of discipline. Compliance with orders was achieved by the exercise of power; whether or not the men were willing was a matter of secondary importance to some commanders and of no importance to others. But the Roman soldier had the same human nature and desire to excel as his Greek counterpart. Greatness was always latent in the legions, awaiting the call to life from a leader of genius. Caesar was such a leader. Under Caesar's eye the Roman legions became 'an unconquered and unconquerable army.'

Julius Caesar. The greatest of Rome's generals who developed his gift for leadership by hard study and through arduous experience.

Caesar's very presence seemed to transform ordinary professional legionaries into men of extraordinary valour. 'Soldiers who in other campaigns had not shown themselves to be any better than average,' wrote Plutarch, 'became irresistible and invincible and ready to confront any danger, once it was a question of fighting for Caesar's honour and glory.' Plutarch cited examples, such as this one:

'There was an occasion in Britain when some of the leading centurions had got themselves into a marshy place with water all round and were being set upon by the enemy. An ordinary soldier, while Caesar himself was watching the fighting, rushed into the thick of it and, after showing the utmost daring and gallantry, drove the natives off and rescued the centurions. Finally, with great difficulty, he made his own way back after all the rest, plunged into the muddy stream, and, without his shield, sometimes swimming and sometimes wading, just managed to get across. Caesar and those with him were full of admiration for the man and shouted out to him in joy as they came to meet him; but the soldier was thoroughly dejected and, with tears in his eyes, fell at Caesar's feet, and asked to be forgiven for having let go of his shield.'

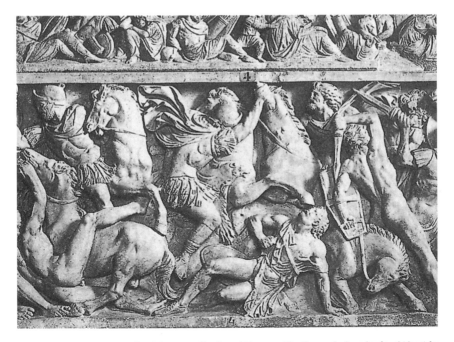

Battle between Gauls and Romans. The Roman legionaries fought best for leaders who shared their dangers, hardships and exertions to the full.

Apart from his open-minded generosity with the rewards of victory – a trait which British tribal war-leaders would recognise – Caesar led by example. There was no danger which he was not willing to face, no form of hard work from which he excused himself. Like Alexander, his great exemplar, Caesar had a passion for distinction which enabled him to overcome disadvantages of a slightly built physique, and a proneness to migraine and epileptic fits. 'Yet so far from making his poor health and excuse for living an easy life,' continued Plutarch, 'he used warfare as a tonic for his health. By long hard journeys, simple diet, sleeping night after night in the open, and rough living he fought off his illness and made his body strong enough to stand up to anything.'

When Caesar's army in Gaul faced the German tribes whose incursions threatened the province, Caesar saw that many of this officers – particularly those young men of good families who had come out from Rome under the impression that a military campaign would mean comfortable living and easy money – were nervous at the prospect of fighting the formidable and frightening Germans. So Caesar summoned them and told them to go back to Rome; they must not run any undue risks, he suggested, in their present cowardly and soft state of mind. Caesar himself proposed to take just the Tenth Legion with him and to march against the Germans. He did not expect to find the enemy stronger than the fiercest of Gallic tribes had been, he declared, and he would not be thought a worse general than Marius. As a result of this speech it is recorded that the Tenth Legion sent a deputation to thank him for his compliment, and the men of other legions were furious with their own commanders. The whole army was now willing and eager for action and they followed Caesar once more to victory.

Marius, whom Caesar mentioned in this speech, had been responsible for a major reorganisation of the Roman Army in the second century BC. He was cast in the Spartan mould. As a young man, Marius served on the staff of a Roman army then campaigning in North Africa. Although lacking in wealth and eloquence, he had an intense confidence in himself, coupled with a great capacity for hard work. In writing about this period of Marius' life Plutarch made some comments about Roman soldiers which are both illuminating and generally applicable to all soldiers, if not to all workers:

> 'It was a hard war, but Marius was not afraid of any undertaking, however great, and was not too proud to accept any tasks, however small. The advice he gave and his foresight into what was needed marked him out among the officers of his own rank, and he won the affection of the soldiers by showing that he could live as hard as they did and endure as much. Indeed it seems generally to be the case that our labours are eased when someone goes out of his way to share them with us; it has the effect of making the labour not seem forced. And what a Roman soldier likes most is to see his general eating his ration of bread with the rest, or sleeping on an ordinary bed, or joining

in the work of digging a trench or raising a palisade. The commanders whom they admire are not so much those who distribute honours and riches as those who take a share in their hardships and dangers; they have more affection for those who are willing to join in their work than for those who indulge them in allowing them to be idle.'

Marius did get himself elected Consul seven times, the first Roman in history to do so. But he was no political leader. In the Senate, when his victories had already brought him a huge reputation, Marius used to behave quite timidly if hecklers attacked him. All the steadfastness and firmness which he showed in battle seemed to drain from him when he stood up to speak in a popular assembly, so that he could not cope with even the most ordinary compliments or criticisms. Clearly his style of military command was not transferable to the world of politics, where essentially equal citizens look up to someone for a lead. Marius lived to be seventy, his harsh nature turning savage and vindictive by the possession of supreme power. He gave the Romans their first real taste of tyranny. It was the fear of another dose of such tyranny that led to Caesar's assassination.

These examples of Roman leadership, gathered from the books of such authors as Virgil and Livy, Caesar and Plutarch, were not wasted. Milton's definition of a good book – 'the life blood of a master-spirit, embalmed and treasured up to a life beyond life' – applied supremely to these classical works. Later generations in Western Europe would feed upon them, learning from the best and worst examples of Roman leadership, becoming aware of themselves as spiritual heirs to the masters of a great empire. As time went on, Europeans would reach behind the Roman shield to the Greek legacy of stories and thought about the nature of authority and leadership in civilised society. In this treasure chest of classical literature they found much that mirrored – and much that might correct – their own ancient tribal customs of democracy and leadership.

The Tribal Legacy

The thirty or so large tribes which the Romans found in Britain had their own tradition of leadership, which they shared with their cousins on the mainland of North-Western Europe. The Roman historian Tacitus has left us some clear glimpses of how they organised themselves. 'About minor matters, the chiefs consult; about greater matters, all consult. But even those things which are kept for the general opinion are fully considered by the chiefs,' he wrote. The tribes had no fixed times for their general assemblies, and two or three days could be lost in calling all the men together. They came to the meetings fully armed. After the priests called for silence, the first to speak in debate would be the king, a chieftain or some other wise elder. Vote was by voice and acclamation.

The German tribes – Angles, Saxons, Wends and others – who invaded and settled in Britain after the departure of the legions, practised much the same system. So did the tribes from Scandinavia, collectively known as the Danes or Vikings, who later invaded England (land of the Angles). Their councils or assemblies were called *things*; one held in the *hus*, or house of a king or war-leader, as opposed to a general tribal assembly, was called a *hus-thing*, which gave us the word 'hustings' – used now of any place where politicians make election speeches.

Tribes tended to have two kinds of leader: the chief and the war-leader. There are considerable variations on this theme, but it is remarkably constant. The tribal chief was more permanent, whereas the war-leader could be temporary. There could be more than one potential war-leader vying for a following among the tribesmen. In some tribes, the position or role of war-leader did become an office. Where the tribes were constantly at war, of course, the war-leader tended to be the tribal chief as well.

The chief exercised more peaceful functions. His main responsibility was to administer justice according to tribal law or tradition. A wise chief judged in a firm and impartial way, impressing those who sat with him in his informal court of tribal counsellors and holy men. If the tribe was large, as Tacitus said, the chief would consult about major matters with the heads of its major clans or family groups. By maintaining the common laws and traditions that bound them together, the chief preserved the unity of the tribe. He also personified its spirit and life. For its part the tribe owed him their loyalty and, on occasion, their lives.

The Bedouin Sheikh

In her account of her travels in *Bedouin Tribes of the Euphrates*, the Victorian writer Lady Anne Blunt described the Bedouin tribe as 'the purest form of democracy to be found in the world.' A later authority on the Bedouin, Wilfred Thesiger, described the role of the tribal chief thus:

'A Bedu sheikh has no paid retainers on whom he can rely to carry out his orders. He is merely the first among equals in a society where every man is intensely independent and quick to resent any hint of autocracy. His authority depends in consequence on the force of his own personality and his skill in handling men.'

Arabian Sands (1959)

From the account of Tacitus and from our knowledge of later tribes, it is clear that a tribal chief had to have considerable personal ability as a leader in order to lead the tribe effectively. That necessity faced tribes with the perennial problem of succession. Tribesmen did seem to believe that the attributes of fathers were inherited by their sons (mothers may have been regarded as mere vehicles in the process, not genetic contributors). Moreover, a chief's son had the advantage of being able to learn the art, so to speak, by his father's example and tuition. But experience taught them that a number of things could go wrong with natural succession. Despite their birth and upbringing, some crown princes simply lacked the necessary personal authority and qualities which the tribe needed in its leader. The wiser tribes chose their chiefs with some care from among the relatives of the king, a brother or a younger son for example, or from certain pre-eminent families – the forerunners of the nobility. The process was fraught with difficulty, however, for the 'dispossessed' heir-presumptive could become troublesome.

In Ireland, today, the prime minister's title is *Taoiseach*, tribal chief. Succession in the Irish Celtic tribes, too, was not necessarily hereditary, although it tended to run in certain families. The deputy prime minister's title, *An Tanaiste*, is also a relic of those tribal days, for it means the one next in line, the heir apparent to the tribal chief.

The bond between the English tribal warrior and his war-leader was extremely close. As warriors could choose whether or not to accompany him, they had to make a judgement about his leadership, courage, and abilities as a soldier before venturing the lives. For his part, a war-leader would only choose men who would not betray or desert him in battle. He also had the useful prerogative of dividing out the booty and could therefore offer them the incentives of reward. Men loved a generous leader, one who gave out spoils fairly and according to each man's just deserts, or beyond them. In war, the mutual loyalty engendered between war-leader and follower took precedence over even the closest family ties. It was lasting dishonour to run away, even when the leader lay dead on the field.

Apart from gifts of captured horses and weapons, wrote Tacitus, a tribal chief would reward his men with gold or silver rings and other personal ornaments. These symbols of honour, forerunners of the orders of chivalry on their chains or medals-and-ribbons, were especially coveted. In Anglo-Saxon poetry, written in England, the war-leader was often called 'the giver of rings' and 'the bestower of treasure.' The English word 'lord' comes from *hlaford*, 'loaf-giver.' The war-leader gave bread to the warriors who brought their own spears, swords and shields to fight under his leadership.

Relations between the tribal chief and the war-leader could become a major issue in tribal politics. Young and successful war-leaders, for instance, could become arrogant, especially if their followers flattered them overmuch in those victory feasts into the night, the great log fires crackling on the hearth, when silver-mounted drinking-horns were filled many times with the potent beer which the Germanic tribes in particular loved to drink. The beginnings of future troubles and dissensions could often be traced back to such feasts.

Alfred the Great

The first Christians to reach Britain were probably men serving in the Roman legions. Like the Jews, the early Christians claimed exemption from military service, but before the end of the second century many Christians were serving in the army. The enterprise of sowing more seeds in ground ploughed up by the Roman conquerors attracted some remarkable teachers and preachers in the Word. Their courage as much as their faith must have impressed the chiefs of the pagan tribes of Europe. The decision to change the tribe's religion, thereby abandoning immemorial custom, must have been a momentous one. It called for considerable leadership from the tribal chief or king, and a certain amount of compromise from the Christian missionaries.

Alfred the Great. A thirteenth century statue which captures
something of the energy of this remarkable leader.

As the sun of Rome, gradually losing energy, sank ever lower in the sky,
new Christian stars began to appear in the firmament of Europe. Roman
missionaries converted almost all Saxon tribal kingdoms in Britain. But
when they first invaded England, the Danes came as exuberant pagans,
worshippers of Wodin, Thor and Freya, who live on today in our names
of three weekdays. Therefore the Norsemen posed a double threat to body
and soul of Christian England.

Anglo-Saxon kings – Alfred, Edgar and Ethelred. Christianity and classical
learning made further headway in the parts of England they controlled.

At first, the Vikings came in their longships to rob, plunder and pillage.
Then they began to winter in England, and finally they made more permanent settlements. To cope with the crisis posed by their presence, the English
needed a leader with the wisdom of Pericles and the tenacity of Caesar.
They found him in Alfred, King of Wessex. Like his predecessors and successors as kings of Wessex, Alfred was destined to spend much of his life as
a war-leader. He served his brother in that capacity and, upon his death,
was chosen to be king in his place, despite the fact that he was not next
in line of succession. With Danish longships hunting in packs like wolves,
and the annual invasion fleets growing ever larger, this was not a time to
sit the dead king's heir – a young boy – on the throne of Wessex. Already
the kingdoms of Northumbria and East Anglia had fallen to the Danes,
while Mercia was under threat. Wessex alone remained free and defiant.

Asser's use of the sea analogy takes us back to the fundamental meaning of the Anglo-Saxon word for leader. A helmsman in those days was usually both captain of the longship and leader in battle. At sea, the English warriors or their Viking opponents, having stored weapons and hung outboard their painted shields, would man the oars and work the sail. The steersman guided the ship by a steering oar over the right hand or *starboard* side. The helmsman-leader also had knowledge of the stars and could use it for navigation. He was in direct contact with the sea, the environment of the ship's company; in a storm he had to wrestle with his oar in the white-foaming high seas, proving himself worthy of his trust. It required some mastery of nature in the form of a subtle and sensitive exploration of how to extract the most power from wind and water. Still, today, the best helmsmen are those who find and hold that invisible line of balance along which the elements seem to join in driving the boat forwards.

Alfred's incessant campaigns against the Danes, fight after fight where he led his soldiers in person, gave England the respite it needed so badly. In 886, the year Alfred entered the old Roman capital of Londinium, all the English people, except those in land captured by the Danes, submitted to his rule. Alfred set about uniting them with a common law for all the land.

Having first collected the laws of Wessex, Mercia and Kent, he had a new code drawn up incorporating the best practice in them which would be acceptable to all.

Alfred changed the culture of England. He did so by promoting classical learning and Christianity, which in those days went hand-in-hand. Here, as on the battlefield, Alfred led by example, first by learning to read and write in English, and then by mastering the Latin language. Among other works, he translated from Latin into English Bede's *Ecclesiastical History*, Pope Gregory's *Cura Pastoralis*, and the universal history of the Church Father named Orosius, adding notes to it from his own knowledge. He wrote a letter to each of his bishops exhorting them to foster learning. He ordered that all the sons of free Englishmen should, if they had the means, go to school and be educated in the English tongue. As another sign of the breadth of his interests, the notes Alfred made on two voyages of exploration have survived.

Alfred translated the first fifty psalms from Latin into English. He must have often reflected upon their author, King David, who like himself had fought against the heathen, and who, also like himself, had gone into hiding from his enemies before emerging to win victories for God. Alfred vested himself in David's integrity. He, too, sought to be 'a man after God's own heart.'

It was Englishmen in the seventeenth century who bestowed on Alfred his proud title 'the Great' – the only English king to be so honoured. They saw Alfred as their true spiritual ancestor, intent upon making the nation both Christian and learned in Latin – the only gateway in those days to a knowledge of the civilizations of Greece and Rome. They attributed to Alfred the foundation of Oxford University; to another Christian king, Sigebert of the East Angles, they gave the credit for planting the sister university beside the River Cam.

Alfred's great-nephew, Edgar was the first acknowledged King of all England. At his coronation in Bath Abbey, in 973, the earliest form of the Coronation Service still used at the crowning of England's monarchs was introduced. Its solemn rites included the royal prostration and oath, the consecration and anointing, the anthem, 'Zadok the Priest' (which linked the Anglo-Saxon kings with those of ancient Israel), and the investiture with sword, sceptre and rod of justice. Behind these rites lay the idea that an anointed king and his people formed a partnership under God. After that sacramental act, loyalty to the Crown became a Christian obligation. The ideal of patriotism, centering round the Crown, began to take shape in men's minds, superseding the old loyalties to tribal chief or war-lord.

The Round Table of King Arthur. This version was made for the use of King Edward III and the Knights of the Garter at Windsor Castle. It is now displayed on a wall in the Castle Hall at Winchester.

The Roots of British Tradition

CHAPTER REVIEW

Summary

In King Alfred the three major strands of cultural tradition in the West symbolically come together: tribal, classical and biblical. His leadership in war and peace also helped to ensure that they would continue to infuse together in the cauldron of English society. In the tribal society of his day men saw themselves as essentially equal. No chieftain could dominate a tribe by force; he had to lead it by prestige, persuasion and example. The classical tradition was only slowly assimilated, not least because few Englishmen before the days of Alfred could read Latin. As that door into the past gradually opened, English leaders could match themselves against such great leaders as Julius Caesar. But Christianity held up to them the ideals of leadership: moral integrity, humility before God and service to one's fellow men. From these materials, as we shall see next, the English forged a new and richer concept – the gentleman leader.

Key concepts

- Part of human nature is the desire to excel – very often this latent 'greatness' needs to be merely sparked into life by a leader.

- Great leaders go further and draw from ordinary peoples extraordinary performance.

- Great leaders lead by example – often sharing in the difficult conditions, hardships and physical toils of their people.

- Leaders can win valuable support by seeking as much consensus as possible in decision-making. Wise leaders always do!

Further reflection

- How far is the old tribal tendency to separate the roles of Chief (preserving the unity of a tribe and personifying its spirit) and War-leader now echoed in calls to separate the Chairman and Chief Executive roles?

- How important do you consider it to be that a leader sees him or herself as 'first among equals'?

EIGHT
The Gentleman Leader

'He has a look upon his face that I would fain call master.'
'What is that?'
'Authority.'

SHAKESPEARE, KING LEAR

During the centuries that followed Alfred the Great the concept of leadership was both refined by further thought and spread more widely to 'commoners' as opposed to the feudal nobility. The more natural leaders forced their way to the front despite the dominance of a ruling class. Like the Greeks, however, the English in the age of the Renaissance believed that a good education had a vital part to play in producing such natural leaders, gentlemen who were fitted by their qualities and abilities to govern in peace or war. Such an education, in contrast to the pernicious doctrines of Machiavelli, was moral and Christian in its guiding assumptions about leadership. By the reign of Elizabeth these developments had become clear. Some of the more adventurous commoners would take this new understanding of leadership with them to the New World.

The Elizabethan society that Shakespeare portrayed in his plays was a hierarchical one. It was far removed from the democratic tribal culture recorded by Tacitus more than a millennium earlier. England was ruled by the monarch who gave the age her name. She was supported in council by her lords and bishops – successors to the tribal chief's council of lesser chiefs, elders and holy men. The gentry came next and were largely responsible for local government in the shires. Then came the lesser merchants, followed by tradesmen, and, at the bottom, the lower orders of labourers. There were even social uniforms, for sumptuary laws laid down what kind of clothes could be worn by each station.

Democracy was limited to property owners in shire and borough electing representatives to the House of Commons. Parliament met at the monarch's will, however, and it enjoyed only limited privileges and responsibilities. Everyone knew their place. Deference and obedience to one's betters was encouraged from the cradle upwards. As a very old rhyme used to teach manners, says:

'Speak when you're spoken to,
Come when you're called.
Shut the door after you –
And that will be all.'

Despite internal troubles and external threats, caused mainly by the splitting of Christianity into Protestant and Catholic camps, England was a not unhappy country during Queen Elizabeth's reign, and indeed during the centuries that both preceded and followed it. English society worked. The English became more aware of their good fortune. Shakespeare expressed that consciousness in glowing patriotic verse:

'This royal throne of kings, this scept'red isle,
This earth of majesty, this seat of Mars,
This other Eden, demi-paradise,
This fortress built by Nature for herself
Against infection and the hand of war,
This happy breed of men, this little world,
This precious stone set in the silver sea,
Which serves it in the office of a wall,
Or as a moat defensive to a house,
Against the envy of less happier lands;
This blessed plot, this earth, the realm, this England.'

As in Athens, it was possible in England to move up the social ladder. As Thomas Fuller wrote, 'An English Yeoman is a gentleman in ore.' The Church had provided the first means whereby poor but bright boys could better themselves. The City of London provided other routes for the Dick Whittingtons of England. Thus two of Shakespeare's contemporaries, a humble cloth-worker in Guildford and his wife, could produce a son, George Abbot, who became Archbishop of Canterbury. Of his brothers, Robert ended his days as Bishop of Salisbury, and Maurice served as Lord Mayor of London.

The Impact of Education

Again as in Athens, it was free education that created the new opportunities for young men to rise to positions of leadership in society. The Elizabethans took seriously the dictum of Diogenes: 'The foundation of every state is the education of its youth.'

Without the free grammar school in Guildford, for example, George Abbot would not have gone to Oxford, where he became Master of Balliol College and Dean of Winchester at the age of thirty-five. Guildford Grammar School was one of the numerous new schools which had been founded in the reign of Elizabeth's half-brother, Edward VI. It borrowed its statutes from St Paul's School, which John Colet, Dean of St Paul's, had refounded with the help of his friend Erasmus in the previous reign. These Renaissance scholars were leaders of a European educational revolution, with England in its forefront. Under the patronage of the Tudors, they intended to transform English society into a Christian Athens. Like so many revolutionaries, these learned men and their patrons could not have foreseen all the consequences that would flow from their reforms.

Ad fontes – 'Back to the fountains' – was the personal motto of one of their colleagues, Thomas Linacre, an eminent doctor and founder-member of the Royal College of Physicians. But it can stand equally well as the slogan of both Renaissance and Reformation. Both movements sought to recover golden ages. St Paul's School, for example, was the first in the country to teach Greek as well as Latin to the sons of the nobility, gentry and merchants. Its 153 free places (the number of fish in the miraculous draught recorded in St John's Gospel) were open to children of all nations. For the leaders of the Renaissance wanted to transcend nationality. They saw themselves, like Socrates, as citizens of the world and pioneers of a new universal order of peace, religion and harmony.

The progress of the Reformation destroyed the hope of that vision being realised in the lifetime of Colet, Erasmus, More and Linacre. Through emphasis on the Bible (now widely translated into the vernacular language) as the only source and authority for true Christianity, Protestants in Europe studied what Jesus and Paul had to say about the nature of leadership in church and state. The revolutionary impact of the return to Scripture was already evident on the continent: the progress of the Reformation swept away a whole segment of the medieval hierarchy – Pope, bishops and abbots – and pronounced that all Christians were equal before God; there were to be no priests, but leaders in the form of 'ministers', or servants, and 'pastors', or shepherds. The English compromised on this point. They abolished the Pope's authority and privatised the monasteries, but left intact archbishops and the bishops, archdeacons and deans.

Richard Baxter

Men such as Richard Baxter, a famous Puritan minister in the seventeenth century, came to look for Christ-like leadership in the Church. Writing of bishops who persecuted separatists and drove them out of the land to America, he said:

'I saw that he that will be loved, must love; and he that rather chooses to be more feared than loved, must expect to be hated, or loved but diminutively. And he that will have children, must be a father; and he that will be a tyrant must be content with slaves.'

The new grammar schools that sprang up, made possible by the growing wealth of England, were intended to provide the nation with both educated rulers and educated subjects. The philosophy or purpose behind them is well summarised in the statutes of Halifax Grammar School, founded in 1591 by a Puritan wool-merchant and his son – 'There is nothing that can more advance the flourishing and constant happiness of any kingdom or commonwealth, than in the advancement of divine and human knowledge, the undoubted mother of all good policy in the magistrate, and of all right obedience in the people.' Evidently, mutual understanding was fostered between gentlemen and the ranks immediately below them. As a whole the grammar schools, unlike the colleges of Oxford and Cambridge, did not suffer the fate of being recast in the gentleman's image. Within their walls, as one celebrated Elizabethan headmaster put it, the 'cream of the commons' associated together, be they sons of gentlemen or tradesfolk. Some of the grammar schools (which we now perversely call public schools) were indeed later recast in the gentleman's image.

Harrow School, founded by John Lyon, yeoman farmer of Preston, for poor boys, was gradually changed until all free places were eliminated. The Lower School of John Lyon was then founded to make amends, but it also became a fee-paying public school. On the other hand universities continued to give places to poor students, even some who had to wait on wealthier students to earn their keep.

John Brinsley, in his book *A Consolation for Our Grammar Schools* (1622), quite clearly recognised the responsibility of the nation's schools for developing leaders. As Brinsley, a leading schoolmaster of the day, wrote to his fellow teachers:

> *'We are they who help to make or mar all. They that are the flower of our nation, and those who become leaders of the rest, are committed to our education and instruction.'*

For those who could not read Greek or Latin authors in the original, Elizabethan authors offered a plethora of translations. Shakespeare's plays, such as *Julius Caesar, Anthony and Cleopatra,* and *Timon of Athens,* served to popularise still further the personalities and political issues of the Greek and Roman worlds. The actors in Shakespeare's plays wore Elizabethan clothes; but, by identifying with them, the Elizabethans saw themselves in white togas as Greeks and Romans reborn.

Within the context of education in grammar school and university, the instruction on leadership was mainly through the medium of classical history and biography. But Elizabethan teachers also drew upon the philosophical tradition of Greece, where there was the beginnings of a more analytical approach. It was dominated by Aristotle, Plato's great pupil. His teaching on leadership had a direct and profound influence on the English concept.

Frontispiece of *The Boke named the Governour.* Sir Thomas Elyot's book was part of a growing literature aimed at educating leaders.

Leadership Qualities

In the *Cyropaedia* Xenophon had listed the qualities of an ideal ruler as: temperance, justice, sagacity, amiability, presence of mind, tactfulness, humanity, sympathy, helpfulness, courage, magnanimity, generosity and considerateness. Aristotle reduced the qualities of leadership to just four: justice, temperance, prudence and fortitude. In the sixteenth century they became the starting point for the English exploration of the nature of leadership. The Renaissance writer Sir Thomas Elyot, for example, used them as a framework in his book *The Governor* (1555). Elyot had served the Crown as a diplomat, in central government and as a magistrate. Therefore he could write from experience. He also wrote his book in English, which gave it a wide circulation.

Governors, Elyot reminded his readers, should be good examples to the people. All their actions will be observed. For governors or leaders 'sit, as it were, on a pillar on the top of a mountain, where all people do behold them'. The 'noble example of their lives,' and the way they act as justices of the peace or sheriffs, as crown ministers or royal ambassadors, is decisive for the nature of their state. 'Such as be the governors, such be the people.'

In the footsteps of Aristotle, Elyot took *justice* to be the chief virtue in a governor. He saw it primarily as the guide of men and women in their relations with one another, giving to each his or her right, and thus binding all together in a cohesive society. From it sprang fidelity. Drawing on the English and French tradition of chivalry, Elyot saw fidelity as encompassing loyalty to the sovereign and trustworthiness in one's dealings with all men.

It is not surprising that the second main virtue necessary in a good governor, *prudence,* was sometimes thought to be an intellectual quality rather than a moral one. For it translated (by way of the Latin) the Greek word *phronesis,* practical wisdom. Elyot defined it correctly as knowledge applied to practical affairs, by which a man might know what to do and what not to do. A quality of the mind and temper is also implied: self-control, a lack of rashness as well as the ability to concentrate the mind on a problem before acting. Prudence had many branches, according to Elyot, – such as acumen, foresight, resourcefulness, circumspection, diligence in execution, discretion – all necessary to right thinking and right acting. As the application of knowledge to conduct, it involved three steps: deliberation, decision and action. In the phase of deliberation, probable and possible outcomes have to be carefully weighed.

Sir Philip Sidney

The statesmen, courtiers, adventurers, and soldiers in Elizabethan England embodied in different ways and in varying degrees the ideal of the governor or leader. Contemporaries esteemed Sir Philip Sidney, the 'president of noblesse and chivalry.' He was a poet, courtier, diplomat and soldier. It was an age in which men strove for many-sided perfection, but few could rival Sidney as a universal Renaissance gentleman.

On Thursday 22 September, 1586, Sir Philip, as Governor of Flushing, took part in a fight in the Lowlands at Zutphen. When the fog cleared that morning, a small force of some 500 Englishmen found themselves face-to-face with an enemy body of Spaniards, Italians, and Albanians five times their number. The English could have withdrawn, but that possibility was not considered. "For the honour of England, good fellows, follow me!" shouted the young Earl of Essex. A musket ball struck Sidney in the left leg early in the first charge. His mount took flight and galloped away from the field to the English camp a mile and half distant.

There Sidney was lifted off his horse and laid upon a pallet. Overcome with thirst, he called for a drink. A bottle was brought, and he hastily put it to his lips. But at that moment a soldier was being carried past; the dying man fixed greedy eyes upon the flask. Sidney handed it to him. "Your necessity is yet greater than mine," he said. Two weeks later Sidney died of his wounds.

'A brave captain is as a root, out of which, as branches, the courage of his soldiers does spring.'

Sir Philip Sidney

English writers such as Elyot interpreted the third quality, *temperance*, to mean self-control or 'inner governance.' Self-control enabled a man to find the mean between extremes, to see both himself and the world in which he lived with objective justice, and to apply such justice. If he permitted reason to rule, his abilities would become virtues. If, on the other hand, he was driven by the lower part of his soul, if his emotions and passions ruled without the bridle of reason, then his abilities would degenerate into vices. But Elyot and his fellow teachers of the classical virtues were conscious that temperance was not an easy ideal to sell to the English in an age of extravagant display, prodigal spending and habitual excess at the table. The importance of generosity and equanimity, which they also advocated, were much more to the English taste.

The last of the four classic virtues was *fortitude*. That word smacked too much of forbearance or stoic passivity – most un-English traits – so Elyot called it courage or valour. Unlike temperance, which was inward-looking, valour was a more outward-looking virtue. In fact it looked both ways, for courage was shown both in a person steeling himself or herself to patient endurance or misfortune and in a person embarking upon a great enterprise fraught with risk. But Elyot chiefly praised courage as a necessary companion to action.

Courage was especially necessary in governors or leaders, argued Elyot, because they might be called upon at any time to defend their country. The English had a reputation for their ferocity in war, but they were not a militaristic nation. Lord Burghley, Elizabeth's principal minister, even warned his son against training a boy for the wars, since he who lived by that profession 'can hardly be an honest man and a good Christian,' while 'soldiers in peace are like chimneys in summer.' As an island people, the English employed their courage more in daring voyages and adventures on the high seas than warlike exploits on land. Sir Philip Sidney again epitomised the age by his fervent and courageous desire to join Sir Francis Drake on a projected voyage of exploration; he chose to soldier in the Netherlands only after the Queen forbade him to venture his person on the high seas.

Sir Philip Sidney. Poet and soldier, Sidney was born at Penshurst in Kent in 1554.
He personified the qualities of an English gentleman leader.

Sir Francis Drake

The need to create teamwork is perennial. Drake showed himself a true leader by creating unity out of disharmony. During his epic voyage in which he circumnavigated the globe, Drake faced persistent troubles among his crews. A long period of cold, miserable, stormy weather accentuated one source of discord. In order to train officers for future operations against Spain's colonies, Drake had brought with him a large number of young gentlemen. They scorned to work with their hands, much to the sailors' displeasure. Behind the general low morale lay a deeper cause: Drake had not told the crews why the enterprise had been mounted in the first place. He had not won their hearts. Sensing the need, Drake decided to take action. Having mustered the three ships' companies on shore, Drake told them plainly that their mutinies and discords must cease:

'For by the life of God it does even take my wits from me to think on it. Here is such controversy between the sailors and the gentlemen and such stomaching between the gentlemen and the sailors, that it does even make me mad to hear it. But, my masters, I must have it left. For I must have the gentlemen to haul and draw with the mariner and the mariner with the gentleman. What! let us show ourselves all to be of a company and let us not give occasion to the enemy to rejoice at our decay and overthrow.'

Drake then offered the *Marigold* to any who would sail home rather than work as a team. He added, however, that he would sink that vessel if it chanced into his way. Not a man raised his voice for going home. Drake then startled his captains and officers by discharging them. One or two of the worst offenders he now reprimanded by name; they humbled themselves on their knees before him. Having justified his recent controversial proceedings (in circumstances of doubtful legality he had had one gentleman beheaded), and having communicated to them fully the reasons behind the voyage, Drake appealed to their patriotism. Finally he restored the officers to their positions and once more impressed upon them all that they served the Queen, not himself. Thus he secured the willing obedience of all. Not long afterwards, Drake changed his flag ship's name to *Golden Hind*; it was an act that symbolised the new beginning.

Sir Francis Drake. Began his career as apprentice on a coasting vessel and rose to become England's outstanding leader of sea expeditions.

Beyond the four qualities emphasised by Aristotle, Elyot and other English writers especially commended *courtesy* as a virtue which would win men's hearts and inspire their willing obedience. Courtesy consisted of two parts: knowing what behaviour was fitting to each person including oneself, and graciousness in giving to each his or her due. The particular form of courtesy which should characterise a leader or governor is called *majesty* in Elyot's book. He defined it as follows:

> *'In a governor or man having in the public weal some great authority, the fountain of all excellent manners is majesty; which is the whole proportion and figure of noble estate, and is properly a beauty or comeli-*

ness in his countenance, language and gesture apt to his dignity and fitting to time, place and company; which, like as the sun does his beams, so does it cast on the beholders and hearers a pleasant and terrible reverence. In so much as the word or countenances of a noble man should be instead of a firm and stable law to his inferiors. Yet is not majesty always lofty or fierce countenance, nor in speech outrageous or arrogant, but in honourable and sober demeanour, deliberate and grave pronunciation, words, clean and facile, void of rudeness and dishonesty, without vain or inordinate jangling, with such an excellent temperance, that he, among an infinite number of other persons, by his majesty may be espied for a governor.'

The gentler side of majesty Elyot called *affability*. He contrasted vividly the contrary effects of arrogance and affability:

'How often have I heard people say, when men in great authority have passed by without making gentle countenance to those which have done to them reverence: "This man afflicts us with a look to subdue all the world. Nay, nay, our hearts be free and will love whom they please." And thereto all the others do consent in a murmur, as it were bees. But when a noble man passes by, showing to men a gentle and familiar face, it is a world to behold how people take the comfort, how the blood in their face quickens, how their flesh stirs and hearts leap for gladness. Then they all speak as it were in a harmony. The one says, "Who beholding this man's gentle countenance will not with his heart love him?" Another says, "He is no man, but an angel, so how he rejoices all men that behold him." Finally, all do grant that he is worthy all honour that may be given or wished him.'

Such, then, are the effects of what Shakespeare in *King Richard II* called 'humble and familiar courtesy.'

For Sir Thomas Elyot and his fellow writers and teachers, good birth and noble family are desirable but not essential. A governor or leader has to demonstrate that he possesses the qualities or virtues which are naturally necessary in one who aspires to rule others. These attributes and traits alone will enable him to rule justly, inspire obedience, and inculcate right ways of living among the people. Such a natural gentleman would be an honourable man. Originally, honour was understood by the Greeks to be simply a just reward of virtue. In time it came to mean fame or glory. Finally, used in the plural, honours signified the outward signs of that fame: dignities, offices, titles and orders of chivalry.

For his son, Lord Burghley succinctly summed up this new code of the English gentlemen leader. 'Towards your superiors, be humble, yet generous,' he wrote. 'With our equals, familiar, yet respectful. Towards your inferiors show much humanity and some familiarity…The first prepares the way to advancement. The second makes you known for a man well-bred. The third gains a good report; which, one got, is easily kept.'

The Renaissance gentleman, then, was fit to lead in peace or war. Justice, liberality, prudence, courtesy and self-control equipped him as a magistrate in peacetime. But when the trumpets of war sounded, he could don his armour and draw his sword on the field of Mars, showing there other facets of his character: courage, endurance, patience, foresight, flexibility of mind, and magnanimity towards the foe. Graceful in speech and resolute in action, master of himself, in prosperity or adversity, equipped with practical reason and useful knowledge, he was indeed the 'man for all seasons.'

Machiavelli and Leadership

The emerging English concept of the gentleman leader was both classical and Christian in its inspiration. In sharp contrast stood the teachings of Niccolo Machiavelli, who died in 1527. Machiavelli's works were not translated into English until the following century and few could read and understand the Italian original (among them were Thomas Cromwell, Henry VII's minister – an early disciple of Machiavelli – and Queen Elizabeth herself). Yet his name soon became a byword for a doctrine of rulership totally at odds with the English understanding of leadership.

Machiavelli's theme was power: how to attain it and how to hold it. By power he meant the subjection of people to the will of the ruler. Machiavelli subscribed to the ancient Roman saying: 'Let them hate as long as they fear.' Seneca had denounced that proverb as a vile, detestable, deadly sentiment. The English tradition sided with Seneca; Machiavelli did not. 'It is far better to be feared than loved,' he wrote. 'The bond of love is one which men, wretched creatures that they are, break when it is to their advantage to do so; but fear is strengthened by a dread of punishment which is always effective.'

Englishmen in the sixteenth and seventeenth centuries loathed the name of Machiavelli for one main reason. They detested anything that smacked of tyranny. Although Machiavelli, a citizen of the Florentine Republic, in theory did not regard absolute monarchy as the best form of government, in practice he did. His historical situation – an Italy riven with internecine warfare and dominated by its powerful neighbours – largely explains his desire for a strong, masterful dictator. But the ideas underlying absolute monarchy were not English; their root was foreign, and British soil did not prove congenial to their growth. Machiavelli came to be regarded as their promoter and prime mover; for his English readers of that time abstracted from his writings only the arguments supporting the absolute rule of the prince. Thus Machiavelli seemed to his contemporaries to be the apologist of tyranny, the teacher of subtle and ruthless methods of how to enslave a free people. 'Men ought to be well treated or utterly crushed,' he wrote, 'since they can avenge small injuries but not great ones.' That was the flavour of Machiavelli.

Machiavelli also threatened to rip apart one seam of the Western tradition concerning leadership, where the classical and Biblical traditions had been stitched together over the centuries. Machiavelli did not deny Christianity; he merely saw it as irrelevant to the work of governing people. A ruler should free himself from its restraints, however privately he might regret the necessity for doing so. He should not, of course, practise the wanton cruelty of Nero, but nothing must stay his hand from the actions that must be taken to achieve his task. Necessity, not morality, should be his sole guide. 'A prince who wants to hold his own,' he wrote, 'must know how to do wrong when necessary.'

Machiavelli taught that princes or governors need to actually possess the qualities or virtues associated with leadership, as long as they seem to have them. 'It is unnecessary for a prince to have all the virtues, but very necessary to appear to have them.' But humility was one virtue that a prince need not even simulate, because it had no place in statecraft. For rulers

Machiavelli advocated a return to the values of Greece and Rome. As he wrote in his *Discourses on Livy*:

> 'The old religion did not beatify men unless they were full of worldly glory: army commanders, for instance, and rulers of republics. Our religion has glorified humble and contemplative men, rather than men of action. It has assigned as man's highest good humility, abnegation and contempt for worldly things, whereas the other identified it with magnanimity, bodily strength and everything else that tends to make men very bold.'

The 'old religion' then, was best for the preservation of the state and the encouragement of the many facets of virtue as Machiavelli conceived it – strength, will-power, valour, high spirit, technique and efficiency. Its morality was political and secular, not personal and Christian. The chief god of that pagan religion's pantheon was Fortune.

To be ruthless, which means literally to have no pity or compassion, ran contrary to the Christian understanding of leadership, or indeed to what constituted Christian morality. Nor did the idea that private and public morality can and should be kept in separate compartments commend itself to Christian humanist thinkers in Europe. It is a doctrine which helped to produce the horrors of Hitler's gas-chambers in the concentration camps of the Third Reich.

Some English writers also rejected Machiavelli because he advocated what they called subtlety. A leader deceiving his followers or colleagues by artful methods seemed to them a contradiction in terms. But this aspect of Machiavelli's teaching in the use of craft or cunning in political life did win some converts in England.

Queen Elizabeth was certainly a Machiavellian in that respect, as her first Archbishop of Canterbury, Matthew Parker, discovered painfully as he tried to establish good order in her newly-established Church of England. 'Her Majesty counts much on Fortune,' wrote his friend, the Puritan Sir Francis Walsingham, to him, 'I wish she would trust more in Almighty God.' Her restless and calculating mind was always at work, plotting a course forwards through a tangled maze of possibilities and dangers. She observed men closely and played upon their emotions as if they were the keys of her harpsichord. She alternated royal severity with a feminine touch. On one occasion, when Elizabeth had said some 'hard words' to Parker in council the day before, it fell to his duty to meet her on Lambeth Bridge. 'She gave me very good looks,' wrote the bemused Archbishop, 'and spoke secretly in my ear, that she must needs countenance mine authority before the people, to the credit of my service.' On reflection Parker felt himself to be in a well-nigh impossible situation, as he complained to Lord Cecil: 'Her Majesty told me that I had supreme government ecclesiastical, but what is it to govern cumbered with such subtlety?'

Integrity, in the sense of plain speaking and above-the-board dealing, was the ideal set before English leaders by their school teachers and the writers of the day. As Shakespeare wrote in *Hamlet*:

> 'This above all: to thine own self be true,
> And it must follow, as the night to day,
> Thou canst not then be false to any man,'

Leaders who resort to cunning or crafty methods of manipulating people to their will may gain short-term advantages, but in the long run they forfeit trust. 'Subtlety may deceive you,' wrote Cromwell in a letter to Robert Barnard in January 1642, 'integrity never will.' For integrity implies adherence to moral standards – especially truth and goodness – that lie outside oneself.

The Great Rebellion

When Cromwell wrote the words quoted above England was drifting towards a civil war. When it broke out that summer the Parliamentarians firmly believed that they were taking up arms to save England from a tyranny in the making.

The English Civil War revealed that England had bred gentleman leaders in plenty. Divided upon the political, constitutional and religious issues though they were, both Cavaliers and Parliamentarians demonstrated a common quality of leadership, modelled on the concept that they had acquired from their classical education and by reading such books as Sir Thomas Elyot's *The Governor*.

One such leader was John Hampden, one of the first great leaders of the House of Commons. Hampden, who had first attracted public attention by his refusal to pay the illegal Ship Money tax, emerged as a leader in the Long Parliament which met in November 1640. The reformist majority in the Lower House, leavened by the Puritan group led by John Hampden and John Pym, clearly enjoyed overwhelming support in the country. 'When this Parliament began,' wrote the Earl of Clarendon in his *History of the Great Rebellion* 'the eyes of all men were fixed on Hampden as their *Patriae pater* (father of his country), and the pilot that must steer their vessel through the tempests and rocks which threatened it. And I am persuaded that his power and interest at that time was greater to do good or hurt than any man's in the Kingdom, or any man of his rank has had in any time. For his reputation for honesty was universal, and his affections seemed so publicly guided that no corrupt or private ends could bias them.'

Although he was a Royalist, and therefore on the opposite side in the House, Clarendon clearly admired and observed him closely. He imputed to Hampden a considerable degree of Machiavellian subtlety, but recognised also his gift for leadership. Hampden, he wrote, 'was not a man of many words, and rarely began the discourse, or made the first entrance on any business that was assumed; but a very weighty speaker, after he had heard a full debate and observed how the House was like to be inclined, took up the argument and shortly and clearly and craftily so stated it that he commonly conducted it to the conclusion he desired.' Hampden, he added, always showed civility and modesty, listening to others as if he mistrusted his own judgement. He summed up John Hampden as 'a very wise man', and of great parts, and possessed with the most absolute spirit of popularity, that is the most absolute faculties to govern the people, of any man I know.'

John Hampden. He had the misfortune to die in battle in 1643, otherwise his fame as a leader would have eclipsed that of his first cousin, Oliver Cromwell.

Following the deaths of Hampden and Pym, the control of the war against King Charles passed into the hands of a coterie of leaders among whom Hampden's cousin, Oliver Cromwell, soon emerged as the man of strength. After the establishment of the New Model Army in 1645, Cromwell's rise was meteoric. He had a talent for military leadership. Not only did he have a burning fervour for the cause but he could also sense its presence – or absence – in others. Even as Colonel of his regiment of horse known as the 'Ironsides,' Cromwell had paid much attention to selection. As he wrote in a letter, he looked for 'such men as had the fear of God before them and made some conscience of what they did... the plain russet-coated captain that knows what he fights for and loves what he knows.'

Once Cromwell had found the right officers and men, he inspired them by his words and example. Like the best leaders of those times and all times, he led them in battle from in front.

Promotion in the New Model Army was by merit and character, not birth or patronage. Consequently it widened the social ladder of advancement upwards. Thomas Shelbourne, for example, was John Hampden's shepherd on the Chiltern Hills 'in which capacity he served him for many years.' His military career began early in the Civil War in Hampden's Greencoats and ended in the New Model as Colonel of Cromwell's old regiment of Ironsides. Such men as Shelbourne had natural leadership potential, which the war gave them occasion to develop. They believed in Major-General John Lambert's words, that 'the best of men are but men at their best.'

Thus the English Civil War gave fresh impetus to the doctrine that leadership should go to those who are able and qualified to exercise it, regardless of birth or lineage. In the following centuries Britain's schools continued to produce an abundance of such men. Britain's expanding colonies, the green shoots of empire, would give them both opportunity and responsibility as governors. They constituted what Edmund Burke in 1791 called a 'natural aristocracy,' the essential core of any nation. 'Men, qualified in the manner I have just described,' he wrote, 'form in nature, as she operates in the common modification of society, the leading, guiding, and governing part. It is the soul to the body, without which the man does not exist.

The American Experience

The foundation of Britain's colonies in America opened up new opportunities for the gentleman leader. John Winthrop, for example, the first Governor in Massachusetts, brought to his responsibilities in the New World the qualities of a leader as outlined by Elyot, except that he was no soldier. He was inspired with the Puritan vision of creating a new Christian commonwealth in the wilderness of North America, to be like a city set as a beacon upon a hill for the whole world to see. Winthrop actually governed Massachusetts much as if it had been an English shire. With their monarch so distant, and with no one else above them in the social hierarchy – no bishop set foot in New England and even the more Puritan nobles decided against emigrating – commoners such as Winthrop found themselves to be virtually sole rulers in their Puritan states, checked only by the bill of their councils and public opinion, often roused and shaped from the pulpit.

DAVID CROCKETT.

I am happy to acknowledge this to be the only correct likeness that has been taken of me.

David Crockett

David Crockett, the American folk-hero, was one of the many natural leaders who emerged later as the frontier moved westwards.

A Source of American Democracy: The Town Meeting

The New England colonists revived the ancient tribal practice of general assembly, either from folk memory or by consciously adopting the civilised form of it in Athens – where the word 'democracy' – rule by the people – was first coined. These extracts from the regulations of Springfield, Massachusetts, are typical:

'May the 14th, 1636.

'We whose names are underwritten, being by God's providence engaged together to make a plantation, at and over against Agawam on Connecticut, do mutually agree to certain articles and orders to be observed and kept by us and by our successors, except we and every one of us, for ourselves and in our persons, shall think meet upon better reasons to alter our present resolutions.

'We intend by God's grace, as soon as we can with all convenient speed, to procure some godly and faithful minister with whom we purpose to join in church covenant to walk in all the ways of Christ.

'We intend that our town shall be composed of forty families, or if we think meet after to alter our purpose, yet not to exceed the number of fifty families, rich and poor…

'For the better carrying on of town meetings it is ordered that whensoever there shall any public notice be given to the inhabitants by the select townsmen…it is expected that all the inhabitants attend personally such meeting so appointed. And in case the time and hour of meeting be come, though there be but nine of the inhabitants assembled, it shall be lawful for them to proceed in agitation of whatever business is there propounded to them; and what the major part of the assembly there met shall agree upon, it shall be taken as the act of the whole town and binding to all.

The first Tuesday in November yearly is mutually agreed on and appointed to be a general town meeting for the choice of town officers, making, continuing, and publishing of orders etc., on which day it is more especially expected that each inhabitant give his personal attendance, and if any shall be absent at the time of calling, or absent himself without consent of the major part, he shall be liable to a fine or two shillings sixpence.'

The conditions in the frontier towns favoured this kind of democracy. In its early days, of course, New England towns such as Springfield were on the frontier. The constitution of Rhode Island has the distinction of first using the actual word 'democracy' in the New World. Those who framed its political constitution in 1641 understood democracy to mean 'popular government,' by which they meant that 'it is in the power of the body of freemen orderly assembled, or a major part of them, to make or constitute just laws, by which they will be regulated, and to depute from among themselves such ministers as shall see them faithfully executed between man and man.' In other words, Rhode Island – which was then a small community made up of those who had rejected (or been rejected by) the main Puritan colonies – would be governed by an enlarged version of the town meeting.

This concept was different from the predominant Western version of democracy, which was defined by Alexander Hamilton in 1777 as representative democracy. Here citizens meet in conditions of free speech to elect representatives who would in turn choose some of their number to exercise executive and legislative functions. In such a form of democracy, which rapidly became the dominant strain in America as eventually in many other parts of the world, sovereignty was conferred on the people, but did not give them rule. That responsibility remained with their elected representatives or leaders.

When men and women moved to the frontier in America, the old fixed social hierarchies became irrelevant. Stripped of uniform or rank, they were measured by their fitness to lead in the new conditions of life. Inequalities developed, but they reflected evident differences of ability and they were neither great nor rigid enough to create classes on the European model. For pioneers on the frontier, socially speaking, started with a clean slate. They came together and then invented their social institutions. If they organised themselves and elected leaders it was because they saw the need for organisation and leadership. The notion that a social order existed as a divinely ordained and hallowed entity, and that men must accept the station within it allotted to them by birth or custom, made no sense in the frontier's trackless forests, valleys and mountains, the 'State of Nature' in which the pioneers now found themselves.

A Kentucky Frontiersman

Daniel Boone was an outstanding frontiersman. He was a master of woodcraft, able to find his way hundreds of miles through unbroken forests, able to maintain himself alone for months on end by his rifle, tomahawk and knife; and this in the face of hostile Indians. He was a man of vision, for he felt ordained by God to, as he said, 'conquer the wilderness.' Calmness and serenity seem to have been characteristics in all his human relations. Where most men were Indian haters, Boone harboured no rancour against his foes; he treated them honourably in peace and war. He was trustworthy, loyal and ever ready to help others.

During a long siege by Indians of the stockaded settlement of Boonsborough, Daniel Boone emerged as the natural leader of the defenders. He had unrivalled knowledge of Indian warfare. Yet Colonel Callaway, senior regular officer in the fort, had Boone court martialled after its close, on the grounds that he held no military rank and had unsurped his own authority. A court martial speedily acquitted Boone. Not long afterwards he was made a colonel in the militia.

Parties of settlers migrating across the continent in the next century were advised in the guidebooks to organise themselves into a company and elect a commander. They should sign an obligation to abide in all cases by his orders and decisions. In addition they should undertake to aid each other, so as to make the individual interest of each in the company the common concern of the whole company. With the prospect ahead of Indian attacks on the plains, together with natural hazards and obstacles, the pioneers stood in need of good leadership and teamwork. A typical agreement of this sort is described in the Journal of one Silas Newcombe:

> 'At a meeting of a Company of Californians on the Banks of the Missouri, May 6th, 1850, the following Preamble and Resolutions were unanimously adopted:

> 'Whereas we are about to leave the frontier, and travel over Indian Territory, exposed to their treachery and knowing their long and abiding hatred of the whites; also many other privations to meet with. We consider it necessary to form ourselves into a Company for the purpose of protecting each other and our property, during our journey to California.

'Therefore Resolved, that there shall be one selected from the Company, suitable and capable to act as Captain or Leader.

'Resolved, that we, as men, pledge ourselves to assist each other through all the misfortunes that may befall us on our long and dangerous journey.

'Resolved, that the Christian Sabbath shall be observed, except when absolutely necessary to travel.

'Resolved, that there shall be a sufficient guard appointed each night regularly, by the Captain.

'Resolved, that in the case of a member's dying, the Company shall give him a decent burial.'

Daniel Boone blazed the pioneer trail in 1775 from East Virginia to Kentucky, which was followed by settlers in the first large-scale migration westwards.

This familiar experience, inaugurated by the Mayflower Compact of 1620, gave America a tradition of a free association for the meeting of common emergencies. And with this method of voluntary co-operation is associated the appearance of natural leaders, such as George Washington, Daniel Boone, Davy Crockett, John Sevier, James Robertson, George Robertson, William Clarke, Sam Houston, Andrew Jackson, and – greatest of all – Abraham Lincoln. Thus, as the American frontier moved further westwards and away from the social conventions of the east coast, a distinctive ethos of a natural rough-and-ready leadership began to emerge in the new territories; it remained with them long after they achieved statehood. George Washington represented a marriage of the frontier virtues with the tradition of the gentleman leader.

George Washington

Washington's great-grandfather, John Washington, stepped ashore in Virginia in 1657 and acquired for himself a handsome estate. George was born in 1732, third son of a second wife. He trained as a surveyor and at sixteen journeyed to the Shenandoah Valley and the region of the Blue Ridge Mountains. He grew to be a tall man of 6'2", with blue-grey penetrating eyes and a commanding countenance, acquired while leading Virginian companies in the wars against the French and Indians. In 1775 he was appointed to command the American forces struggling against the British Redcoats.

The American soldiers deserved such a leader for they had shown already a greatness of spirit. Washington found his army besieging Boston, about to be attacked by a British force of regulars under orders to raise the siege. Crouched behind their crude fortifications, in the sweltering June heat, the Americans were not dismayed. An old man even prayed: 'I thank thee, Lord, for sparing me to fight this day. Blessed be the name of the Lord.' In the battle of Bunker's Hill that followed, the Americans suffered a defeat, but inflicted heavy casualties on the British.

George Washington. Re-elected President in 1793, Washington refused a third term.
He died in 1799 and was buried at Mount Vernon, Virginia.

Unity among the revolutionary army was essential. It was not an easy task to create it. At the outset of the war, for example, many units refused to obey orders from officers who did not come from their own colonies. Patrick Henry, Governor of Virginia, spoke as a stateman when he declared: 'the distinctions between Virginians, Pennsylvanians, New Yorkers and New Englanders are no more. I am not a Virginian, but an American'! Washington established his authority slowly, carefully and firmly in the army largely through the power of his personality. Virtually everyone who met him found him dignified and modest. Abigail Adams, for instance, who met most of the leaders of the Revolution and approved of few of them, was deeply impressed by Washington. To her husband, she wrote: 'You had prepared me to entertain a favourable opinion of him, but I thought the one half was not told me. Dignity with ease and complacency, the gentleman and soldier look agreeably blended in him. Modesty marks every line and feature of his face.'

Another friend recalled: 'There was so much native dignity in his deport-ment, that no man could approach him without being impressed with a sensation that he accosted a superior being: yet there was a small mixture of timidity in his general demeanour, lest he might commit an error, and this modesty was exceeding prepossessing. It gave a mildness and kindness to his manner...'

As the fortune of the Revolutionary War ebbed and flowed they brought criticism and doubts of Washington's generalship, which he bore with dignity. But his personal courage and leadership could never be called into question. One volunteer – the Marquis de Lafayette, a major-general at the age of 20 – saw him intervening to stop the American soldiers running away at Monmouth, New Jersey. Lafayette saw him riding 'along the lines amid the shouts of the soldiers, cheering them by his voice and example and restoring to our standard the fortunes of the fight. I thought then as now that never had I beheld so superb a man.'

On April 30 1789, Washington took the oath of office as the first President of the United States. To his old artillery commander he confided that he faced 'and ocean of difficulties, without that competency of political skill, abilities and inclination which is necessary to manage the helm.' His high office brought him little joy. He once confided, Thomas Jefferson said, that it represented 'the extreme wretchedness of his existence.' Yet he served the nation conscientiously, realising that everything he did would affect history. 'I walk,' he said, 'on untrodden ground. There is scarcely any part of my conduct which may not hereafter be drawn into precedent.'

The Gentleman Leader

CHAPTER REVIEW

Summary

The Renaissance rekindled the belief that the natural qualities and abilities of leadership could be developed. The strong strand of egalitarianism in the hierarchical society of England supported a growing belief that leadership should be given to those who are fit to exercise it by their character, knowledge and skills. The classical virtues of justice, prudence, temperance and fortitude were widely seen to be the foundations of such leadership, but other attributes – notably courtesy – were also regarded as important in the English context. A leader was expected to have integrity and gentleness as well as strength, two qualities strikingly absent in Machiavelli's rival portrait of the effective and powerful ruler. If English writers normally expected such gentleman leaders to be of gentle birth, no such expectation was held in the frontier regions of the American colonies. The necessities of that rugged environment encouraged natural leaders to emerge. The United States of America, however, still drew upon gentleman leaders, such as George Washington, for its early rulers. The more traditional world of Georgian England also produced some fine examples of that school, notably Horatio Nelson, who merits a chapter to himself.

Key concepts

- Good educational systems produce the context in which great leaders emerge.

- Valuable lessons in leadership can be learnt from studying great leaders throughout history and understanding the qualities they exhibit. Even in 1555, the classical attributes were seen as justice, prudence, temperance (self-control), fortitude and courtesy with each quality carefully defined..

- Leadership can be established through power of personality.

- Leadership belongs to those who are able and qualified to exercise it – regardless of birth or lineage.

Further Reflection

- Creating teamwork is vital in exercising effective leadership. If faced with low morale and poor management, what lessons from his famous voyage of circumnavigation does Sir Francis Drake have for the modern business leader?

- How far does Lord Burghley's advice to his son (on the new code of the gentleman leader) apply to current times?

- Can ruthlessness and fear ever be the hallmarks of a great leader?

NINE
Nelson

Perhaps once or twice in its history every nation produces a person with a genius for leadership. Horatio Nelson was such a genius. His leadership style was particularly remarkable given that it was being exercised in the Royal Navy in the conditions of the late eighteenth century, but of course Nelson, like all geniuses, transcends both his times and the limited military context. As long as the British are interested in leadership they will always study Nelson.

For, apart from epitomising the gentleman leader discussed in the last chapter, Nelson reveals almost all the core qualities of leadership identified in Part One. He had the authority of knowledge and personality, as well as of rank and position. He gave clear directions; he built teams; and, he showed a real concern for the individual. As Nelson's career unfolded, it also became clear that he possessed a great leader's gift of drawing out the best from people. These are the reasons why Nelson's story is worth telling again in this context.

Early Life

Nelson's family and social background was relatively humble. His father, a country vicar in Norfolk, had eleven children. His paternal grandfather, another rector, who had been educated at Eton and Emmanuel College in Cambridge, had married the daughter of a butcher in Petty Cury. His mother, a relative of the Walpole family, kept up her links with the Walpoles, but she had other relatives nearer to home, notably the Suckling family. When Spain threatened the Falkland Islands and Horatio's uncle Captain Maurice Suckling was making ready for sea, he invited one of his Nelson nephews to accompany him. Horatio, the younger of the two, a well-spoken boy with a certain charm of manner, accepted with alacrity. As a midshipman, he sailed with Suckling to the West Indies. He also voyaged to the Artic, and finally to the East Indies where he was stricken by a fever.

On his way home to England in the *Dolphin* – the voyage took over six months – Nelson suffered a severe depression, caused first by his fever and then by his apparent lack of prospects. Under the kindly eye of the captain his health returned and his spirits revived. Nelson thought he perceived a radiant orb which beckoned him on. 'A sudden glow of patriotism was kindled within me,' he would tell his officers later, 'and presented my King and Country as my patron. My mind exulted in the idea. "Well, then," I exclaimed. "I will be a hero, and confiding in Providence, I will brave every danger."'

This simplicity of purpose remained his strength. Nelson's values were henceforth clear for the rest of his life – King and Country, God and the pursuit of glory. It was all straightforward. Later, in language appropriate to his age and rank, he advised a young midshipman to steer a similar course. 'There are three things, young gentleman,' said Nelson, 'you are constantly to bear in mind – first, you must always implicitly obey orders, without attempting to form any opinion of your own respecting their propriety; secondly, you must consider every man as your enemy who speaks ill of your King; and thirdly, you must hate a Frenchman as you do the devil'! Although Nelson did not follow his own advice in the first respect for he did not practise blind obedience, he knew that all entrants to the military profession must learn to obey orders.

With Captain Suckling as his patron, Nelson rose fast in the service. Nelson was extremely ambitious; he had a gift for not only getting noticed by those who mattered in his career but also for establishing excellent relations with most of his superiors without any hint of subservience or servility. He was captain of a 32 gun frigate at the age of 21 years, but then he endured five years on the beach with half-pay in England, fretting for action. Like Alexander the Great, Nelson thirsted for battle. He desperately desired a great name and all the honours that accompanied success.

Nelson's impatience becomes more intelligible when it is remembered that he had yet to take part in a major sea battle. His enforced stay on land came to an end in 1793, when he was appointed to command the *Agamemnon* of 64 guns, under Lord Hood. Two days later England declared war on France. His new command brought him sudden glory, the loss of his right arm at Tenerife, and, from 1798 onwards – after the Battle of the Nile in Aboukir Bay – general fame. Such universal popularity might have been unwelcome to a man of different temperament, but Nelson loved it. He basked in the limelight of England's hero-worship. Nelson's enjoyment of his success was marred only by the effects of the nasty wound above the eyebrow he received in Aboukir Bay (Lady Emma Hamilton taught him later to cover up the scar by combing his hair forwards). He had lost his right eye in Corsica, and the sight in his remaining eye was beginning to fail.

The Man and the Legend

Later, Nelson took care to foster his own legend. He understood and practised the art of public relations. After actions at sea he excelled at writing what he called 'a famous account of your own actions.' He arranged for these despatches to be leaked immediately to the press, directing that where he had written 'I' and 'my' the third person should be substituted, to give the impression that some other hand had written them. He loved having his portrait painted. One of his mentors, the crusty old Lord St Vincent, told some ladies that Nelson, 'foolish little fellow, has sat to every artist in London.' (Nelson was only 5'2" in height.) Soon Nelson's image, drawn from these portraits, appeared everywhere: on souvenir jugs and mugs, patriotic handkerchiefs, and swinging inn-signs. In Yarmouth, when the landlady of the Wrestlers Inn asked leave of Nelson to rename her hostelry the Nelson Arms, he smiled and replied: 'That would be absurd, seeing that I have but one'!

People seldom forgot their first meeting with Nelson. It was in Admiral Hood's ship the *Barfleur* that Prince William, son of the reigning monarch and later England's eccentric sailor king, met Nelson, than a 23 years old frigate captain. His appearance made the straitlaced Prince stare. The Prince was midshipman of the watch on deck 'when Captain Nelson, of the *Albemarle*, came in his barge alongside, who appeared the merest boy of a Captain I ever beheld: and his dress was worthy of attention. He had on a full-laced uniform: his lank untidy hair was tied in a stiff hessian tail, of extraordinary length; the old fashioned flaps of his waistcoat added to the general quaintness of his figure, and produced an appearance which particularly attracted my notice; for I had never seen anything like it before, nor could I imagine who he was, nor what he came about. My doubts, however, removed when Lord Hood introduced me to him. There was something irresistibly pleasing in his address and conversation; and an enthusiasm, when speaking on professional subjects, that showed he was no common being.'

That youthfulness and enthusiasm never left Nelson. But in his later years his sandy-grey hair turned almost white. His face with its irregular features became lined with suffering, looked older than his years. Nelson improved his dress. In later life he customarily wore his blue naval uniform with gold epaulettes, adorned with his four orders of chivalry, the ribbons of two of them, and the gold medals awarded to all captains of ships-of-the-line after the battles of Cape St Vincent and the Nile.

During the long war with France, when at one point Britain was threatened by Napoleon's Grand Army, the nation needed a saviour. In fact it found two – Wellington and Nelson. The two men possessed very different backgrounds and characters.

Nelson Meets Wellington

It was where he was not known that Nelson wished to impress. The classic instance occurred during his chance meeting with the future Duke of Wellington, then Sir Arthur Wellesley. This took place in September 1805, immediately before Nelson left England for the last time. Wellington was eleven years younger than Nelson, but even at the age of thirty-six he had acquired a great reputation in India. Ahead of him was a succession of victories in Europe, culminating in Waterloo.

'Lord Nelson was, in different circumstances, two quite different men,' Wellington said later. 'I only saw him once in my life, and for, perhaps, an hour. It was soon after I returned from India. I went to the Colonial Office in Downing Street, and there I was shown into the little waiting-room on the right hand, where I found also waiting to see the Secretary of State, a gentleman, whom from his likeness to his pictures and the loss of an arm, I immediately recognised as Lord Nelson. He could not know who I was, but he entered at once into conversation with me, if I can call it conversation, for it was almost all on his side and all about himself, and in, really, a style so vain and so silly as to surprise and almost disgust me.

'I suppose something that I happened to say may have made him guess that I was somebody, and he went out of the room for a moment, I have no doubt to ask the office-keeper who I was, for when he came back he was altogether a different man, both in manner and matter. All that I had thought a charlatan style had vanished, and he talked of the state of the country and of the aspect and probabilities of affairs on the Continent with a good sense, and a knowledge of subjects both at home and abroad, that surprised me equally and more agreeably than the first part of our interview had done; in fact, he talked like an officer and a statesman.

'The Secretary of State kept us long waiting, and certainly, for the last half or three-quarters of an hour, I don't know that I ever had a conversation that interested me more. Now, if the Secretary of State had been punctual and admitted Lord Nelson in the first quarter of an hour, I should have had the same impression of a light and trivial character that other people have had, but luckily I saw enough to be satisfied that he was really a very superior man; but certainly a more sudden and complete metamorphosis I never saw.'

Rear Admiral Sir Horatio Nelson, aged 39 years. Nelson sat for this portrait by Lemuel Abbott in October 1797 at the Royal Hospital, Greenwich, after the loss of his arm but before the stump had healed.

Wellington came from the aristocracy. He had a certain aloofness about him, together with a lordly indifference to what people thought or felt about him – especially his social inferiors. He practised the virtue of self-control to the point of being taciturn. Wellington won victories and he won respect, but did he also win hearts? Wellington always seemed more at home with his officers, in their red-coats and gold epaulettes, than the rank-and-file, those scourings of society – the 'scum of the earth,' as he once called them. The British Army, he added, had turned these men into fine soldiers. Popular as 'Old Nosey' was for winning victories, for the good administration and even-handed discipline he maintained in his army, Wellington remained a commander rather than a leader.

In strange company Nelson usually said very little, although occasionally he could be boastful. He disliked any form of public speaking. Among friends Nelson spoke in a simple and unaffected way, his face animated. One of his nephews said that, 'at his table he was the last heard among the company, and so far from being the hero of his own tale, I never heard him allude voluntarily to any of the great actions of his life.'

As Wellington's story illustrated, Nelson could switch from one part to another with rapidity. Vanity and modesty fought for position in him. For Nelson's soaring ambition for glory and honour was confronted by a genuine humility before God – to whom he prayed night and morning – and before his fellow men. One of his captains, Sir Alexander Ball, tells the story that after the glorious battle of the Nile, he and he fellow captains commissioned an artist to paint Nelson's portrait. The artist had difficulty in even getting started. At last he admitted that the task was beyond his powers. 'There is such a mixture of humility and ambition in Lord Nelson's countenance,' he said, 'that I dare not risk the attempt.'

Achieving the Task

'Nothing can stop the courage of English seamen,' wrote Nelson exultantly after one fight against the French in the Mediterranean. Nelson exemplified physical courage. He gave evidence in childhood that he had little sense of fear. As we have noted, he had an abnormal thirst for action which recalls Alexander the Great. The odds against him seldom mattered. Luck and the devotion of his colleagues and subordinates saw him through – at least until Trafalgar. In the boat attack on Cadiz in 1797, he and a crew of thirteen men attacked a Spanish barge with a crew of thirty. They fought it out with swords and pistols. John Sykes, the coxswain, twice saved Nelson's life with his cutlass; a third time he dived forwards and received on his own head a slash meant for Nelson. 'We all saw it,' wrote one soldier. 'We were witnesses to the gallant deed, and we gave in revenge one cheer and one tremendous rally. Eighteen of the Spaniards were killed, and we boarded and carried her, there not being one man left on board who was not either dead or wounded. "Sykes," said Nelson as he caught the gallant fellow in his arms. "I cannot forget this," But my wounded shipmate only looked him in the face, and smiled as he said, "Thank God, Sir, you are safe."'

On 25 July 1797 Nelson attacked Santa Cruz and had his right elbow shattered. The amputation of his arm without an anaesthetic proved to be an agonising ordeal, but according to an eyewitness Nelson bore it with 'firmness and courage.'

'Authority flows from the man who knows', says the proverb. Having gone to sea at the age of twelve, after briefly attending three schools, Nelson had little formal education but he read voraciously while he was at sea. He applied himself, too, to mastering his profession, passing his Lieutenant's Certificate at 19, one year below the permitted age (it helped having his mentor, Captain Suckling, on the examining board!) 'I have been your scholar,' Nelson wrote to William Locker, captain of the *Lowestoffe* on which he served as a lieutenant, 'it is you who taught me to board a Frenchman…and my sole merit in my profession is being a good scholar.'

Sea battles usually consisted of two long lines of stately white-sailed wooden ships sailing in parallel and pounding each other with broadsides. Nelson showed his flair and imagination in varying this theme. He spent much of this time thinking – thinking hard – about how to best use his 'grey-geese,' as he sometimes called his beloved ships. Off Cape St Vincent his self-confidence and flexibility of mind led him to ignore conventional tactics and turn his ship the *Captain* out of line and across the head of the enemy column. At the Battle of the Nile, Nelson surprised the French fleet by attacking them at anchor on the landward side where their gunports were inoperative. At Trafalgar he approached the French line at right angles with two columns of ships. 'What do you think of that?' he had asked one of his captains to whom he had explained the plan while they strolled in the gardens of his Merton house before leaving England. 'Such a question I felt required consideration, I paused,' recalled Captain Keats. 'Seeing it he said, "But I'll tell you what *I* think of it. I think it will surprise and confound the enemy! They won't know what I am about. It will bring forward a pell-mell battle, and that is what I want."'

Nelson was exceptionally good at communicating his ideas and plans to his officers. After joining the fleet off Cadiz before Trafalgar, he gave a dinner for fifteen commanding officers in his stateroom aboard the *Victory* on 29 September, his birthday, and to as many other captains on the succeeding day. 'I believe my arrival was most welcome, not only to the Commanders of the Fleet, but to almost every individual in it,' he wrote to Lady Hamilton, 'and when I came to explain to them the "*Nelson touch*" (his idea of bringing on a confused fight) it was like an electric shock. Some shed tears, all approved – "it was new – it was singular – it was simple!" and, from Admirals downwards it was repeated – "It must work, if ever they will allow us to get at them. Your are, my Lord, surrounded by friends, whom you inspire with confidence."'

The only meeting between Nelson and Wellington – Britain's greatest soldier and greatest sailor – which took place by chance in 1805.

Bringer of Harmony

In all his command, Nelson both inspired confidence and created harmony. Whether it was with an individual ship, a squadron or a fleet, he demonstrated that he was a natural team builder. Nelson began with an unusually high opinion of his fellow officers and seamen. He trusted them and they in their turn resolved not to let him down. Months after the Nile, in a letter to him of congratulations, Lord Howe said how notable he thought it was that *every* captain had done his duty on that day. Alas, he added, in his long experience, that had not always been the case. Nelson replied: 'I had the happiness to command a Band of Brothers; therefore night was to my advantage. Each knew his duty, and I was sure each would feel for a French ship.'

This gift of creating or enhancing harmony wherever he went extended to the lower deck. He had the knack of finding the golden mean as far as discipline was concerned. The harshness of some naval commanders, who relied overmuch on fear and corporal punishment to enforce their orders, often caused dissension and even mutiny within the fleet. That unimaginative disciplinarian Prince William, when he commanded a ship under Nelson, was quite indiscriminate on occasion: he once had a visiting German journalist whipped with a cat-o'-nine tails for some remarks which were not to his liking. Nelson eschewed such brutality. On one occasion in the West Indies, he courted unpopularity with his seniors for saving from the hangman's noose a drunken deserter called Able Seaman William Clark. Nelson had powers to suspend the court martial sentence, but not to pardon or discharge the man: he did both. Lord St Vincent, one of the old school, commented: 'he used a hatchet where I would have used a penknife.'

Once a crew was working as a team and was infected with the right spirit, Nelson gave them his whole-hearted and warm affection. 'Nobody can be ill with my ship's company,' he wrote of the *Agamemnon*, 'they are so fine a set.' He turned down the offer of a bigger ship in order to stay with them in what he regarded as 'the finest ship I ever sailed in.' During a time when Spain allied itself somewhat uncertainly to Britain, Nelson paid a friendly visit to the Spanish fleet in Cadiz. 'Very fine ships, but shockingly manned,' was his professional judgement. 'The Dons may make fine ships,' he remarked, 'but they cannot, however, make men.' By contrast, the Royal Navy, like Wellington's army, did make men out of unpromising and sometimes unwilling material. 'My seamen,' he once wrote to his wife, 'are now what British seamen ought to be…almost invincible: they really mind shot no more than peas.'

Nelson once told a friend that at the Battle of the Nile his daring plan rested upon the outstanding abilities of his captains and crews. 'Without knowing the men he had to trust, he would not have hazarded the attack: there was very little room, but he was sure each would find a hole to creep in at.' 'Having caught sight of the French fleet,' Nelson added, 'I could not help popping my head every now and then out of the window (although I had a damned toothache) and once, as I was observing their position, I heard two seamen quartered at a gun near me, talking, and one said to the other, "Damn them, look at them. There they are, Jack, if we don't beat them they will beat us." I knew what stuff I had under me, so I went into the attack with a few ships only, perfectly sure the others would follow me, although it was nearly dark and they might have had every excuse for not doing it, yet they all in the course of two hours found a hole to poke in.'

Meeting Individual Needs

Nelson's early life in a country rectory in Norfolk had taught him to care for others. His financial generosity to those who had some claim on him was one expression of it. Nelson had plenty of that liberality which Sir Thomas Elyot had expected an English governor or leader to show. He was always an affectionate man, especially to children such as his youngest sister Kate, or, later, to his future wife's five years old son. A friend of hers once surprised the 'great little man of whom everyone is afraid,' at play under the dining room table with young Josiah.

Like any good Naval officer of the day, Nelson concerned himself with the sailors' material needs, on one occasion providing one crew with fifty blankets at this own expense. He insisted that the men's quarters were properly ventilated and kept as free from damp as possible. He encouraged music and dancing, and any other activity which could help to sustain morale. He obtained Bibles and other Christian literature for the sailors. But such good works do not explain his extraordinary effect upon the lower deck. That was much more to do with his personality and charm.

Apart from Nelson's reputation, which preceded him like an ever mounting bow wave, the seamen loved him for his humanity and fellow-feeling. At Aboukir Bay, when a piece of iron shot ripped across his forehead above the eye leaving the bone white and skin hanging over his face, Nelson was carried down to the cockpit. He was convinced that he was a dead man, for the spurting blood had blinded him. In spite of being in intense pain, when the surgeon broke away from a sailor he was attending in order to dress the wound, Nelson stopped him, 'No,' he said, 'I will take my turn with my brave fellow.'

Thomas Rowlandson's drawing of guns being worked during a sea battle. The Royal Navy's victories owed much to the skills and teamwork of the sailors on the gundecks.

After Nelson's early days as a lieutenant, the seamen of the *Lowestoffe* presented him with an ivory model of their frigate, filled with dominoes. Later it was a familiar sight in Nelson's cabin, a valued token of affection from his 'brave fellows'. In his despatch after that first major success off Cape St Vincent, Nelson added in a postscript that one sailor from his ship the *Captain* had come up to him on board the captured *San Joseph*, and shaken him warmly by the hand, saying he might not soon have such another place to do it in, and 'assuring me he was heartily glad to see me.'

As Captain of the *Boreas*, an officer on that ship recalled, he used to call the midshipmen his children. He never rebuked the more timid of them, but always wished to show them he desired nothing of them he would not instantly do himself. 'I have known him say – "Well, Sir, I am going a race to the mast-head, and I beg I may meet you there." ' The officer added that Nelson never seemed to notice the timid boy's lack of alacrity in climbing the mast, but 'when he met at the top, began instantly speaking in the most cheerful manner, and saying how much a person was to be pitied who could fancy there was any danger, or even anything disagreeable in the attempt.' Who could resist a Commander-in-Chief who, asked by a fond mother to deliver a last-minute note to a midshipman on his first voyage, requested her to kiss it, so that he 'might take the kiss to him too'?

Trust in his colleagues and subordinates was the key to Nelson's leadership. It is summed up in the original form of his famous flag signal at Trafalgar. He ordered this signal to be hoisted on to the *Victory* yardarm high above the amber-and-black sides of the ship as the two British columns inched towards the waiting French lines at an agonisingly slow speed of two knots. It was to read as follows: **NELSON CONFIDES THAT EVERY MAN WILL DO HIS DUTY**. He agreed to an officer's suggestion with commendable modesty – that **NELSON** should be changed to **ENGLAND**. As **CONFIDES** would have had to be spelt out letter by letter, Nelson also accepted the suggested substitute of **EXPECTS**. At least on one quarter-deck the response was characteristically British. 'What is Nelson signalling about?' grumbled Admiral Collingwood at the head of the other column, 'We all know what we have to do.'

After Nelson's death at Trafalgar the sense of elation which swept through the British fleet at its great victory was tempered by the great shock of losing such a leader. 'I never set eyes on him,' wrote a sailor in his letter home, 'for which I am both sorry and glad, for to be sure I should have liked to have seen him. But there, all the men in our ship who have seen him are such soft toads. They have done nothing but blast their eyes and cry since he was killed. God bless you! Chaps that fought like the Devil sit down and cry like a wench.'

Nelson on board the *Victory* at Trafalgar. His admiral's dress and glittering decorations made him a target for French marksmen.

The Power of Example

Paul Nicholas was scarcely sixteen when he embarked on the 64 gun *Belleisle* in October 1805 as an ensign in the Royal Marines. He wrote a vivid account of his experience at Trafalgar which included his first discovery about leadership:

'At half-past ten the *Victory* telegraphed 'England expects every man will do his duty.' As this emphatic injunction was communicated through the decks, it was received with enthusiastic cheers, and each bosom glowed with ardour at this appeal to individual valour...

continued…

'The determined and resolute countenances of the weather-beaten sailors, here and there brightened by a smile of exultation, were well suited to the terrific appearance which they exhibited. Some were stripped to the waist; some had bared their necks and arms; others had tied a handkerchief round their heads; and all seemed eagerly to await the order to engage. My two brother officers and myself were stationed, with about thirty men at small arms, on the poop, on the front of which I was now standing. The shot began to pass over us and gave us an intimation of what we should in a few minutes undergo. An awful silence prevailed in the ship, only interrupted by the commanding voice of Captain Hargood, "Steady! Starboard a little! steady so! echoed by the Master directing the quartermasters at the wheel. A shriek soon followed – a cry of agony was produced by the next shot – and the loss of the head of a poor recruit was the effect of the succeeding, and as we advanced, destruction rapidly increased. A severe contusion on the breast now prostrated our Captain, but he soon resumed his station. Those only who have been in a similar situation to the one I am attempting to describe can have a correct idea of such a scene. My eyes were horrorstruck at the bloody corpses around me, and my ears rang with the shrieks of the wounded and the moans of the dying.

'At this moment, seeing that almost every one was lying down, I was half disposed to follow the example, and several times stooped for the purpose, but – and I remember the impression well – a certain monitor seemed to whisper, "Stand up and do not shrink from your duty." Turning round, my much esteemed and gallant senior [Lieutenant John Owen] fixed my attention; the serenity of his countenance and the composure with which he paced the deck, drove more than half my terrors away; and joining him I became somewhat infused with his spirit, which cheered me on to act the part it became me. My experience is an instance of how much depends on the example of those in command when exposed to the fire of the enemy, more particularly in the trying situation in which we were placed for nearly thirty minutes from not having the power to retaliate.'

Nelson's Legacy

Apart from his physical frailty, Nelson had other human weaknesses. Some would describe them as flaws of character. At Leghorn in 1794, for example, he is known to have shared his captain's cabin with an untidy and slovenly woman – 'he makes himself ridiculous with that woman', wrote a brother officer. Some critics thought that Nelson had made a fool of himself with Lady Hamilton too, but there was a depth and permanence in their relationship which balanced his outward adoration of her and silenced all but a few critics. Among them, alas, was his sovereign, King George III, for whom he had ventured so much loyalty. According to a friend of Lady Hamilton's, she said that his besetting sins were 'venery and swearing,' but neither faults were untypical of the sailors of his, or any other, day. Besides, in the military, political and industrial fields, leaders have what has been called an 'idiosyncrasy credit': grateful for success, their colleagues discount human failings and peccadilloes. The British nation, and certainly the Navy, had no difficulty in overlooking his affair with Emma, for he was careful to observe the conventions of propriety. In this respect his charm helped him, for he remained on excellent terms with Emma's lawful husband, Sir William Hamilton, who actually died in Nelson's arms. Such faults may have made him less of a paragon, but paradoxically they make his virtues more accessible to those who would emulate him as a leader.

Of course Nelson had luck – lots of it. So many of his successes could have turned into disasters, and branded him forever as foolhardy. But most of the risks he took were carefully calculated. Nor could he have achieved his pinnacle of fame unless he was supported by other superb leaders, captains and commanders in the Royal Navy, who fell not far short of him in courage, professional knowledge and even leadership. Ovid's words in *Heroides* again come to mind: 'He was a leader of leaders.' Nor should his glory detract from the real heroes, those seamen who endured the long blockades at sea with him and fought their guns in the infernos of smoke and flame between decks. What distinguished Nelson was his rare combination of leadership qualities and abilities. Fused together, and with a certain but indefinable personal charm, Nelson achieved excellence as a leader.

None of the portraits quite capture Nelson's personal magnetism, nor do any of the descriptions of him convey it. It is best deduced from the extraordinary effects he had upon others. Yet the memory of his inspirational leadership is central to the legacy he left to the British Navy. 'Not the least glory of the Navy is that it understood Nelson,' wrote Joseph Conrad. 'He brought heroism into the line of duty. Verily he is a terrible ancestor.' By that last remark Conrad meant that, for officers of the Royal Navy in particular, Nelson was a very hard act to follow.

'May humanity after victory be the predominant feature in the British Fleet'.

Nelson, 21 October 1805.

Nelson

CHAPTER REVIEW

Summary

The chapter itself is a short summary of Nelson's life, achievements, personality and legacy, so a further summary is not warranted.

Key Concepts

- Nelson possessed a genius for leadership, just as Mozart – born two years before him – had a genius for music. In his life and career as a leader most of the strands of leadership identified so far, and more besides, come together in harmony.

- A combination of patriotic fervour – a sense of duty and love of England – blended in Nelson with an extraordinary ambition for personal fame, yet he established and maintained excellent relationships with his colleagues as well as his superiors and subordinates. He did promote his own reputation by every means at his disposal, not always wisely. He was an odd mixture of humility and ambition.

- Possessed of boundless natural courage, Nelson led from the front in battle. He mastered his profession by study and experience, acquiring thereby the authority of knowledge. He could think quickly and from first principles, giving him a confidence, clarity and flexibility of mind.

- Nelson believed in communication through channels of command and in small groups, but oddly enough there is no record of him making a speech to a ship's crew or a large gathering. He was no public speaker.

- As a builder and inspirer of teams, Nelson was without equal. He showed considerable humanity in his treatment of individuals, balancing firmness and fairness on the one hand with understanding and empathy on the other. He was as proud of his 'brave fellows', the sailors, as they were proud of him.

Further Reflection

- One of Nelson's captains who survived Trafalgar refused to travel on the first steam-engined train journey on the grounds that it was too dangerous! The world of Nelson's navy may seem far distant from the grimy factories and mills of his own day, let alone the business world of today but the Royal Navy was the largest industry in Europe of its day – the National Health Service presently holds that title. Do you think Nelson would have been equally effective today in the National Health Service? How would you translate his example into practice today in industry or commerce?

- Why are there no leaders of genius in industry and commerce? Is it to do with the nature of the common task – the apparent lack of a sublime cause or purpose that evokes the best from human nature? Or is it more due to cultural factors that have deflected natural leaders away from careers in management? That situation is changing, but is it changing fast enough?

- Despite the legacy of Nelson as a hero and role model, the Royal Navy takes pains to train its officers in leadership. Against that benchmark, what is your organisation doing to train or develop its leaders for tomorrow?

TEN
Polar Explorers

'Had we lived, I should have a tale to tell of the hardihood, endurance, and courage of my companions which would have stirred the heart of every Englishman.'

CAPTAIN ROBERT FALCON SCOTT

'Great God! This is an awful place,' wrote Scott in his journal on 17 January 1912, having reached the South Pole. Polar expeditions placed groups of men in the worst physical conditions on earth. The difficulties caused by weather, terrain and isolation called for great leadership – especially if things went wrong. The three case-studies in this chapter illustrate different aspects of leadership by British explorers in the extreme tests posed by the polar regions.

Of the three, the names of Captain Scott and Sir Ernest Shackleton are well-known. The name of the third – Gino Watkins – may not be so familiar. He was a young explorer in the 1930s who pioneered a new style of leadership on expeditions, one which could be transferred to many other kinds of enterprise in modern life. All three men, however, stand within the tradition of the British gentleman leader. They both epitomised that concept and added to its fullness by their lives and examples.

Captain Robert Falcon Scott

At the beginning of this century, Captain Robert Scott received command of the *Discovery* and sailed for the desolate regions of Antarctica. His famous expedition to the South Pole set out in June 1910. Six months later, accompanied by four companions, he reached the Pole, only to find that the Norwegian explorer Amundsen had beaten him to it three weeks before. The full story of the terrible return journey, revealed when Scott's journals were published in 1913, made him a national hero. But was Scott a good leader?

Captain Scott was certainly in command. He governed the scientific expedition in the style of a naval officer and gentleman. His subordinates, as he regarded them, were expected to be as deferential and as obedient as junior naval officers or ratings. He and his more senior colleagues ate their meals in a separate mess. Scott does not seem to have been open to ideas from any quarter, least of all his men. But even in those days 'the governor' was expected to know all the answers; to appear not to do so might be interpreted as a sign of weakness.

On Consultation

The tradition that superiors should not seek the advice of their inferiors goes back a long way in British history. In the early nineteenth century, for example, William Cobbett remarked upon how foolish it was for an owner ever to consult his men before making a decision. 'Let me exhort you,' he wrote in a book on forestry 'to give simple and positive orders, and never, no, never to encourage, by your hesitation, even your bailiff or gardener so much as to offer you advice.' And again, 'Above all things, avoid asking their advice, and even telling them your intentions. If you do this, even with the foreman, they will soon become councillors. They will deliberate ten times a day; and those who deliberate know not any sense in the word obedience. As many hands as you like, but only one head.'

By contrast, an old Roman proverb says more wisely: 'Many times has even a labouring man spoken very much to the purpose.'

Captain Robert Falcon Scott. Scott entered the Royal Navy in 1882 and was forty-four years old in 1912 when he reached the South Pole shortly after Amundsen.

Other methods of travel over snow and ice Captain Scott does seem to have ignored the advice generously offered to both him as well as his compatriot, Amundsen, by Fridtjof Nansen, the most experienced living polar explorer of the day. Amundsen, a better listener than Scott, decided to take his advice and use dog teams for his dash to fame. Scott persisted with his erroneous decision to rely on ponies for transporting their food and gear to the South Pole. The two expeditions also reflected the different values and class structures of their respective countries. Scott appears, for example, to personify the cult of the amateur when compared to the much more professional approach of the Norwegians to Artic journeys. On these grounds Scott has been justly criticised by modern biographers.

In the scientific field, however, the primary purpose of his expedition, Scott did succeed in his task as a leader. He enabled the scientists to achieve a great deal of useful research. Moreover, he had colleagues and subordinates of the highest quality with him. He expected them to behave like English gentlemen, and to remain calm in disaster. They did not fall short of these standards. As he lay in the blizzard-bound tent on 16 March, Scott recorded the end of Lawrence Oates thus: 'He said: "I am just going outside, and may be some time." He went out into the blizzard, and we have not seen him since…We knew that poor Oates was walking to his death, but though we tried to dissuade him, we knew that it was the act of a brave man and an English gentleman. We all hope to meet the end with a similar spirit, and assuredly the end is not far.'

For Scott to have written thus about his team members does perhaps reveal something of his leadership. He could do nothing for them, but in his pencilled notes he expressed his sense of their worth. No leader has left such a moving testimony to his companions. Faulty though Scott's judgement may have been in some respects, he had shared all the consequences of his decisions with them. Such men of calibre offered him no recriminations. They died together – leader and companions – as great exemplars of a national tradition.

Scott's story illustrates the need for leaders to be clear about their aim. Scientific research, not being first to reach the South Pole, was the task of his expedition. That error was compounded by his relative lack of technical or professional knowledge about long Arctic journeys on foot, and his unwillingness to listen to those who could give him good advice on the matter. Scott's real qualities as a leader – courage, endurance, coolness and calmness in crisis, and thoughtfulness for others – only emerged in the terrible days of that last journey. So often on any journey it takes extreme adversity to draw out the best in leaders and companions.

Sir Ernest Shackleton

Shackleton was also called upon to face a crisis in Arctic regions as potentially fatal as that which befell Scott. Born in Ireland and educated at a British public school, Shackleton became a merchant navy officer, and later accompanied Scott upon his early Antarctic expeditions. Scott found it difficult dealing with the merchant navy personnel, who were not accustomed to the rigid discipline of the Royal Navy. As his lieutenant, Shackleton stepped in on one occasion and used his fists on an insolent seaman. Scott wanted to send this man home for his disobedience and because he was a bad influence, but the fellow obstinately insisted on staying put. Shackleton kept knocking him down until he agreed to go home. In those days that sort of behaviour was common in the merchant navy, where men prided themselves on their toughness. The sailor ended his days with high regard for Shackleton, both as a man and as a leader. In fact, it was Shackleton himself who was sent home in the end. Apparently, Scott thought that Shackleton had let him down by falling ill on one of their journeys into the hinterland. The experience stirred him into forming and leading his own expedition.

In 1908 Shackleton sailed south from New Zealand in the *Nimrod*, in command of an expedition which came within 100 miles of the South Pole. Upon Shackleton's return he was knighted. He then embarked upon an attempt to cross the south polar continent from sea to sea. In fact, the crossing never took place, for his ship, the *Endurance*, was crushed by pack-ice and sank ten months later, in November 1915. For five months the whole party of 28 men drifted on a huge ice floe, which gradually shattered into segments and diminished in size as time passed.

'Shackleton displayed his superb leadership during this period – keeping everyone busy, making alternative preparations for any eventualities, and maintaining morale with jokes, entertainments and special treats,' wrote Sir Edmund Hillary in his introduction to the eyewitness account by his fellow New Zealander Frank Worsley, skipper of the *Endeavour*. 'His spirit never seemed to flag, although his diary reveals his deep concern for the men and their situation.'

One evening, Worsley tells us, Shackleton even cheerfully discussed taking an expedition to Alaska when the present one was finished. 'We look up all the maps and books on the subject that we can lay our hands on and are enthusiastic about our next trip before we can definitely settle how the devil to get out of this one...'

On the 9 April 1916 the pack-ice broke up and the three boats salvaged from the *Endurance* were quickly launched. Seven hazardous days and nights in the ice field later, they landed on desolate Elephant Island. Shackleton then took the largest boat, a twenty-two footer, and together with five others crossed some 800 miles to South Georgia. The epic voyage lasted for sixteen days over those inhospitable seas, through wild and furious weather. After his landfall, Shackleton had to cross the mountains of South Georgia on foot to reach the whaling stations. After thirty-six hours, he and two others struggled into the nearest whaling station. Shackleton's thoughts turned immediately to the men left on Elephant Island. Upon the fourth attempt, on 30th August, he found a way through the pack-ice and found all twenty-two of his men safe and well. The 'Boss', as Shackleton was called, had not failed them and not a man was lost.

Shackleton (second from left) on board the *Nimrod* in 1909. He died on board the *Quest* in 1922 on another expedition to the Antarctic.

Shackleton proved to be unsuccessful on all his major journeys – in so far as success is measured by whether or not the goal is achieved. As a leader of men, however, and as an overcomer of appalling obstacles, Shackleton was undoubtedly outstanding among the polar explorers. The enormous respect, trust and affection he engendered in his expedition members shines through their diaries and writings. One of his men called him 'the greatest leader that ever came on God's earth, bar none.' Another declared: 'For scientific leadership give me Scott; for swift and essential travel, Amundsen; but when you are in a hopeless situation, when there seems no way out, get down on your knees and pray for Shackleton'!

Gino Watkins

The advent of the 1920s and 1930s saw a relative change in the climate of social relations – less hierarchy, more informality and a greater sense of democracy. Polar exploration both mirrored the changes and to some extent blazed the trail for a style of leadership which would suit modern circumstances. One attractive exponent of it was Gino Watkins, who led expeditions to Edge Island (near Spitzbergen), Labrador and Greenland. Watkins died in 1933, drowned in a Greenland lake while out hunting in a kayak, which is still to be seen to this day at the Royal Geographical Society in London. Posthumously he was awarded the Polar Medal with Arctic clasp. The passage from J.M. Scott's biography of Gino Watkins concerns his travels in Greenland during 1930; it is a classic description of a leader in action. The average age of the fourteen members of the party, twenty-five years, was eighteen months older than Watkins himself, and so he had the challenge of leading men who for the most part were senior to him in years.

'As quietly as if it had been a Scottish shooting-party Gino had organised the greatest British expedition to the Arctic for half a century, and he was carrying it through in the same unofficial, heroic spirit... When he sailed for Edge Island he had no first-hand knowledge of the conditions. He was successful because he could sum up positions quickly and act without hesitation, and he was a tactful and popular leader because he asked the opinions of the members of the party who had each some special knowledge to impart. In Labrador it had been the same. Everyone he came in contact with was gratified by his respectful interest in all they said and, without fully realising it, they did what he wanted them to do and taught him all the useful knowledge they possessed. In England he had read widely and had asked pertinent questions whenever he met well-travelled men, so that by now he knew a great deal about polar technique; and although he was no scientist he understood clearly enough what the specialists were after...

'He did what he enjoyed and visited the places that he wanted to visit, but, being there, he used all the resources in his power to bring back every-thing he could. By knowledge he was best qualified to lead in Greenland quite apart from the fact that he had created the expedition. Most of the party had seen little of him before they sailed, and they were ready to treat him at least with the outward deference they were accustomed to show with a commander. If he had enjoyed that sort of thing he could very easily have kept it up. But his sense of humour made it absurd. He took trouble to climb down from this uncomfortable eminence by telling stories against himself, flirting with the Eskimos, posing as an utter Philistine or joining in every menial task...

'Besides, he gave himself no privileges at all. His bed was no more comfort-able than ours; probably it was less so, judging by the dog harness and rifles which were piled on top of it. His clothes were no better and his private possessions far less numerous. His dogs I had given to him after selecting what I considered the best team for myself. Only his native hunting instruments were superior because he had taken great trouble in acquiring them. I was reminded that once in Labrador I heard a man call him Boss, and Gino had been a little embarrassed and very much amused. That was not his name, so why address him so?

'As unemotionally as one is conscious of a fact of life, he knew that he would lead in any circumstance. Neither familiarity nor conventional disci-pline could alter that, and he preferred familiarity because he had no wish to be lonely. He was a young man who set out to enjoy himself and to make others enjoy themselves as well, because he believed that people work better when they are happy.

'All that was comparatively easy. Almost anybody with a sense of humour could have done as much if his sole object was to be accepted as a member of the party. But to one who was responsible for making people do unpleasant tasks it was a self-imposed handicap which could only be overcome by a very high type of personality. There could be no bluffing such leadership; it would either prove magnetic by its inspiring originality or lead to chaos by its non-existence.

'At first there was some argument as to Gino's wisdom in following the course which he had chosen. People like the Bedouin are used to such methods: they expect a leader to be one of themselves and recognise a strong character most easily in contrast to circumstances which they themselves experience... One or two of the Service men in particular were upset by the apparently casual suggestions which passed for commands. Gino said it was absurd to write to a man you could talk to; but even so, they would have appreciated the comfortable definiteness of written orders, if only to assure them that they had done all that was expected. Others, although they could not have admitted it, had looked for something more in exploration: a consciousness of adventure and romance. All this was so straightforward and matter-of-fact that if one so much as grew a beard one felt theatrical. Gino's plans and his rebellious why-not? points of view were exciting enough if one could swallow them; but without experience we had no personal standard to judge by; and could anyone so casual have taken trouble to prepare the best equipment?

'As time passed and experience brought knowledge, these doubts were laid one after another. It very soon became apparent that the equipment was extraordinarily good. The clothing was light and warm, while the sledging rations – Gino's most striking innovation – were excellent; no one had been really hungry on any journey and there had only been one serious case of frostbite. The sledging tents, lighter and easier to pitch than the older Antarctic models, had withstood considerable storms. The dome-shaped tent at the ice-cap station, which was designed somewhat on the lines of an Eskimo igloo with a tunnel entrance and small tube venti-lator at the apex, had so far proved efficient, though it had not yet had to withstand the hardest test of all. The Base hut, with its double walls and central kitchen, was warm and well designed. These facts and a thousand little things bore proof of care and foresight.

'The work of the first season proved remarkably successful. Luck played a part, as in the absence of heavy ice at Kangerdlugsuak, but luck is a valuable addition to a leader's reputation. In detail the journeys had not developed exactly as expected; but the acting leaders, unrestricted by precise directions yet understanding very clearly the general objective, had used their initiative to achieve a useful end. In the course of our work we had done things that we had never done before – we had driven dogs and navigated small boats through ice – and we had found these things remarkably easy. Knowing that so much had depended upon ourselves, our self-confidence increased and with it our confidence in Gino; for his plans were only alarming when we doubted our ability to fulfil our part in them. Having discovered the surprising fact that we were as good men as Gino thought we were, we accepted him as a splendid leader. He was exacting, he was ruthlessly indifferent to small discomforts like cold or unvaried fresh meat diets at the Base, he was disconcerting in his words and actions, but he would never be at a loss and would never blame. Once only Gino remarked that a man was beginning to behave badly and that he thought he would have to have a row with him. He had his row, in a roaring temper, so it seemed, and afterwards they were far stronger friends than they had been before.

'If he told inexperienced men to do what they thought best, and if they made some fatal blunder, the responsibility would be his just as surely as if he had expressly ordered that disastrous action. The world would see it thus and so would he. It was a risky policy, but for his purpose the risk was unavoidable.

'Briefly, his method of leadership was to train each man to be a leader; his ideal exploring party consisted of nothing else. These were young men and he was looking ahead towards other, more perplexing, quests.

'In Gino's opinion, initiative and self-confidence were all-important and so he would keep nobody in leading-strings. The boy who stood on the burning deck seemed to him nothing but a fool. Once, too, he had gone to a film about the sinking of a great liner. When he saw the last brave men, who had put the women and children in the only boats, standing to attention to sing "Nearer, my God, to Thee", he turned to his neighbour in the darkness and in a urgent whisper said, "Why the hell don't they build rafts instead of wasting their time being heroic?" From the same coldly practical point of view he had told me on our last journey that if the food ran out and he himself should die he would naturally expect to be eaten; and, when I demurred, he added, "Well, I'd eat you, but then, of course, you are much more fat and appetising!"

'He did not preach this philosophy which I attempted to explain. He followed the path which he had chosen, enjoying every step, quick to shock, slow to offend, but caring nothing how his words and actions were interpreted when he felt their aim was right, leading without looking back because he knew that we would follow him. Both as a friend and a leader he had always something in reserve, some depth which gave occasional proof of its existence, but which even he did not understand. The one aspect aroused interest and the other confidence.'

Gino Watkins. This young British explorer personified the qualities of natural leadership which were in demand as democracy advanced.

Polar Explorers

CHAPTER REVIEW

Summary

Scott, Shackleton and Watkins show us different facets of leadership. The story of Scott underlines the need for leaders to be clear about their aim and to stick to it. The purpose of Scott's expedition was scientific research, in which it was outstandingly successful; it was not to be the first to reach the South Pole. Scott's shortcomings as a thinker and decision-maker contributed to the disaster that followed. Yet in that mortal crisis Scott rose to the heights as a leader. He remained calm and encouraged his team. Shackleton displayed the same qualities. Moreover, by prudent planning and decisive action, he rescued his party from what must have seemed certain death. Watkins had the inner confidence to live on the same level as people and to work alongside them. He led from within, not from above like Scott. All three, it must be added, had the advantage of leading hand-picked and highly-motivated teams.

The contrasting styles of Scott, Shackleton and Watkins reveal, too, how British society was changing. The deferential ethos was giving way to a more democratic climate, which placed much more emphasis upon leadership as opposed to paternalistic or benevolent command. Change, the theme of the next chapter, heightened the awareness of the need for leaders who could give direction. Their mission was to turn change into progress. Tennyson had this wider journey of mankind in mind when he wrote the words 'To strive, to seek, to find, and not to yield' that now stand over the graves of Scott and his companions in Antarctica.

Key concepts

- Great leaders know when to seek and, as important, when to take heed of advice from others and thus to value their subordinates.

- Extreme conditions are the real test of great leadership.

- Great leaders share the consequences of their decisions with their subordinates.

- Great leaders show courage, endurance, calmness in a crisis and thoughtfulness for others.

Further reflection

- Is great leadership always characterised by achieving the initially formulated goal? Or is it more a question of how the constantly changing sequence of events is handled that gives the stamp of great leadership to an individual leader? How far, for example, should great business leadership be tested by whether the survival of a business during inclement economic circumstances is secured rather than by its failure to achieve the previous year's budget?

- Put it another way, if Scott and Shackleton are heroic failures (by some standards) can you name parallels in the business world of chief executives who are regarded as great leaders even when they failed to achieve their goals? Or parallels in the armed forces where defeat in a battle does not detract from a general's reputation as a great leader?

ELEVEN
Leadership in a Changing World

'The business of life is to go forwards.'

SAMUEL JOHNSON

During the early part of the last century a climatic shift took place in human awareness in the West. Across a broad front of human activity – philosophy, religion, politics, art and science – people felt the dawning consciousness that change was the order of the day. This feeling of the reality and inevitability of change cheered some and depressed others. For it heralded the end of a more leisurely, more static and more privileged age.

Change and leadership are closely linked. Change tends to throw up the need for leaders; leaders seek to create change. The first of these two processes is much stronger than the second. For it is actually quite difficult for a leader to bring about change within an institution or organisation which, from inside and outside, is untouched by the need for change.

In the nineteenth century the greater awareness of change did bring a new sense of need for leaders across a broad range of political, religious, educational, social and industrial fields. Contrary to the Marxist theory of how change happens in history, it became evident that good leaders – and leaders for good – formed a key factor in progress. The experiences of the First and Second World Wars led to better methods of selecting and training such leaders, at first in the armed services and then in other fields of human enterprise.

The New Climate of Change in the Nineteenth Century

Technology had much to do with the new climate of change as the nineteenth century unfolded. The Industrial Revolution was in full swing. The Great Exhibition of 1851 presented to the British nation the fruits of remarkable progress. Under the great glass greenhouse of the Crystal Palace were arranged all the products that could be gathered from the fertile soil of British inventiveness. But Victorians had no need to travel to London in order to see progress, for it was all around them and its momentum was increasing every day. Progress was a word much on their lips. Originally it had been used to describe royal journeys around the country, tours marked by pomp and pageantry. Now it was applied to any journey in the sense of forward or onward movement.

Change for the better is progress. The gradual betterment of life became a central integrating purpose. As Tennyson wrote:

> 'Yet I doubt not thro' the ages one increasing purpose runs,
> And the thoughts of men are widen'd with the process of the suns.'

The concept of progress on such a grand scale – the progressive development of mankind – came just in time: it was pressed into service as the spiritual rational of the British Empire. That Empire was already the largest in history. A belief in progress and commitment to service informed the minds of the best of its governors and civil servants. 'While we are here,' said Stamford Raffles, founder of Singapore, 'let us do all the good that we can.'

The Hebrew tradition, mediated to the West through Christianity, had fed the water-table from which the new fountain flowed. Biblical writers assumed that history has a beginning and an end; it moves forward under the guidance or providence of an omniscient and omnipotent God, who is also the Shepherd or Leader of Israel. The Christian Church, as the New Israel, had claimed the right to form the vanguard in that marching army of humanity. The Puritans in England and New England even saw themselves at the head of the vanguard. For they felt that they had a special relationship with God. 'What does He then but reveal Himself to His servants, and as His manner is, first to His Englishmen?' asked John Milton in the midst of the English Civil War, not without an assurance bordering on arrogance. 'Let not England forget her precedence of teaching nations how to live.'

In a more secular form this vibrant faith now animated the Victorians. They congratulated themselves that they belonged to a European culture where change was the order of the day. Meanwhile, in the Orient, the notion of progress was still unknown. The East clung to the idea that history went in cycles. Europe had made much the same sort of assumption in the middle ages; hence the excitement around the year 1500 when the golden age of Greek and Roman culture seemed about to dawn again. But in the European case, the Renaissance and Reformation – the twin rebirths of the classical antiquity and New Testament Christianity –did not swing Europe backwards upon an orbit of time. Rather, they gave direction and impetus for a new trajectory of progress, one which ultimately would have surprised Erasmus and Luther.

Tennyson, Poet Laureate to the Victorian Age, gave voice to this new sense of forward-looking and positive purpose, in the music of words. In his poem *Locksley Hall*, he set forth his vision for Western man. The prophecy had its dark side:

> 'For I dipt into the future, far as human eye could see,
> Saw the vision of the world, and all the wonder that would be;
> Saw the heavens fill with commerce, argosies of magic sails,
> Pilots of the purple twilight, dropping down with costly bales;
> Heard the heavens fill with shouting, and there rain'd a ghastly dew
> From the nations' airy navies grappling in the central blue.'

A hundred years later, in 1942, the skies over Europe would indeed see the rival fleets of warplanes locked in combat. As Tennyson wrote some sixty years even before the Wright brothers made the first powered flight in 1903, it was a remarkable act of foresight.

Wars would continue. The prospect of such conflict, however, might induce, wrote Tennyson, 'a palsied heart' and 'jaundiced eye'. Progress was so slow! 'Science moves but slowly, creeping on from point to point'. No wonder the Orient, untouched by the spirit of change, looked so inviting:

> 'There methinks would be enjoyment more than in this march of mind,
> In the steamship, in the railway, in the thoughts that shake mankind.'

But there could be no escape from destiny. For Milton's heirs the road backwards – or sideways – to Paradise Lost was barred by the Angels of Progress and Science. They heralded the dawning of a new future that beckons, golden with promise that dims all the lustre of former ages. Tennyson sounded the clarion call:

> 'Not in vain the distance beacons. Forward, forward, let us range,
> Let the great world spin for ever down the ringing grooves of change.
> Thro' the shadow of the globe we sweep into the younger day:
> Better fifty years of Europe than a cycle of Cathay.'

Tennyson could not foresee that the philosophy of a contemporary of his would eventually change even the cyclical mentality of Cathay (China). In the decade in which he wrote *Locksley Hall*, Tennyson could conceivably have met Karl Marx in London, for Marx arrived in 1849 as a political refugee from Prussia.

Mark claimed to have established a science which could give understanding of change in history, just as Darwin had suggested the mechanism of change in the evolution of species, which he called natural selection. Marx, however, believed in revolution rather than evolution. Because the privileged classes would not surrender power easily, the proletariat must rise, throw off their chains and seize it from them. The iron laws of change in history would assure them of victory. For power and economic might always march together. The proletariat had the economic muscle; therefore power would come to them – if they took it. The 'Age of the Common Man' was about to dawn.

Thus, in the clothes of Communism, the Judaeo-Christian belief that history moves forward in a line, not round in circles, was imported by Lenin into Russia and by Mao Tse-tung into China. In the first half of the twentieth century, revolutions in both these vast countries overthrew regimes whose rulers had shown themselves insensitive to the need for change and repressive of those who had demanded it.

Alfred Tennyson, poet laureate of the Age of Change. He actually succeeded
Wordsworth as poet laureate in 1850 and lived until 1892.

How Progress Happens

A year before Tennyson's *Locksley Hall* appeared in 1842, the Scottish author Thomas Carlyle published a series of successful lectures he had given, which he entitled *On Heroes, Hero-Worship and the Heroic in History*. 'No sadder proof can be given by man of his own littleness than disbelief in great men,' he wrote. For the history of the world, he believed, is the biography of great men – poets, prophets, priests and kings.

For Marx, however, the history of all hitherto existing society was the history of class struggle. He held that this struggle necessarily led to the dictatorship of the proletariat. The natural laws of movement in society are economic in character. Economics, not great men, change history.

But Carlyle's and Marx's views now seem to us to be simplistic. In the process of change we can discern a number of factors at work: individual leaders, groups, organisations, movements, general trends – social, economic or political, and cultural values. In order for more significant change to happen, two or three of these must align themselves together. It is the linkages and interactions of some or all of these factors that constitute the stuff of history. Leaders are needed to personify the desired change, to direct and organise it. If external factors – social, economic and technological – support that direction, then the winds of time will propel the leader and his or her team rapidly forwards.

The history of Communism in Russia supports that theory. As Marx pointed out in the preface of *Das Kapital* (1865), even when a society accepted this interpretation of the natural laws of its movement, it could not thereby avoid the obstacles posed by its own history: knowledge would only shorten and lessen its birth-pangs. In other words, knowing the theory was not enough. 'The philosophers have only interpreted the world in various ways,' he wrote later, 'the point is to change it.' But that needed leaders, cells of revolutionaries, parties, all linked arm-in-arm in a world-wide fraternal movement of man marching forwards to a new utopia. Marx, like Moses, could see the Promised Land, but it needed a Joshua to bring down the walls of Western capitalist civilisation.

Lenin is held in veneration by Communist Russia as its founding father. In 1922 his embalmed body was laid in a mausoleum in Red Square, Moscow.

Lenin, the pseudonym of Vladimir Ilyich Ulyanov, brought such executive leadership to the Communist movement. When Marx died he was still a boy of thirteen living in Russia. After briefly practising law, Lenin devoted himself to revolutionary propaganda. The imperial authorities banished him to Siberia for five years. Upon his release Lenin worked abroad, visiting London several times. In *What is to be done?* (1902), he maintained that the revolution would not take effect unless it was led by a disciplined party of professional revolutionaries. At the 1903 congress of the Communist Party in London, this lead was accepted by the majority of delegates, who hence became known as Bolsheviks ('majority'). Lenin led by example. 'There is no else,' wrote a friend, 'who for the whole twenty-four hours of every day is busy with revolution, who thinks and even dreams only of the revolution. What can you do with a man like that?' He took an active part in the 1905 revolution in Russia, but after its defeat he again had to leave the country. On the outbreak of the revolution in March 1917 he returned to Russia and eventually emerged as the chief leader of the first Soviet government.

For significant changes to happen, then, there usually have to be general factors or trends working together in a direction, and a movement, organisation or small group pioneering the way with an effective leader or leaders at their head. If one or more elements in the combination was missing, then change either did not happen or it came about very slowly. Increasingly, leadership was seen to be a key ingredient in the process of change.

Captains of Industry

'The Leaders of Industry,' Carlyle wrote in 1843, 'are virtually Captains of the World.' Their contemporaries saw the new industrialists as leaders in the vanguard of progress. Their products seemed self-evidently good. 'Railways exhibit the grandest organisation of capital and labour that the world has yet seen.' According to Samuel Smiles in his *Lives of the Stephensons* (1868). The immense advantages of the railways to mankind profoundly impressed him. 'As tending to multiply and spread abroad the conveniences of life, opening up new fields of industry, bringing nations nearer to each other, and thus promoting the great ends of civilisation, the founding of the railway system by George Stephenson and his son must be regarded as one of the most important events, if not the very greatest, in the first half of this nineteenth century.' Smiles did not live to see the First World War, in which vast armies were mobilised and moved to the various fronts largely by railway. Without Europe's railways war on such a scale could not have happened. For the successors of such men, Samuel Smiles wrote a number of books, notably *Self Help* (1860), in which he taught them the virtues of industry, perseverance and self-culture. But he had nothing to say about the management of people. Nor, for the most part, had the new breed of engineers been educated in public school or university to be gentlemen leaders.

In British industry in the nineteenth century it was commonly the engineers who provided the leadership of technological change. They did so mainly by virtue of having the authority of professional knowledge. Yet there were natural leaders among the new 'Captains of the World.' Isambard Kingdom Brunel, Victorian England's most celebrated engineer, was such a leader. His father, Marc Brunel, was a French engineer who had served in the French navy until 1792, when he went to New York. Coming to England, he was knighted for his engineering works, such as a tunnel under the Thames from Wapping to Rotherhithe. His son assisted him in the Thames tunnel project. In his own career Isambard laid some one thousand miles of railway in Britain, including the Great Western Railway between Bristol and London, then the longest in the world. He also designed and built docks, suspension bridges in iron, and steamships of great size.

In the five years it took to build the Great Western, Brunel gave his attention to every detail of the line, bridges and stations, solving countless problems as the thousands of navvies inched the track forwards in all weathers. When progress fell behind the timetable, Brunel increased the work-force to 4,000 men. Like a true leader, he inspired willing work by occasionally rolling up his sleeves and working alongside them. When the two gangs of navvies tunnelling through Box Hill near Bath met in the middle (it took more than two years to bore the 3,212-yard tunnel), Brunel was so delighted with the accuracy of their work that he took a valuable ring from his finger and gave it to the foreman.

Brunel had in good measure one essential leadership quality – a capacity for exceptionally hard work. Such was his energy and prodigious industry that he became known as 'The Little Giant.' Writing instructions alone took four or five hours a day when he was working on the Great Western – 'I fear I sometimes pump myself dry and remain for an hour or two utterly stupid.' For four months at one stretch he worked rarely less than twenty hours a day. Brunel's other main attribute as a leader was his vision. But the general impression one gains from studying Brunel and the other great engineers of the day is they were very task-orientated. They were not people-orientated as well, in the sense that, for example, Nelson had been. Technical knowledge equipped them to lead in a limited sense, but they lacked most, if not all, of the more general leadership abilities. The great industrial entrepreneurs who set themselves the task of matching capital and labour to opportunity, tended to regard work people as a commodity to be bought and sold. It was plentiful and cheap. Supported by their managers and under-managers (mostly recruited from the ranks of engineers and accountants), the industrial entrepreneurs pressed on with their profitable campaigns in the cause of progress, mindless of the casualties among their workforces.

Isambard Kingdom Brunel in front of the enormous chains of the *Great Eastern* (1858), a great ironship with a screw propeller which he designed.

Like machines, people were seen essentially as means to ends, and not primarily as ends in themselves. In cotton mills women and children supplied the cheapest labour, working twelve or more hours a day in an inferno of noise and heat. In coal mines women were harnessed to trucks and hauled them by chains like pit-ponies. Children of five and upwards were used to pull trucks through spaces too small for men or women. Thousands of boys worked in the Potteries for up to fifteen hours a day, dragging moulds to the furnaces.

Not all employers were so callous. The Welshman Robert Owen, who became partner and manager of the textile mills in Lanark in 1800 at the age of twenty-eight, would not employ young children and instead provided an infant school for them. He also opened schools for the older ones. He demonstrated that an employer could improve working and housing conditions, wages and general welfare, and still make a profit. He introduced a co-partnership system and a co-operative store, in contrast to those mill-owners who compelled workers to take part of their wages in the form of over-priced goods from the company shop on the premises. He also encouraged thrift and cleanliness.

Factory reforms, and the opposition of Trade Unions, provided some check on their freedom of action, but for the most part entrepreneurs and their under-managers remained task-centred. With an eye ever upon the ledger books, they regarded their labourers as a set of numbers, a cost to be set against profit, an expendable human resource. 'It is the Age of Machinery, in every outward and inward sense of the word,' wrote Thomas Carlyle in *Signs of the Times*. By that he meant that the temptation grew to see industrial workers not only as minders of machines, but as actual cogs in a machine, things or 'hands' rather than as people.

If the Luddites smashed machines because they posed an economic threat to their livelihood, others feared and hated them as the new enslavers of man. In 'Prayer before Birth,' the twentieth century poet Louis MacNeice voiced these lingering fears as he prayed against:

> '...those who would freeze my
> humanity, would dragoon me into a lethal automaton,
> would make me a cog in a machine, a thing with
> one face a thing, and against all those
> who would dissipate my entirety...
> Let them not make me a stone and let them not spill me
> Otherwise kill me.'

Attitudes changed slowly. Some industrialists, like the Quaker families such as the Rowntrees, Cadburys and Frys, did show a social conscience and humanitarian concern for those who worked for them. Others belatedly followed Owen's path of enlightened self-interest. They took the view that people, like machines, need to be looked after, cared for and maintained if they are to give efficient, reliable and long-lasting service. Paternalistic though this approach may now seem to us, at least it has led employers to do the right things for the wrong reasons. But, as the twentieth century dawned, even those following this limited policy were still no more than a growing minority. The majority of industrialists still saw themselves as owners and masters, bosses and managers, but not as leaders. The great business tycoons on both sides of the Atlantic – such as Rockefeller, Carnegie and Ford in America or Mond, Leverhulme and Austin in Britain – were not memorable for their powers of leadership. But times were changing, and the experience of two World Wars led to a revolution in social expectations, bringing with it a demand for better leadership at all levels of management.

Management Through Leadership

The growth of the Trade Union movement, which came into being to protect the individual and to promote his or her needs over and against the needs of the task and the organisation, was symptomatic of the lack of leadership in industry. Clearly entrepreneurs and directors, the new captains of industry, had no access to the English tradition of leadership. If they had done so, they probably could not have translated it into language that applied in their own novel situation. No wonder that industry had to re-invent the wheel of leadership. In fact, the first significant modern thinker about leadership in industry was a Frenchman, Henri Fayol.

Fayol, who was born in 1841, was a French mining engineer and became the director of a large group of coal pits before retiring in 1918. He published *General and Industrial Administration* two years earlier. In it Fayol divided the activities of an industrial company into six main groups:

- **Technical** – production, manufacture, adaptation.

- **Commercial** – buying, selling, exchange.

- **Financial** – search for and optimum use of capital.

- **Security** – protection of property and people.

- **Accounting** – stocktaking, balance sheet, costs, statistics.

- **Administration** – forecasting and planning, organising, commanding, co-ordinating and controlling.

Fayol defined command as 'getting the organisation going' and he gives some examples of what it means in practice. A person in command should:

- Have a thorough knowledge of employees.

- Eliminate the incompetent.

- Be well versed in the agreements binding the business and its employees.

- Set a good example.

- Conduct periodic audits of the organisation and use summarised charts to further this review.

- Bring together his chief assistants by means of conferences at which unity of direction and focusing of effort are provided for.

- Not become engrossed in detail.

- Aim at making unity, energy, initiative and loyalty prevail among all employees.

Fayol's analysis of managing in terms of functions has withstood more than a half century of critical discussion. L.F. Urwick, an early British exponent of Fayol's theory, in his *The Elements of Administration* (1947), made use of the more appropriate English word leadership for this aspect of management.

When Fayol's book appeared in 1916, the nations of Europe were locked in a Great War, which the machines and mass production of their industries made possible. But as industry altered the face of war, so war accelerated change in industrial society. The Great Depression damped down the fires of change, but the Second World War brought them again to furnace heat. By the time the first English translation of Henri Fayol's book appeared in 1949, the 'Management through leadership' revolution was underway. That was the title of a series of six lectures given in the previous year to 1200 British managers in Sheffield City Hall, under the auspices of the new British Institute of Management. Some words by Bertran Braley are printed on the title page of the first lecture:

> 'Back of the beating hammer, by which the steel is wrought,
> Back of the workshop's clamour, the Seeker may find a thought:
> The thought that is ever master of iron and steam and steel,
> That rises above disaster and tramples it under heel.
> Back of this, the Direction that plans and drives things through,
> Back of it all, the Thinker who's making the thought come true.'

The Lord Mayor of Sheffield opened the series by reading a telegram from Sir Stafford Cripps, Chancellor of the Exchequer, declaring that 'the country urgently needs a great demonstration from management of inspired and progressive leadership in industry if we are to avoid the perils of uncontrolled inflation and if we are to compete successfully in world markets. 'Decades later, those words have a familiar ring!

A Factory of Democratic Leaders

The concept of management through leadership owed much to the Second World War. Indeed, two of the speakers in Sheffield – General Sir William Slim and L.F. Urwick – argued persuasively that the principles of leadership applied successfully in armies could also be put to work with as good effect in British industry. In order to understand their case it has to be remembered that the British Army had undergone radical internal changes during the Second World War. It had become a factory for democratic leaders.

For the British Army in 1945 was very different from the British Army of 1939. The British Expeditionary Force which evacuated the continent from the Dunkirk beaches in 1940 contained some shocking officers as well as some good ones. At the outset of the war, after a fairly long period of peace, such variable equality is not unusual in any army. Back in Britain the regulars formed the cadre for a vast army of civilians-in-arms. Though these new recruits were eager to do their bit for King and Country, and to end the days of the Third Reich, they entered the army with trepidation, as visitors in an alien world. Those with socialist and trades union backgrounds, such as many veterans of the General Strike in the bitter class war, regarded officers as yet another manifestation of the dominant ruling class. These officers, they believed, owed their rank to having gone to the right school or having the right father. The social hierarchy of the army – the privileges of the officers, the social distance from the men – appalled them. They noted that some officers only allowed soldiers to speak to them through the intermediary of a non-commissioned officer. Such officers seemed to lack any interest or concern for their men. Practices such as saluting, and each officer having a servant, struck them as relics of a bygone age. These antipathies – actual or latent – touched directly upon the issue of leadership in that they affected people's attitude to their leaders.

By 1944 the climate had changed for the better. The anonymous author of a book entitled *A Solider Looks Ahead*, published in that year, perceptively charted this change. Captain "X", as he signed himself (his identity remains a mystery), explained that he had become a socialist at sixteen. At university he spent all his spare time on practical activity for the Labour and Trade Union movement, which he continued when he subsequently became a journalist. He was in his mid-twenties when he joined up in September 1939 – an 'arch-civilian' as he called himself. He served in a tank regiment in England and wrote his book while training for the impending invasion of Europe. His book was about 'how to make the army better than it is or how to fit it for our democratic age.'

After stating what sort of army would be needed after the war and clearing away some of the misconceptions about what a democratic army should be like, Captain "X" spelt out clearly his four requirements for a democratic army:

- The Best Possible Officer.

- Democratic Spirit and Education.

- An Efficient Channel for Suggestions and Complaints.

- Good Pay and Conditions.

The Right Leader

Alan Moorehead, than a war reporter with the British Eighth Army in North Africa, made this perceptive observation:

'On the battlefield the individual vanishes. Men turn with absolute trust to one another; they need one another as they seldom do in the even time of peace. The leader should be the product and best expression of the system; not an individual experimentalist. The system should be flexible and inspired enough to throw up the best men into leadership so that when the leader comes to take a daring decision it will be just the decision all his men would have taken.'

From *The Desert War* (1965)

A tank crew being briefed in 1941. The technology of the tank threw officers and men into close proximity and called for leadership and teamwork.

'If the officers are not enthusiastically democratic, then the rest of the army cannot be,' he argued. 'If the officers are bad officers, then the very fact that they have been able to acquire leading positions will make the rank and file cynical and apathetic. Bad officers make a bad army and good officers make a good army. An officer's job is to lead; therefore if you have good officers they will so organise the army that most of the other democratic requirements are fulfilled.'

Captain "X" proposed the continuation of the rule, introduced in 1939, that all officers should have served for at least several months in the ranks. There must be no short cuts in future to officers' training colleges. There were several things that made this principle important. In the first place, service in the ranks would give the future officer an understanding of the life of the men he was going to lead (which any sane community, he believed, would regard an indispensable condition of leadership). Secondly, service in the ranks tested a man's soldierly qualities over a fairly long period. Thirdly, the men, by observing that good soldiers were chosen from among themselves and made into officers, would see that the choice of officers depends on merit alone and that there is no favouritism or string-pulling. It is indeed very important, he argued, not only that officers are well selected, but that all ranks are convinced of it.

It should be noted, in passing, that the army was way ahead of industry in this respect. Recruits to management from university or college were not invariably asked to work on the shop floor; but that requirement grew as the influence of the army's example spread after the war, only to disappear as a general practice later.

How would the selection of an army officer be made? A suitable candidate should go before a War Office Selection Board, a method of assessment introduced in 1940. Captain "X" warmly approved of these new Boards. These were an important step in the story of leadership.

In the first year of the war, the British Army relied upon the interview for choosing officers. Questions of the type, "What school did you go to?" and "What does your father do"? were customary. Such interviews, conducted by amateurs, were poor tools for predicting leadership performance. Twenty-five per cent (and in one case fifty per cent) of those picked out by this way were subsequently returned to their units from the officer training schools as being unfit to lead platoons.

Alarmed by the high rate of failure and its effects on the individuals concerned, the Adjutant-General of the day, Sir Ronald Adam, assembled a working party of senior officers and psychologists, including an American called W.R. Bion, who later made a distinguished contribution in the field of social psychology. Together they developed a new method of selecting leaders, called the War Office Selection Board (WOSB). It was the grandfather of all the assessment centres we know today.

A WOSB was spread over several days. It was based upon the principle of selecting leaders for groups by placing candidates in groups with tasks to perform. The tasks were developed to include outdoor exercises, such as getting a barrel over a stream with limited equipment. Various aptitude tests, role plays, giving a talk and leading a group, and an assault course were all fitted into three days. The pace and demands of the programme introduced an element of stress, no bad thing when one is selecting leaders for battle. The selectors then watched the 'command tasks' with particular attention, to see how far each candidate performed the necessary functions to help the group to achieve the task and to hold it together as a working team. In other words, the working group used an embryo form of the three-circles approach (see p.66), together with the concept of functions meeting these needs. This was a different concept from that which assumed a leader was born with certain leadership qualities, such as patience and determination, which would equip him or her to lead in any situation.

A War Office Selection Board for officers in progress. Candidates wore numbers, and were known by them, as an aid to fairness.

The WOSB system was a spectacular success and it is still used by the British Army and the other armed services that soon adopted it. Apart from the Civil Service, which introduced its own version of the WOSB during the war, hardly any other organisation showed interest in this method of selection. In recent times a rash of assessment centres catering for industry and commerce made its appearance on both sides of the Atlantic. But the full potential of the WOSB method has yet to be realised by industry and commerce, education and public services.

The WOSB system tested a candidate's potential in a practical way. Captain "X" saw leadership as the essential ingredient in the best possible officers. He had these pertinent things to say on the subject:

> 'From the moment a man starts to be trained as an officer he must be taught to regard himself as someone who has voluntarily accepted a huge responsibility and who has a very high standard to maintain in everything he does.

> 'Lawrence of Arabia said, "No man can be a leader except he eats the same food as his men, wears the same clothes, leads the same life and yet appears better in himself." This must be the spirit of the corps of officers in a People's Army. If the weather is very cold and the main worry of the men is how to stand up to it, then it is the duty of their officers to set them an example of how to bear the cold and remain cheerful and active in spite of it. They cannot do this if they dress themselves up in sheepskin coats and fur-lined gloves that they have bought for themselves and which the men are not able to obtain. If the men are suffering from shortage of food and drink, it is altogether wrong for the officers to go over to the Officers' mess lorry for a glass of whisky. They must inspire their men by accepting the same hardships and yet bearing them better and being less weighed down by them. And this will be very difficult for them, for no one is more cheerful under hardship than the British soldier.

> 'The officer must know his men really well. He should see them regularly in private and talk to them about any troubles they may have and about their ambitions – whether it is to become a more skilled tradesman or an NCO or an officer. He must be on good, intimate terms with his men and he must inspire them with a realisation of what a democratic army is.

'The officer must be the master of his weapons. He must not "leave it to the sergeant-major." He must be able to strip his guns, tune his wireless, read his map and hit his target better than any of his NCOs. His men must realise that he is a professional soldier who has made it his duty to understand the weapons, vehicles, equipment and personnel under his command.

'Men's Attitude to the Officers. The men in a democratic army should therefore feel about their officers rather what we all feel these days when we meet a parachutist or a member of a submarine crew: "Here is someone I admire because he has taken on himself responsibilities which I doubt if I could fulfil myself." The men will not feel this by being told to feel it. They will feel it only if the officers themselves earn such a reputation. It will be the duty of all officers in a People's Army to set about earning this reputation for themselves as a corps and to expect stern punishment and even reduction to the ranks if they ever do anything that might delay the attainment of such a reputation.

'Those who want a cushy life, doing what is expected of them and no more, must not aspire to commissioned rank in a People's Army.'

Captain "X" had no experience of active service when he wrote and published this book. Had he fought with either of Britain's main field armies in 1943 – the Eighth Army in North Africa or the Fourteenth Army in South-East Asia – he might have found the officers even less aloof than they were already becoming in England as D-Day approached – especially in tank regiments where officers and men were thrown together in close confines. The commanders of those armies – Generals Montgomery and Slim – both believed passionately in the values of good leadership and good communication. Their examples and precepts did influence and encourage the development of communications, by leaders in the units below them. Captain "X", pondering these matters while his tank trundled over Salisbury Plain, would have heartily approved.

Leonard Cheshire

The modern technology of war brought officers and men physically close together in submarines and destroyers, tanks and aircraft. In these circumstances, there could be no artificial distance maintained. In the air, leaders of Fighter Squadrons and Wings flew and fought. Douglas Bader and 'Johnny' Johnson were outstanding leaders here, as was Adolf Galland in the *Luftwaffe*. Bomber Command also threw up leaders, among them Guy Gibson and Leonard Cheshire. Cheshire took command of 617 Squadron. This was the unit which had earned glory for Wing-Commander Guy Gibson VC in the costly but successful raid on the Eder and Mohne dams. Guy Gibson had since been killed, but the memory of him was still very much alive in his old squadron, and Gibson's was a hard act to follow. One of the squadron's veterans, Dave Shannon, recalled:

'Leonard was a first-class pilot. There's no doubt about that…He was a very good leader in a very different fashion, I think, from Guy Gibson. Gibson on duty was very much the disciplinarian; he could be a bit of a small martinet in a way and specifically so once airborne. Leonard, I think, led by example and led by persuasion and led by the air of calmness that he gave off in knowing that things could be done; and persuasion that if everybody went along with him any raid would be a success. He had a tremendous knack of persuading people to his way of thinking, and the wry sense of humour that was always coming through from Leonard meant, I think, that in a very short space of time the squadron really took to him as a first-class leader.'

The Victoria Cross awarded to Leonard Cheshire was offered for sustained courage over four years of extremely dangerous operations, for inspired tactical thinking and for qualities of leadership which made others willing to follow him wherever he led. In the words of another colleague, Jock Moncrieff:

'He was a natural leader. He was compassionate, he took care of everyone, he appealed to people and he knew what was going on in his squadron…He had a terrific sort of power over other people, a kind of, what do you call it – magnetism, charisma? Heaven knows what it was but he certainly had it.'

continued...

As for courage, who can doubt that Leonard Cheshire needed courage and a high degree of confidence in his own judgement to take the many risks involved in setting up the early Cheshire Homes?

It was the RAF at war which first taught Cheshire what could be achieved by a group of people working towards a common goal. It was war which first awakened him to his own capacity to lead and inspire others and to make change happen. It was war which demonstrated to him the need to work for international peace, and the good of mankind.

The votes of the British Army proved decisive in the 1945 General Election. To many people's surprise, Winston Churchill was ousted from office not long after his triumph. The new Labour Government came in with a far-reaching mandate to make Britain a more democratic society. The soldiers had voted Labour in such large numbers because they wanted to create a better world for their children after the war. Possibly their experience, too, of social change in the army – greater quality and more democratic leadership from officers – had helped to persuade them that real democracy in society was attainable. As all soldiers could apply for commissions and be judged on merit, why could their sons and daughters not go to university if they merited places? Thus the kind of leadership advocated by Montgomery and Slim, as a necessity to win the war, helped Labour to win the election. It was also transferred to industry by at least some of the many thousands of officers and men who returned to their old jobs as managers and supervisors, foremen and Trade Union leaders. Vic Feather, a General Secretary of the Trades Union Congress in the 1960s, voiced their conviction when he said, 'What industry needs now is not bosses but leaders.'

Slim on Leadership

After the war, the new Prime Minister in Britain was Clement Attlee. Like Slim, he had once served as an officer in the Gallipoli campaign during the First World War. Attlee tabled for the Cabinet consideration a paper by Slim suggesting that 'management through leadership' was the way forward for British industry and commerce. Perhaps Slim could introduce democratic leadership in the factories? As a first step, in 1947, Attlee appointed him as Vice-Chairman of British Railways, so that he could prepare himself for becoming Chairman in due course. Yet not six months after Slim started work, Attlee asked him to leave British Railways in order to be Governor-General of Australia.

Slim was a most effective communicator on the subject of leadership, which he believed in so deeply. Firms such as ICI frequently called on him to speak to their managers. Later he reached an even wider audience on the radio. Slim took immense care in writing these speeches and broadcasts. The natural teacher in him, together with a simple and natural style of speaking and writing, made what he had to say on leadership both profound and memorable. The following extract comes from one of his best speeches, given to a large audience in Adelaide in 1957. The Governor-General had this to say about leadership:

> To begin with, we do not in the Army talk of "management" but of "leadership". This is significant. There is a difference between leaders and management. The leader and the men who follow him represent one of the oldest, most natural and most effective of all human relationships. The manager and those he manages are a later product, with neither so romantic nor so inspiring a history. Leadership is of the spirit, compounded of personality and vision; its practice is an art. Management is of the mind, more a matter of accurate calculation of statistics, of methods, time tables, and routine; its practice is a science. Managers are necessary; leaders are essential. A good system will produce efficient managers but more than that is needed. We must find managers who are not only skilled organisers but inspired and inspiring leaders, destined eventually to fill the highest ranks of control and direction. Such men will gather round them close knit teams of subordinates like themselves and of technical experts, whose efficiency, enthusiasm and loyalty will

be unbeatable. Increasingly this is recognised and the search for leadership is on…

'I have talked so far about those destined for the higher appointments but the Army in which the only leaders are the generals will win no victories. All down the line there must be leaders. We have the equivalent of the supervisors and foremen of industry; they are our Warrant and Non-Commissioned Officers. You will note we call them officers. They are very definitely a part of the management, feel themselves that they are and are recognised by others as such. The position of the equivalent ranks in industry, suspended as they often are, between management and workers must be terribly difficult. The American system, where they are made to feel much more a part of management, has advantages.

'The greater the size of an army, or an organisation, the more difficult it becomes for the leaders to make their ideas and intentions clear and vivid to all their thousands of subordinates. All sorts of ways of doing this have been attempted. There has even grown up in industry a special class of officer whose job roughly is to keep touch between management and workers. I think there is some danger they may interpose rather than connect. Leadership is a very personal thing and like some germs it is weakened by passing through other bodies.

'There are many things that can be done to keep touch, but to be effective they must all be based on two things:

- The head man of the army, the firm, the division, the department, the regiment, the workshop must be known as an actual person to all under him.

- The soldier or the employee must be made to feel he is part of the show and what he is and what he does matter to it.

'The best way to get known to your men is to let them see you and hear you by going among them and talking to them. The head man should be able to walk on to any parade-ground in his command or into any factory in his firm and be recognised –even if it's only "Here come the old so-and-so." It's surprising how soldiers and workmen can use an uncomplimentary expression as an endearment. The boss should talk to individuals as he moves about and occasionally – only occasionally as it should be something of an event – assemble all his staff and workers, mixed together for preference, and tell them something of what he is trying to do. To talk to men doesn't require great eloquence; only two things are needed – to know what you are talking about and to believe in yourself. The last is important.

"To make anyone feel part of a show you have to take them into your confidence. Soldiers have long grown out of the "theirs-not-to-reason-why" stage. Any intelligent man wants to know why and for what reason he's doing things. Personally I believe a good system passing on to every man information of what is going on outside his immediate view is worth more than such things as joint consultation which really only reach a few. Security I know may enter into this as it does in military matters but a little risk with security is more than repaid by the feeling chaps get that their leaders have confidence in them, that they are let into the know and that they belong.

'From washing machines to electronic brains we live increasingly by technology. Technicians are vital to our industry. But we don't make a man a general in the field because he is an expert in explosives; the most brilliant surgeon is not necessarily the best man to run a hospital; nor the best-selling author to run a publishing business. The techni-cally trained man is not the answer to the management problem. There has in some quarters been a tendency to make managers out of technical men. Some of them may make good managers because they have in them the qualities of leadership, but the better the technician, the better to use him in his own field.

'We anxiously calculate stocks of raw materials, seek new minerals, study technical advances overseas and push them on at home; we devise new processes, we equip our factories with new machinery. In all these matters we take great thought for the morrow. Yet too often we just hope that tomorrow's leaders will, by some miracle, bob up when needed.

'The only way in which the growing need for leadership in manage-ment can be met is to find the potential leader and then start his training and give him his chance to lead.

'Here in Australia, believe me, there is no lack of potential leaders – the climate, the freedom, the tradition of this country breed them: leader-

ship material is lying around in every factory, office and university in Australia. Unless we spot it and give it a chance, a lot of it is doomed to rust. That would be a tragedy but a greater would be that our expanding industry should lack leadership.

'The raw material of leadership is there and the Australian worker, properly led, from what I have seen of him, is as good as any and more intelligent than most. But the words "properly led" are vital. Australian industry deserves and will need leaders not just efficient managers.

'In industry you will never have to ask men to do the stark things demanded of soldiers, but the men you employ are the same men. Instead of rifles they handle tools; instead of guns they serve machines. They have changed their khaki and jungle-green for workshop overalls and civvies suits. But they are the same men and they will respond to leadership of the right kind just as they have always done.

'Infuse your management with leadership; then they will show their mettle in the workshop as they have on the battlefield. Like me, they would rather be led than managed. Wouldn't you?'

Managers or Leaders?

Slim first posed the issue – managers or leaders? He also suggested that leadership is a much older concept than management. By comparison with *leader* and *leadership*, *manager* and *management* are indeed relatively young words. They entered the English language about three or four centuries ago. Their root is the Latin word *manus*, a hand. The father of our words manager and management was the Italian verb for handling or 'managing' a war horse. English soldiers then brought the words back from the Italian riding schools and applied them to handle armies in the field, handling swords and handling ships. In the late 18th and 19th centuries the terms 'manager' and 'management' were applied to employees appointed by entrepreneurs to run their businesses. As we have seen, these managers and under-managers were selected largely from the ranks of the professional classes already employed by the entrepreneur-owners; principally they were drawn from engineers and accountants. Both have a tendency to be systems-minded.

The words *direct* and *director* stress guidance and the exercise of leadership. They suggest a stronger overall control, while *manage* often refers to operational control, to the actual running or handling of specific affairs. Clearly the concept of leadership is much closer to change than the old idea of management – now almost gone – as the occupation of running an unchanging organisation in a static environment.

In industry today, throughout the world, the nature of management has shifted perceptibly and irreversibly in the direction of leadership. All industrial and business enterprises are launched upon a journey, if only a journey of survival. Managing is now about taking change by the hand before it takes one by the throat. Managing change needs to be done effectively at two broad but overlapping levels. The strategic work has become the prime leadership responsibility of the chief executive officer or managing director, together with the board of directors. Operational responsibility for making it happen ought to be shared by executive directors, managers of all levels, and all other members in the organisation.

The Manager-Leader

'I'm just a hired hack – a professional manager, I'm proud of that – I'm not a proprietor, not dominant. I lead by example and persuasion and a hell of a lot of hard work. Not on the basis of power or authority. My skills are to help a large number to release their energies and focus themselves. It is switching on a lot of people and helping them achieve a common aim. People only do things they are convinced about. One has to create conditions in which people want to give of their best.

'The board of directors should be, in Nelson's phrase, a "band of brothers". We should be so aware of one another's views that any one of us could act for the lot of us.'

Sir John Harvey-Jones

Sir John Harvey-Jones, appointed Chairman of Imperial Chemical Industries in 1982, an outstanding British business leader.

Leadership in a Changing World

CHAPTER REVIEW

Summary and Key Concepts

- Continuity and change are the warp and weft of life. In the nineteenth century people became far more conscious of change. They became committed, too, to changing things for the better.

- Change and leadership are closely linked. Change heightens the need for leaders; leaders tend to be initiators and managers of change, hence the proliferation of leadership in fields far removed from the political and military spheres, the traditional grounds for the exercise of leadership.

- As education becomes more universal, and expectations rise, men and women look for something more than the traditional, authoritarian owner-bosses of industry and their lieutenants, the managers.

- The Second World War indirectly accelerated the general shift towards greater democracy and better leadership in the workplace. Outstanding generals, notably Slim and Montgomery, believed and taught that leadership could prove to be equally effective in peacetime, on the grounds that human nature does not vary.

- Only the crises of the recent decades have begun to bring home the importance of leadership to industry. We are now in the dawn of a new era of management through leadership.

- Across the broad front of human endeavour leaders contribute direction and executive action to the work of progress.

Further Reflection

- Why has industry, commerce and the public service been so slow to learn the value of good leadership, at all levels, from the military field? Why has it placed so little emphasis on selecting and training its managers as leaders?

- Several possible reasons come to mind. A major one is that industry saw leadership as good human relations – the management of people. Not until change became permanent did it begin to see that leaders lead change as well as people. If your task circle includes a lot of change, you need leadership to give direction, hold the team together and care for individual needs. Communication and making the right decisions stop being desirable and become essential. Business survival, as well as business growth, depends on leadership within management.

- You will see that there is currently an even greater need for excellent leaders in every field of human enterprise. How do you think business schools and management courses should be changing now in order to develop leaders?

PART 3

TWELVE
Charisma

'True charm is an aura, an invisible musk in the air; if you see it working, the spell is broken.'

LAURIE LEE

Charisma first became a popular term in America during the 1960s and 1970s. Webster's Dictionary defines it as a 'personal magic of leadership arousing special popular loyalty or enthusiasm for a statesman or military commander.' It has since been applied much more widely to leaders in fields other than politics or war. In industry, for example, the word has often been used about industrialists such as Sir John Harvey-Jones in Britain, Lee Iacocca in American and Carlo Benedetti in Italy. It is now in danger of losing all its distinctive meaning and becoming synonymous with public attractiveness: a mixture of good looks, a striking manner and self-proclamation. So often such 'charisma' proves to be like a coat of unrenewable fresh paint, which shortly reveals lasting inadequacy underneath it.

In this chapter the nature of charisma (in Webster's definition), and the problems associated with it, will be explored by looking at some military commanders who undoubtedly had it, notably Alexander the Great, Napoleon and Lawrence of Arabia. The actual word 'charisma' comes to us from the New Testament. The chapter concludes with an exploration of the Biblical concept signified by the word. It is an example of how the three seams of tradition that lie beneath the Western understanding of leadership – in this case, Judaeo-Christian religion and philosophy – can still be mined for ideas which refresh leadership today.

The Rediscovery of Charisma

Our modern use of 'charisma' stems from the work of Max Weber, a German sociologist who died in 1920. Weber was interested in how authority becomes legitimatised in various societies. He postulated three forms of authority: traditional, charismatic and bureaucratic (or rational-legalistic). According to Weber, charisma is 'a certain quality of an individual personality by virtue of which he is considered extraordinary and treated as endowed with supernatural, or exceptional forces or qualities.' Consequently, charismatic authority was inner generated – it derived from the capacity of a particular person to arouse and maintain belief in himself or herself as the source of knowledge and authority. History showed plenty of examples of such inspired leaders challenging the traditions of their day. Their informal groups of followers, however, tended to move towards the rational-legal basis (bureaucratic) once they grew bigger and when the original leader died. Sometimes, as in the case of St Francis and the Franciscans, it happened before the founder's death, and he could find himself an alien in a large organisation that was rapidly losing his spirit. There are counterparts in every field, not least in industry when the entrepreneur gives way to the manager.

Jim Jones

In 1974 a pastor called Jim Jones established a commune of the People's Temple Sect in Guyana, which he called Jonestown. The Sect originated in San Francisco's black community. Complaints of oppression led to a visit by a United States congressman, who was promptly shot with his companions. Then Jones gathered his disciples together and preached a long sermon which ended with an invitation to mass suicide. Most submitted to him with blind and unquestioning obedience, while his guards coerced those backsliders unwilling to administer the cyanide to the children. In this dreadful deed, one leader was responsible for the deaths of 914 people, including 240 children. Clearly, extraordinary personal authority can be used for misguided ends as well as good ones.

Weber's categories need not detain us any longer, for they are vague and ambiguous and therefore difficult to make operational. In fact, Weber had in turn borrowed the concept of charisma from the writings of Rudolf Sohm, a Strasbourg church historian and jurist. Although Weber was not hostile to religion as were some other nineteenth century German philosophers such as Nietzsche and Feuerbach, he was certainly no Christian and confessed himself to be 'religiously unmusical.' Weber indeed missed the musical overtones of charisma. Through lack of historical knowledge, he also confused it with the pagan phenomenon which Carlyle had aptly named 'hero-worship'.

Undoubtedly there were men and women in the past, as there are today, who exhibited extraordinary courage, firmness, or greatness of soul, in the course of some journey or enterprise. We, as humans, also have a tendency to admire and venerate them for their achievements and noble qualities. That admiration in some people can become inordinate and they come to worship the hero or great man. They even make a fairly ordinary leader into a hero simply because they need a hero to worship. An ambitious and unscrupulous leader, who discovers that he or she has some magnetic power, can capitalise on this aspect of human nature. He or she can present a self-image that emphasises personal powers; among a susceptible group it may arouse admiration, awe and even worship, with its concomitant – blind obedience.

Leadership: A Gift from Above?

In 1841 Thomas Carlyle published a series of his popular lectures under the title *On Heroes, Hero-Worship and the Heroic in History*. 'The Great Man was always as a lightening out of Heaven; the rest of men waited for him as fuel and then they too would flame,' wrote Carlyle. 'He is the messenger sent from the infinite unknown with tidings to us.' The religious overtones in Carlyle's words are immediately apparent. Paraphrasing him, we might say that charisma is a gift from on high. It is a sacred flame that enables a leader to inspire others.

Mount Olympus, identified as the home of the gods in the *Iliad*, stands in northern Thessaly.

But who is the giver? There are three broad answers to that question: the gods, God or Nature. In a secular age such as this one, we are disposed to be noncommittal about religion and the third option, Nature, may attract more support. For Wordsworth, Carlyle's near contemporary, Nature was more than the physical environment: it was the object of reverence and the source of all that is best in man.

The Greeks were specifically religious in the sense that they believed in the existence of divine beings or gods who were distinctly human in some respects. In other words, the distinguishing line between divine and human was not drawn firmly. 'Hero' was the Greek name given to men of super-human strength, courage or greatness of soul, gifts which showed that they were favoured by the gods. Later in Greek history these men were regarded as demigods and immortals. The archetypal hero, Heracles, served as a model for both Alexander the Great and Mark Anthony. Both aspired to become heros in those senses. Alexander once commented that only the needs for sex and sleep made him still feel human.

Now the Greeks as a whole were quite prepared to acknowledge that leadership is a gift of the gods. But, unlike the Romans, they were reluctant to take the step of hero-worship: according divine honours to a human being. The Greeks had sufficient respect for the gods, or fear of their vengeance, to avoid insulting them in this way. On the other hand, despite their sophistication, the Greeks were children of their tribal times. It was an age of animistic belief: divine spirits were seen or felt to inhabit tree, river and mountain. Why not also the heart of a man? An unscrupulous leader could exploit human credulity. Given some accomplices, he could seek to establish himself as a person of divine or semi-divine powers and worthy of the awe, reverence and unquestioning obedience reserved for the gods. In other words, he could invoke hero-worship.

Among superstitious people, for example, the power to hypnotise others might be interpreted spontaneously as evidence of a god at work. In the context of leadership, certain physical characteristics were often taken as evidence of a person's inspired nature. Brightness of eye, and a penetrating gaze which made the recipient feel as if his or her innermost heart was being scrutinised, were especially potent signs of charisma. In turn, the eyes of such leader's followers became riveted on him. A voice which arrested attention, by both its musical rhythm and the content of the message, was another focal point. The aura of such a person, working through eyes and voice, was like the two magnetic forces; one attracted the followers closer, the other made them draw back and keep their distance as unworthy of such company. In so far as listeners succumbed to the spell, they became disciples of the teacher or leader in question. Sometimes they did so against their better judgement.

Alexander wearing the diadem and horn or Zeus Ammon. The idealised features suggest his divinity. Silver coin of his successor Lysimachus, c. BC 290.

There is a useful distinction to be made between invocation and evocation. Evocation happens without design, but invocation is a conscious intention. Charisma could be deliberately invoked (as opposed to being passively evoked) in several ways. A leader might associate himself, for example, with a sacred object. Alexander had a 'sacred shield' – the shield from the temple of Athene at Troy – kept by him and carried before him in battle. The Roman general Sertorius, campaigning in Spain, was presented with a milk-white fawn, which became his pet. 'Little by little,' wrote Plutarch, 'he began to build up the impression that there was something sacred and mysterious about the creature. He declared that she was the gift of Diana and possessed the power of revealing secrets to him, for he knew that the barbarians, are naturally prone to superstition.' After it had strayed off and been found again, the fawn was reunited with its master, leaping upon the tribunal where he was hearing petitions. The stage-managed scene had the desired effect. 'The spectators were dumbfounded at first, and then, breaking into shouts of joy and loud applause, they escorted him to his house,' continued Plutarch. 'They were convinced that he was beloved of the gods and possessed supernatural power, and this assurance filled them with hope and confidence for the future.'

Before one of his early campaigns, Attila the Hun appeared before his troops with an ancient iron sword in his grasp, which he told them was the god of war their ancestors had worshipped. The sword-god had disappeared, but Attila claimed that a herdman tracking a wounded heifer by the trail of blood, had found it standing in the desert, as if it had been hurled down from Heaven. The possession of such a supernatural weapon gave him immense influence over the barbaric Hunnish tribes.

Attila described himself as 'Descendant of the Great Nimrod.' But Alexander claimed not only descent from Heracles but also to be Heracles – or at least a god – in the flesh. It was this kind of claim that provoked a negative reaction from the Greeks. As Herodotus made plain in the earliest extant debate on the relative merits of democracy, monarchy and oligarchy, written more than a century before Alexander's campaigns, the Greeks thought the time was long since past 'for any one man amongst us to have absolute power.' Monarchy was widely regarded as being neither pleasant nor good. 'For wealth and power,' wrote Herodotus, 'lead a king to the delusion that he is something more than human.' The Greek passion for freedom made them wary of kings. A king's claim to be divine invariably preceded a demand for unconditional obedience, with a consequent loss of personal freedom and civil liberties.

When complete personal loyalty and blind obedience enter the picture, it is the end not only of equality and freedom but also of leadership. For the king or politician who achieves absolute rule is no longer a leader. In the conclusion to his book on estatement management, Xenophon had made that distinction clear. He acknowledged that an exceptional leader required great natural gifts. 'Above all, he must be a genius. For I reckon this gift is not altogether human, but divine – this power to win willing obedience: it is manifestly a gift of the gods to the true votaries of wisdom. Despotic rule over unwilling subjects they give, I fancy, to those they judge worthy to live the life of Tantalus, of whom it is said that in hell he spends eternity, dreading a second death.'

Case-study: Alexander the Great

Physical height was deeply associated with superiority in the ancient mind, possibly because tall men had an advantage in hand-to hand fighting and tended to be chosen as war-leaders. Alexander was less than middle height. When he first sat on the throne of Cyrus the Great his servants had to replace the footstool with a table. When he met some Persian emissaries they initially made their obeisances to one of his staff who was the tallest man in the royal party. (The Medes first introduced high-heeled shoes for men to give their leaders extra height.) But Alexander did have physical features which suggested to others his genius for leadership. His portraits emphasised his large staring, luminous eyes. He could evidently speak effectively and move men's emotions with his words. His enthusiasm and energy seemed to be boundless. Add to these assets his royal birth and unbroken string of successes, and it is not difficult to see why an aura of divinity seemed to emanate from the young man. But at the core of it lay his extraordinary gifts as a leader.

As an inspirer or motivator of soldiers it is hard to think of anyone in history who excelled Alexander. He shared in the men's dangers, as the scars of his wounds testified. Alexander would remind them on occasion that he ate the same food as they did. He was highly visible. In the siege preparations against Tyre, for example, when a massive stone pier had to be constructed in the harbour under enemy fire, Alexander was always on the spot. He gave instructions, but he also spoke many words of encouragement backed up by rewards for outstanding effort. In the assault which followed, he fought hard himself but he was ever on the watch for any acts of conspicuous courage in the face of danger amongst his men. As a general, Alexander possessed that all-important power of being able to sum up the inevitably confused situations on battlefields and then to take the appropriate action in a calm, effective way. He had a sure intuition – a feeling for the real situation long before it becomes plain to others.

The source of the troubles that almost broke his matchless army lay in its very success. How often success leads to failure! As victory succeeded victory and the epic unfolded, a group of obsequious courtiers around the young king (Alexander was only twenty-two years old when he crossed the Hellespont) fed him with a heady mixture of proper compliments and insincere flattery. They blew up the bladder of his conceit, ascribing the string of successes and conquests to Alexander's own courage and brilliance as a general, not to the combination of the army's superb qualities as a fighting team and Alexander's leadership. It is a fatal error for leaders to take credit rather than give it.

This inflated self-importance was questioned one night with dramatic and tragic consequences. Some six years had passed since the expedition had set out from Greece, and the army was encamped at Samarkand. Alexander and some of his officers had been drinking heavily. The flatterers were at work plying Alexander with the notion that he was superior to the very gods to whom he had been sacrificing that day, and superior even to the god Heracles. Only envy deprived him of the divine honours due, the courtiers told him. This was too much for Cleitus, commander of the Companion cavalry, who was as drunk as his master. In angry tones he denounced such insults to the gods. Moreover, he continued, they grossly exaggerated the marvellous nature of Alexander's achievements, none of which were mere person triumphs of his own; on the contrary, most of them were the work of Macedonians as a whole. The young king lost his temper and in the ensuing brawl he speared his friend Cleitus to death.

Despite Alexander's subsequent remorse, he had not really learnt his lesson. By this time he was the ruler of the old Persian empire and so Persian noblemen at his court had reason to join the flatterers and encourage Alexander's pretensions to divinity. The Persian and Greek contexts were quite different regarding the cultural forms of leadership. In Persia the Great King had been worshipped as a god. The subjects of his new eastern domains deemed it inconceivable that a great conqueror such as Alexander was not a god in human form.

The Greeks were happy to concede to Alexander the descent he claimed from Heracles and to acknowledge him as a genius. Neither committed them to the doctrine that Alexander was a living god before whom they must prostrate themselves. They preferred a leader who was a companion, albeit better than them in all respects; they wanted to remain on the plain of reasoned argument, not to descend into oriental submission to a despot. Being Greeks they knew how to wait for the right moment and then how to make their points as tactfully as possible to Alexander.

The day for speaking the truth to Alexander about his zeal for wars came eventually on the western bank of the river Hypasis in India. Beyond it lay green jungles and plains, already alive in Alexander's fertile imagination with Indian princes and princesses, with rubies, sapphires and pearls in abundance, lords of the largest herds of the most courageous elephants on the continent...But the monsoon rains, incessant for days, had dampened the men's appetite for more adventure. Some swore that they would march no further, not even if Alexander himself led them. When rumours of this discontent reached him, Alexander called a meeting of his officers. But his plan to cross the river was greeted with a long silence. At last Coenus, a brave Companion, spoke up and told Alexander the truth as tactfully as he could – that the army was now longing to return home. 'No longer in poverty and obscurity, but famous and enriched by the treasure you have enabled them to win. Do not try to lead men who are unwilling to follow you; if their heart is not in it, you will never find the old spirit or courage... Sir, if there is one thing above all others a successful man should know, it is when to stop. Assuredly for a commander like yourself, with an army like ours, there is nothing to fear from any army; but luck, remember, is an unpredictable thing, and against what it may bring no man has any defence.'

A burst of spontaneous applause followed these plain words. With a flash of temper Alexander abruptly dismissed them. Next day he told his officers that, while not wishing to put pressure on anyone, he at least intended to continue the advance. For two days he awaited a change of heart. But officers and men remained silent; they were angry at Alexander's outburst and determined not to let him influence them. Using the excuse of the sacrificial omens, Alexander gave in. His message that the army would turn towards home caused much rejoicing. It is said to have been Alexander's only defeat.

Probably for political reasons, more than out of vanity, Alexander persistently put pressure on his Greek officers to prostrate themselves before him. Maintaining law and order in a vast empire when the ruler is perforce absent is much easier, the Persians had discovered, if the ruler is perceived to be a god by his subjects. The worship of such a single man served to focus loyalty and to create unity amid the diverse tribes and nations that made up the patchwork of empire.

For the most part his Greek officers refused to comply; such an act was completely against their traditions. In the event, Alexander compromised. While accepting the obeisances of his Persian subjects – lying flat on their faces before him – he promised his Greeks that the need to prostrate themselves would not in future arise. To confirm that dispensation, Alexander organised a mass wedding in the Persian fashion for eighty of his Companions. He led the way, as always, by marrying two wives himself. 'Alexander was always capable of putting himself on a footing of equality and comradeship with his subordinates,' wrote Arrian, 'and everyone felt that this act of his was the best proof of his ability to do so.'

The Persians had introduced prostration as part of a novel method of the creation of an aura of divinity around their kings. Herodotus told the story of how it came about. A Mede called Deioces, who lived in the ancient time when the Medes had escaped from under the yoke of Assyria, made a local reputation as an arbiter of disputes by his fairness and integrity. Eventually the Medes chose him as their first king. Deioces ordered his subjects to build him a palace, which became the centre-piece of a new capital city, ringed on its commanding hill seven high walls. As far as possible he than vanished from their sight, surrounding himself with a new ceremonial of royalty and strict protocol. For example, it was forbidden to laugh or spit in the royal presence. 'This solemn ceremonial was designed as a safeguard against his contemporaries, men as good as himself in birth and personal quality, with whom he had been brought up in early years,' wrote Herodotus. 'There was a risk that if they saw him habitually, it might lead to jealousy and resentment, and plots would follow; but if nobody saw him, the legend would grow that he was a being of different order from mere men.'

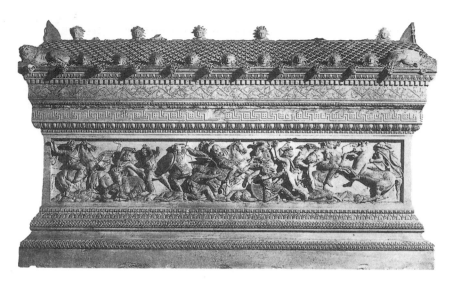

The 'Alexander Sarcophagus'. Alexander, wearing the lion's head helmet of Heracles, attacks Persian horsemen of Issus.

One can see how the Persian method of creating a divine aura by creating *distance* between the ruler and the people is in clear contrast to the Greek tradition of maintaining *closeness* between leader and followers. In the latter, leaders are prized who share the same hardships and dangers, and eat the same food. That principle applied even in such Greek states as Sparta which had kings. In the one culture, the head of state is virtually invisible; in the other, he is expected to be among his people. The drawback of the more democratic concept, of course, is that closeness dispels any notion of divinity. If a man is seen and known at close quarters it is unlikely that people will believe him to be divine. Therefore the Persian method was antithetical to leadership. It was designed to create rulers, not leaders. The logical climax of it was the declaration of the king's divinity.

A direct descendant of Deioces four generations later, Cyrus the Great, is said to be the monarch who introduced prostration into Persia. Incidentally, he balanced the invocation of worship directed towards himself with a remarkable toleration to other religions in his domains, such as the cult of Marduk at Babylon. Cyrus even allowed the Jewish exiles to return from Babylon and rebuild their temple in Jerusalem. Hence, in part, his reputation for wisdom in the Greek world, and why young Greeks like Xenophon revered his memory.

Napoleon crossing the Alps. In fact he crossed the mountains riding a donkey, but the French painter David does capture here his energy and charisma.

The Greeks were too intelligent to recognise Alexander's charisma as anything more than a gift of leadership from the gods, despite his attempts to invoke worship from them. The Persian doctrine, that a great empire could only be ruled by a king-god, was destined to triumph, however, at first among Alexander's successors and then among the Romans. Western European kings, presidents and dictators have applied the same Persian or Eastern formula in their own way with varying degrees of success. One of the dilemmas of modern rulers is that the demands of personal security compel them to distance themselves from their subjects when the democratic ethos calls for a greater closeness between leaders and citizens. Television offers a partial solution to the dilemma, but that medium is open to stage-management for effect.

The Magic of Napoleon Bonaparte

Napoleon clearly possessed charisma, at least as far as the French nation of his day was concerned. Those closest to Napoleon felt his magnetic attraction most powerfully. When, for instance, in Egypt an angry General Davout came to complain about getting an insignificant appointment, Napoleon saw him and, during their conversation, converted him into a devoted follower. From then Napoleon was his god, and Davout became the most faithful marshal of them all. Painful experience revealed to the more intelligent among the marshals and generals the cynical, egocentric and Machiavellian side of Napoleon's personality. 'I have always been the victim of my attachment to him,' wrote a sadder but wiser Marshal Lannes. 'He only loves you by fits and starts, that is, when he has need of you.' And yet the memory of the extraordinary *esprit de corps* created by Napoleon's leadership lingered long. In his retirement, Marshal Marmont wrote. 'We marched surrounded by a kind of radiance whose warmth I can still feel as I did fifty years ago.'

continued...

'The 32nd Regiment would have died for me,' Napoleon once said, 'because after one engagement I wrote "The 32nd was there, I was calm." The power of words over men is astonishing.' Following his defeat at Waterloo, Napoleon abdicated with the apparent intention of going into exile in America. He arrived at Rochefort to find ships of the Royal Navy blocking the harbour. He decided to surrender to the British and went aboard the *Bellerophon* to do so. An English passenger described him thus:

'His countenance is sallow, and as it were deeply tinged by hot climates; but the most commanding air I ever saw. His eyes grey, and the most piercing that you can imagine. His glance, you fancy, searches into your inmost thoughts. His hair is dark brown, and no appearance of grey. His features are handsome now, and when younger he must have been a very handsome man. He is extremely curious, and never passes anything remarkable in the ship without immediately demanding its use, and inquiring minutely into the manner thereof.'

Case-study: Lawrence of Arabia

People today in the West are unlikely to deify a charismatic leader, but we are still fascinated by the rare phenomenon of charisma. One undoubted possessor of it was T.E. Lawrence, known also as 'Lawrence of Arabia'. Lawrence was an almost proverbially complex man. Some of his personal characteristics did evoke a charismatic response; he also deliberately invoked it as well. Opinions may differ about the significance of Lawrence's military achievement but he had an undoubted gift as a leader as this case-study reveals.

'They taught me that no man could be their leader except he ate the rank's food, wore their clothes, lived level with them, and yet appeared better in himself.' So wrote Lawrence about the Bedouin. He fought alongside them during the First World War, while acting as a political and military adviser to the Arab Revolt. Under the leadership of the Hashemite royal family, the Arabs in the Hejaz arose in revolt against the Turks. They moved northwards from Medina towards Damascus, providing a useful ally to the British forces, under Allenby, who were invading Palestine. Thus, with men and money, the British encouraged the Arabs in their fight for independence from Turkish colonial rule.

In this desert war, Lawrence showed an unusual gift for leadership. Of less than medium height, he possessed a penetrating mind and piercing gentian-blue eyes. The traditional classical education of an English gentleman (he was in fact the illegitimate son of an Irish baronet) and his mother's iron version of Christianity were the two major influences on him. As a boy he was deeply interested in medieval military history; at Oxford he joined the Officer Training Corps and became a good shot. Like Winston Churchill, he felt the need to prepare himself for some unknown destiny.

At first, Lawrence found life with the Bedouin to be great fun. 'The Bedouin are difficult to drive, but easy to lead,' wrote Lawrence. It was an accurate judgement. The Bedouin tribesmen would naturally respond to this boyish, brave and enthusiastic young Englishman, who spoke enough Arabic to converse with them around their campfires.

Lawrence of Arabia. According to Lawrence, Augustus John made this sketch of him in just two minutes while he looked out of the window of a Paris flat in 1919.

Lawrence's physical courage was beyond question. Abu Taya, the present sheikh of one of the three major Bedouin tribes in Jordan – the Beni Howeitat – recalled meeting him when he was eleven years old. His father, the redoubtable Auda Abu Taya, became a key ally of the Hashemite army of liberation. 'Lawrence was brave, as fearless as a wolf,' he said. Had his father thought otherwise that judgement could never have been uttered. Lawrence also impressed the British officers and soldiers who served with the Arab revolt. Trooper Moore, a soldier in the Egyptian Canal Corps detachment, remembered that 'we absolutely worshipped him. He was a natural guerilla leader. He was the first commander we had who took his men into his confidence. He personally reconnoitred all our targets for us.'

Further testimony to Lawrence's remarkable qualities as a leader came from the pen of W.F. Stirling, who served as a staff officer with the Arab Army. Writing in *T. E. Lawrence by his Friends* (1937), he said:

> *'Lawrence not only saw the task more clearly than others and how it could be achieved, but also possessed a remarkable intuitive sense of what was happening in the minds of the group. Above all he led by example. He took the limelight from those of us professional soldiers who were fortunate enough to serve with him, but never once have I heard even a whisper of jealousy. We sensed that we were serving with a man immeasurably our superior.*

> *'As I see it, his outstanding characteristic was his clarity of vision and his power of shedding all unessentials from his thoughts, added to his uncanny knowledge of what the other man was thinking and doing...*

> *'How did he gain his power? Chiefly, I think, we must look for the answer in Lawrence's uncanny ability to sense the feelings of any group of men in whose company he found himself; his power to probe behind their minds and to uncover the well-springs of their actions.'*

Lawrence's traumatic experience of war – the exposure to combat, indignities at the hands of the Turkish captor, and the necessity for a Machiavellian duplicity in British diplomacy – induced in him stress, nervous breakdown and a sense of shattered personal integrity from which he never fully recovered. He became a secular equivalent to a monk serving for much of his remaining life in the ranks in the Royal Air Force. In his work on high speed air-sea rescue boats, Lawrence showed another side of his extraordinary intelligence: a flair for mechanical engineering.

The American journalist Lowell Thomas had found Lawrence co-operative when he visited the Arab Army during the desert war: the lantern slides he took later formed the basis for evening lectures in London extolling Lawrence as the 'Uncrowned King of Arabia.' Lawrence came to listen to Lowell Thomas on at least one occasion. He half-believed the imaginative legend he had helped to create. Lawrence had a literary reason for fathering a myth about himself. He aspired to be a great writer. The Arab Revolt and his part in it gave him a subject which he inflated into a Homeric epic and called *The Seven Pillars of Wisdom*. It added immeasurably to Lawrence's fame as a hero and many hailed it as a literary masterpiece.

The British are not usually susceptible to charisma, but many now felt Lawrence's influence and attributed supernatural powers to him (one can see the beginnings of that idea in Stirling's words quoted above). Siegfried Sassoon, for example, felt that Lawrence 'had power over life,' and that in some unique way 'he could make things happen.' John Buchan declared that he would have 'followed Lawrence over the edge of the world.' The Domestic Bursar of All Souls College at Oxford, where Lawrence had a fellowship, found himself spellbound listening one evening to Lawrence's 'quiet, hypnotic voice.' Like so many others, Lawrence's remarkable power of mind impressed itself on him – 'the most remarkable man I ever met.' One of his acquaintances, Winston Churchill, summed up Lawrence as 'one of the greatest beings of our time.'

After his compulsory retirement from the Royal Tank Regiment in 1934, Lawrence said that he wanted nothing more than to become a night watchman in the City. But this decade saw the rise of Fascist dictators and charisma was at a premium. In Britain, Sir Oswald Mosley was preaching the Fascist message to large audiences with clarity and force. His glittering eyes and arrogant demeanour presented a picture of a strong, great man awaiting the nation's call to save it.

The novelist Henry Williamson, a loyal supporter of Sir Oswald Mosley as head of the British Fascists, contacted Lawrence to ask him if he could come down for a meeting at Clouds Hill, Lawrence's home in Dorset. He wanted to discuss with Lawrence a projected mass meeting of ex-servicemen in the Albert Hall. Its aim would be to avoid a war with Hitler. When Lawrence skidded on his motor cycle to a violent death in 1935, he was returning from sending a telegram confirming that lunch meeting. Would Lawrence have become involved in any way with Sir Oswald Mosley? Did he contemplate lending the British Fascists the aura of his support?

Sir Oswald Mosley, the would-be Fascist leader of Britain. Like Mussolini and Hitler, he tried to project an image of charismatic and strong leadership.

These questions cannot now be answered. But Hitler read *The Seven Pillars of Wisdom* and it made a lasting impression on him. The leaders of the British Fascists certainly admired Lawrence's magnetic powers as a public personality, powers which have kept interest in him alive to this day. His brother A.W. Lawrence could see this incipient religious awe on many of the faces in the large crowd that attended his funeral. Afterwards, he received over 500 letters from people begging him to take up the dead man's mantle. 'I had to avoid becoming the new St Paul of a new religion,' said A.W. Lawrence in a television interview. There spoke the voice of British common sense.

Charisma

CHAPTER REVIEW

Summary

Charisma is a kind of personal aura, visible in arresting eyes and audible in a compelling voice. But it is not the essence of leadership. That is not to deny that some leaders do have such magnetic personalities. For there are people who are able to arouse popular loyalty or enthusiasm in their fellows to an uncommon degree. But the tests of leadership are always its fruits or effects: does the task get done successfully; is the team held together, and do individuals feel as much satisfaction as possible? As Mike Brearley, a former Captain of England's cricket team and a man with a talent for leadership, pointed out in his book *Art of Captaincy* (1987):

> *'Charisma does not imply steadiness, patience, concentration, or considerateness, all invaluable in a captain. Above all, placing too much emphasis on charisma might well involve ignoring the central requirement of a captain, namely, that he knows his task. Charisma is not the same thing as leadership.'*

But ought not true charisma to imply these qualities listed by Mike Brearley? Charisma, as originally used in the New Testament, signified an extraordinary power given to a Christian who received the Holy Spirit of God. The Greek word *charisma* meant a 'gift'; it came from *charis*, grace. In his letter to the Galatians, St Paul listed the effects of the gift of charisma of Spirit in a man or woman: love, joy, peace, patience, kindness, goodness, faithfulness, gentleness and self-control. To the Corinthians, he added that famous description of the principal and distinctive charisma of all, the gift of love: 'Love is not jealous or boastful; it is not arrogant or rude,' he wrote. 'Love does not insist on its own way; it is not irritable or resentful…love bears all things, believes all things, hopes all things, endures all things.' Do not these words suggest a certain style of leadership, and an atmosphere in which the task, team and individual needs of today and tomorrow are most likely to be met?

Key Concepts

- Charisma is a personal magic or charm which arouses unusual devotion from others. Leaders who have it attract a special kind of personal loyalty and enthusiasm.

- A charismatic leader may be credited with an almost supernatural inner or personal authority, in contrast to those who derive their authority from knowledge or position and rank in a hierarchy.

- As a form of personal power or influence, sometimes hypnotic in its effects, charisma can be used for evil as well as good ends (see the later section on Adolf Hitler).

- All leadership is in the gift of the followers. You can be appointed a commander or manager in a hierarchy of one kind or another, but you are not a leader until your appointment is ratified in the hearts and minds of those who work for you.

- The charismatic phenomenon is an extension of that principle, in that the followers perceive or endow some superhuman endowment in the leader. Some may unselfconsciously *evoke* that reaction by their looks or appearance or manner. They may, for example, have penetrating eyes or a musical voice. Others may deliberately try to *invoke* that reaction in order to increase their hold over others, for instance, associating themselves with the divine.

- How do you endow ordinary mortals who find themselves kings or queens with prestige and charisma? The Persian method, emulated by the Romans and many others, was to turn them into gods by making a *distance* between the rulers and their people, spreading ideas or rumours of their divinity, and ultimately requiring worship by prostration.

- For political reasons and personal ambitions, fed by unscrupulous flatterers, Alexander half-adopted the Persian approach, but he remained for the Greeks no more than a divinely gifted leader, one who lived, fought, suffered, feasted and died in their midst.

Further Reflection

- One of the dilemmas of modern rulers is that the demands of personal security compel them to *distance* themselves from their subjects when the democratic ethos calls for a greater *closeness* between leaders and citizens. Television offers a partial solution to the dilemma, but that medium is open to stage-management for effect. They are torn between the Persian style of creating distance and Greek style of maintaining closeness.

- Security is, however, not the only issue. How much did the British royal family lose by allowing its members to give very personal interviews on television? Do biographical revelations of extra-marital sex diminish the authority of our national leaders?

- In the New Testament, St Paul argues that the supreme and overriding gift or *charisma* from God is self-forgetful love. It is the touchstone of all other charismas, including the gift of leadership.

THIRTEEN
Women as Leaders

'Even when the path is normally open – when there is nothing to prevent a woman from being a doctor, a lawyer, a civil servant – there are many phantoms and obstacles, I believe, looming in her way.'

VIRGINIA WOOLF

In 1960 Sirimavo Bandaranaike of Sri Lanka became the world's first woman prime minister. Since then, Indira Gandhi, Golda Meir, Isabelita Peron, Margaret Thatcher, Benazir Bhutto and Cora Aquino have all risen to the chief position in their respective countries. Their appointments symbolise a wider trend: the emergence of many more women as leaders in fields normally associated with men. The seeds of this development lie deep within history, although it has taken a century of progress – its pace accentuated by two world wars – to bring women to the fore.

There are, however, problems and obstacles in the paths of women who wish to realise their leadership potential. Most of them are made-made. This chapter outlines the change in values and in society which has opened the door of leadership more widely to women today. That progress has only come about because a number of women – some of whom are described below – were willing to take or make opportunities and so lead the way. Not that the story is yet over. For there are still barriers to the advancement of women as leaders that need to be dismantled, especially in industry and commerce.

The Western Tradition

The river of Western tradition of leadership was fed from classical, tribal and Biblical fountains. What did each of these sources contribute to our understanding of women as leaders?

Socrates said that where women know more than men – for instance, in spinning wool – then they rightly become the leaders. For Socrates grounded authority in having the knowledge appropriate to the situation in which those concerned found themselves. In such circumstances as producing wool, he says, 'women govern the men because they know how to do it and men do not.' In other words, the principle that 'authority flows from the one who knows' applied impartially to women as well as men. But when Socrates turned on to his other tack – arguing that leadership consists of general abilities and qualities, functional activities meeting human need which can be transferred from one working situation to another – he is silent on women. There is no suggestion, for example, that a woman who managed men in making wool could learn to take command of a Greek war trireme.

The tribal strand in our tradition does have examples of women in positions of political and military leadership (the two could hardly be separated in ancient times). For many tribes and tribal kingdoms followed the law that if a dead king lacked sons, his eldest daughter succeeded to the throne.

Some of these queens demonstrated outstanding capabilities as leaders. The Greek historian Herodotus was clearly proud of Artemisia, a former queen of his native city of Halicarnassus in Asia Minor. She commanded her own ships under Xerxes at the battle of Salamis. The Athenians, he tells us, especially resented the fact that a women appeared in arms against them, and offered a reward of 10,000 drachmae for anyone who captured her alive. Women were not generally esteemed. After a later defeat by the Athenians, this time on land, the son of Darius turned upon his Persian general. 'He abused him roundly, and, to crown all, told him his leadership was worse than a woman's,' wrote Herodotus. To call a man 'worse than a woman' was apparently the worst insult one could offer a Persian in those days. The enraged general was barely restrained from killing the prince with his scimitar.

Queen Boudicca. No contemporary image of Boudicca survives, but later
artists have portrayed her as the archetypal female warrior leader.

The Warrior Queen

The Iceni, a Celtic tribe in East Anglia, settled for peaceful co-existence with the Roman invaders of Britain. When King Prasutagus died in AD 60 he nominated the Emperor Nero as co-heir with his widow Boudicca and daughters. But the Romans plundered both his kingdom and his household, scourging his widow and raping his daughters.

The Iceni rose in outrage and stormed Camulodunum, where retired legionaries lived on their plots of land. Led by the vengeful Boudicca, with her daughters beside her, they massacred the small community and its garrison, marched on Londinium and completely destroyed it, and then wrought more destruction in Verulamium (St Albans). Some 70,000 people are said to have died in these three towns. Suetonius Paulinus, the Roman governor of Britain, hastened back from Wales to deal with this threat.

'Win the battle or perish!' So, according to the Roman historian Tacitus, Boudicca exhorted her troops. 'That is what I, a woman, intend to do. Let the men live in slavery if they wish!' The trained legionaries, supported by a large cavalry force, crushed Boudicca's army in battle, and boasted later of slaughtering 80,000 combatants and spectators. The Twentieth legion received the proud title of 'the Victorious' for its work that day. Boudicca committed suicide by taking poison.

Down the ages, history records examples of other Boudiccas. Joan of Arc is well-known as an inspired military leader, but we tend to forget such figures as: Theroigne de Mericourt, an opera singer who led the storming of the Bastille in 1789; Mariya Bochkareva, a Russian who organised an all-women crack corps of 2,000 volunteers, known as the Women's Battalion of Death, during the Russian revolution in 1917; and Salyam Bint Malham, a leading warrior for the prophet Mohammad, who fought with swords and daggers strapped around her pregnant belly.

Christianity brought seeds of change in the perception of the value of women relative to men. St Paul's principle that in Christ all are equal – Jews and Gentiles, male and female, slave and free – was recorded in the Bible, which Christians considered to be the inspired word of God. Those seeds germinated slowly in the soils of Western culture, not least because of the Bible's ambivalence in parts about women. But in time they helped to produce such secular offshoots as the modern feminist movement.

Queen Elizabeth I, a portrait painted at the time of the Armada. The Queen stands on a map of England, symbolising her personal domination of the realm.

Within Christianity women clearly exercised leadership in the churches that Paul visited òr established during his travels from city to city. Later, the institution of monasticism gave women another opportunity, for the abbess or prioress of a large nunnery became the head of a large organisation or community dedicated to worship, learning and service. The reluctance of the Catholic and Anglican churches today to ordain women as leaders is more a hangover from the prejudice against women in classical times, which the Bible does to some extent reflect, rather than anything really intrinsic to Christianity.

The tribal and Christian strands come together in the person of Queen Elizabeth I, who was not only head of the state but also head of the Church of England. A woman of intellectual ability, sharpened by a Renaissance education, she used her intelligence and diplomacy with consummate skill to avoid conflict in both spheres. In 1588, when the Spanish Armada threatened England with invasion, she displayed courage and resolution. Though the Armada was defeated, for a time it was thought that the Spanish army in the Netherlands would still attempt an invasion. In this situation, and despite the fears of some for her safety, Elizabeth resolved to visit her army at Tilbury. As she passed through the army the men fell on their knees. 'Lord bless you all,' she cried. The following day, mounted on a stately horse with a baton in her hand, she witnessed a mimic battle and afterwards reviewed the army. Nothing could surpass the felicity of the speech that she made to them:

> 'My loving people, we have been persuaded by some that are careful of our safety, to take heed how we commit ourselves to armed multitudes, for fear of treachery. But I assure you, I do not desire to live in distrust of my faithful and loving people. Let tyrants fear. I have always so behaved myself that, under God, I have placed my chiefest strength and safeguard in the loyal hearts and good will of my subjects; and therefore I am come amongst you, as you see, at this time, not for my recreation and disport, but being resolved, in the midst and heat of the battle, to live or die amongst you all, to lay down for my God, and for my kingdom and for my people, my honour and my blood, even in the dust. I know I have the body of a weak and feeble woman, but I have the heart and stomach of a king, and of a king of England too, and think foul scorn that Parma or Spain, or any prince of Europe should

dare to invade the borders of my realm; to which, rather than any dishonour shall grow by me, I myself will take up arms, I myself will be your general, judge, and rewarder of every one of your virtues in this field. I know, already for your forwardness you have deserved rewards and crowns; and we do assure you, in the word of a prince, they shall be duly paid you.'

Queen Elizabeth never married. She promoted her image as the Virgin Queen, ruling her community of England like a wise abbess. The prospect of marriage, of course, posed her with major political problems, whether she chose an Englishman or a foreign prince. Quite possibly she did not marry because she disliked the assumption of male dominance in marriage. As Shakespeare's spirited girls and women reveal, that assumption was not unchallenged. Girls educated in the way advocated by Renaissance scholars, such as the daughters of Sir Thomas More or Elizabeth herself, could not submit themselves in blind obedience to a husband selected by their parents.

Leadership in Marriage

The potentially revolutionary nature of Christian thought on the relative values placed on men and women began to emerge – and is still emerging – as Renaissance and Reformation changed the moral climate of Western Europe. John Milton steeped himself in both traditions. He was an uncompromising idealist, both in his work as a writer and in his personal life. In his early years, Milton not only dedicated himself to poetry but exemplified in his life the themes of his pen, such as chastity. 'He who would not be frustrate of his hope to write well hereafter in laudable things,' he wrote in 1642, 'ought himself to be a true poem; that is, a composition and pattern of the best and honourablest things.' The following year, when he was thirty-five, he married Mary Powell, the seventeen-year-old daughter of a Royalist in Oxfordshire, whom he had known as a girl. Within a month of their wedding Mary left him and returned home. Milton struggled in vain to reconcile his experience with the existing teaching on divorce. Therefore he wrote a book on divorce in which he argued for a new doctrine and discipline.

A Non-Leader in Marriage

In 1983 a press report appeared about a divorce case. The judge granted the wife a divorce on the grounds that, in 29 years of marriage, her husband:

- Only gave her two presents – a potato-peeler and a hair-dryer.
- Never took her or their six children on holiday.
- Would not give her housekeeping money but sent her out to work to earn it.
- Never spoke to her unless it was to complain.
- Never asked her opinion on anything because he thought her views were worthless.

When the wife got back from work and tried to talk to her husband, all she got was a grunt. There were never any holidays because her husband thought the house was 'in the fresh air' and that was all they needed. To pay the household bills, she had to take on three part-time jobs.

Her husband was unrepentant. He explained: 'I believe the family is like a ship. You have got to have a Captain and I saw myself as the Captain. You pay the bills and you run the ship. The family can't be run as a co-operative. She told me her views and if I did not agree I did it my way. I felt that as I was paying the bills I was entitled to call the tune and I had vastly more experience.

'If she came back, her attitude would have to change. I feel I am the wronged person. I provided her with a home and looked after her and the children. I fed them, clothed them, housed them and educated them, and at the end of it – well, if you have a family like mine who needs enemies.

'I would still have her back. They say better the devil you know than the one you don't. I never expected much from marriage or life in general. I can't say I have been disappointed.'

When the husband was asked in court if he would give more affection to his wife if she returned, he replied: 'It would have to be earned.'

Milton wrote with feeling about the plight of a chaste man, with little experience of women, who married because the friends of the bride persuaded him that 'acquaintance' will breed love. Such a 'sober man, respecting modesty and hoping for the best, often meets, if not with a body impenetrable, yet often with a mind to all other due conversation inaccessible, and to all the more estimable and superior purposes of matrimony useless and almost lifeless.' Milton argued that even an adulterous wife could be forgiven and taken back, but nothing could be done about 'indisposition, unfitness or contrariety of mind.' Surely here was 'a greater reason for divorce than natural frigidity.'

Milton's concept of marriage is deeply Puritan. A woman's rights were the same as a man's. Authority rested in the husband, except where he acknowledged that his wife was more prudent and intelligent than himself, when 'a superior and more natural law comes in, that the wiser should govern the less wise, whether male or female.' But marriage was above all a spiritual affair, 'a divine institution joining man and woman in a love fitly dispos'd to the helps and comforts of domestic life.' Milton put the social end of marriage first, prizing above the procreation of children 'the apt and cheerful conversation of man with woman to refresh him against the evil of a solitary life.' That 'rational burning' for a companion had its remedy in marriage. It followed that a sexual relationship without what Shakespeare had called 'the marriage of true minds' was virtually worthless. The only course, then, was to divorce and remarry. Influential though this view of divorce has been in our own times, Milton could not prevail against the overwhelming conservative opposition from all quarters to his proposed change in the Christian law. For he did not take it for granted that the man is invariably the leader in marriage. Man and wife were equal before God and equal partners in relation to the world. Leadership went to the partner who had the most natural ability to exercise it.

The English Civil War gave women new opportunities as leaders. The defence of Wardour Castle by Lady Arundel, of Corfe Castle by Lady Bankes, and of Lathom House by the Countess of Derby, showed women acting as equals to men. Within their marriage partnerships some women took the part of leader. The Royalist press accused Lady Anne, General Sir William Waller's second wife, of this usurpation of the traditional male role.

Anne was the unlikely daughter of Sir John Finch, who held high office under King Charles I. 'I humbly besought God to provide such a wife for me,' wrote Waller, 'as might be a help to me in the way of his service, and that I might have a religious woman or none.' Anne Finch was certainly zealous in religion. She proposed that they spend a day together in prayer to seek God's blessing on their marriage. 'It pleased the Lord,' Waller added, 'to answer our prayers in as full a measure of comfort as ever was poured upon a married couple. And though at first there was some little differences in our natures and judgements as to some particulars, yet within a little while that good God wrought us to the uniformity that I may say we were but as one soul in two bodies.'

Lady Anne belonged to the new generation of Puritan women, represented in America by Anne Hutchinson, who wished to participate in the traditional world of men. The Royalist newspaper published in Oxford, *Mercurius Aulicus*, accused her of preaching in public. In the midst of the Civil War, Anne wrote to the editor denying the charge, 'for as yet (she protests) she never preached, but says she knows not what we may drive her to'. According to the newspaper she had only interpreted some difficult passages of Scripture, 'which her Ladyship called undoing hard chapters; according to which phrase her husband's army is quite expounded.' The Royalist newspaper recalled that when the couple attended religious meetings in Winchester Cathedral, Anne took the leading part. If William 'offered to speak about doctrines or uses, her Ladyship would rebuke him, saying, "Peace, Master Waller, you know your weakness in these things."

After his defeat at Roundway Down, Waller fell into a state of despair. 'This was the most heavy stroke of any that did ever befall me,' he wrote later. 'General Essex had thought fit to persuade the Parliament to compromise with the King, which so inflamed the zealous that they moved that the command of their army might be bestow'd upon me. But the news of this defeat arrived whilst they were deliberating on my advancement, and it was to me a double defeat. I had nearly sunk under the affliction, but that I had a dear and sweet comforter. And I did at the time prove according to Ecclesiasticus, Chap. xxvi: "a virtuous woman rejoiceth her husband... As the sun, when it ariseth in the high heaven, so is the beauty of a good wife."' After the Civil War, when Cromwell imprisoned Waller for three years for opposing his despotism, Lady Anne dressed herself in men's clothes and found her way across England to his prison in North Wales.

Lady Anne Waller was one of the many women who exercised leadership during the English Civil War as partners with their husbands.

In the period of English Civil War such women as Lady Anne Waller took part in political demonstrations, grabbed the attention with their religious visions and attempted to make their (generally silent) voices heard in a variety of novel ways. Within marriage, the assumption that the husband would inevitably be the leader was also called into question. Milton had picked up the Socratic tradition, which taught that authority should go to those best fitted to exercise. Within the male domain the English had already accepted that principle in part. According to Sir Thomas Elyot, governors should lead by virtue of having the necessary qualities and abilities that belong to a leader, not by right of birth, rank or even position. The extension of that principle to the family seemed a logical step to men of Milton's stamp.

Great Social Reformers

Prejudice dies hard. Not until the nineteenth century – the age of progress – did women begin to emerge in larger numbers as leaders, often in the face of disapproval. Women with a strong vocation to serve others led the way. Florence Nightingale, for example, transformed the poorly regarded task of nursing the sick into a new profession for women. At the age of twenty-four she began a ten year study of nursing practices in England and Europe, becoming convinced that there was a need for women with a sense of vocation to take up the work. Her first job was the little-sought one of matron in a mental hospital.

In 1854, when Florence Nightingale heard about the terrible conditions of the wounded British soldiers in the Crimean War, she offered to lead a party of women nurses to work in the Military Hospital at Scutari. There she found conditions were appalling. The wounded, lying in disease ridden squalor, died of fever rather than their wounds. Contrary to myth, Florence Nightingale was not known as 'The Lady with the Lamp' by the soldiers she nursed in the Crimean War. She was really 'The Lady with the Hammer', because of an accident when, defying a commanding officer's orders, she broke up a storeroom to obtain supplies. Her image as a saintly figure is also wrong. She was relentless in using influential friends, such as Sidney

Herbert, Minister of War, in order to achieve her ends. A demanding and even fierce person, Florence Nightingale was a highly efficient administrator and a great manager of change. She introduced one important technique of modern reform: the use of statistics.

Florence Nightingale. After her achievements in the Crimean Wars she worked constantly to raise the status and the standards of the nursing profession.

In 1856 the death rate at Scutari fell from 42% to 2.2%. It is no accident that we know the precise figure. For Florence Nightingale, as she said, 'loved to bite on a hard fact;' she added that she found statistics 'more enlightening than a novel.' In her role as a change-agent in society – reforming army medical services, hospitals and nursing education – she discovered the power of statistics and used it to the full. In 1858 she was elected a member of the newly-formed Statistical Society. The main subject of the Statistical Congress two years later was her Uniform Hospital Statistics. That year, a friend wrote to her: 'I have a New Year's Gift for you. It is in the shape of Tables.' Her appetite for such facts and figures was enormous. 'I am exceedingly anxious to see your charming gift,' Florence Nightingale replied, 'especially those returns showing the Deaths, Admissions, Diseases.'

Poverty, Poor Law, Public Health, Factory Legislation, Education, Prisons: there were plenty of opportunities for social reformers who could marshall evidence in the form of compelling statistics. Florence Nightingale and Josephine Butler are the best known of the women who exercised leadership among them. Josephine Butler agitated for the admission of women to higher education, helped to secure the Married Women's Property Act, and worked for the improvement in the lot of 'fallen' women. By acquiring the authority of knowledge, expressed in tables, figures and descriptive passages (Marx culled his picture of the miseries of the English working classes from the Parliamentary Blue Books), women found that they, too, could bring about progress in society. But they still lacked the right to vote.

In October 1906, a respectable mother of five grown up children stood in the dock at Bow Street Magistrate's Court, arrested for taking part in a demonstration by the 'Suffragettes.' Emmeline Pankhurst's upbring was unusual for a young lady of her time. She took part in political discussions with her father and went to Paris to be educated, returning home to Manchester a graceful and elegant young lady, 'wearing her clothes and carrying herself like a Parisienne.' Two years later, at 21 years, she married Dr Richard Pankhurst, a barrister and radical politician. In 1903 she, her three daughters, and a few other women formed the Women's Social and Political Union. Their slogan was simple but powerful: 'Votes for Women.'

Nationwide, women took up the call. But Parliament refused to discuss their demands. Suffragettes who demonstrated for their cause were often imprisoned. When their demands to be treated as political prisoners, rather than common law breakers, were refused, they went on hunger strike and there were even more violent demonstrations. Some women threw stones through the windows of 10 Downing Street, some chained themselves to railings, others lowered themselves down ropes into political meetings which refused to admit them. At the outbreak of the First World War, Mrs Pankhurst called on her followers to support the Government. During the war women worked in factories, on the land, on railways, in hospitals and as ambulance drivers in France. Instead of demanding equality, women demonstrated it. As so often before, war proved to be the matrix for social change.

When the war ended Emmeline Pankhurst continued her work. In 1918 women over 30 won the vote. On the very day in June 1928 that Mrs Pankhurst died, the final Bill giving women the same voting rights as men went through Parliament.

Mrs Pankhurst speaking in Trafalgar Square.

As the twentieth century unfolded, the two World Wars gave further stimulus to women to take up careers. After the Second World War many women began to emerge as leaders in their chosen fields. Dame Ciceley Saunders, for example, gave pioneering leadership to the hospice movement. The hospice of St Luke, which she founded in London, set a new standard in the care of the dying. Apart from showing the way, Ciceley Saunders has given inspiration and encouragement to those who have followed in her footsteps and established similar hospices in Britain and in other countries throughout the world.

Women as Manager-Leaders

'The emergence of more women at senior positions in management will, I believe, be of immense help to industry and commerce,' wrote John Harvey-Jones in *Making it Happen* (1988). 'I am bound to say that young ladies in ICI tend to react somewhat badly when I try and point out that I believe that men and women bring different approaches to thinking, and have different strengths and weaknesses. They feel that such remarks are patronising, whereas I actually intend the reverse. Perhaps the people of the East understand the relative difference between female and male approaches to things better than we. I fervently believe that, as in my family we usually make better decisions when both sexes are involved, so the same applies to industry. Women seem to me to have better intuitive capabilities and a deeper, inbuilt, sense of fundamental responsibility. They are prepared to stick with details longer then men, and to ensure that things are actually done right. They also have a different perception of other people's reactions and, by and large, are more sensitive to them. The best decisions, and the best results, will come where men and women work together as a team, respecting their differences of view, and contributing equally from their own experience and approach to the formation of the policies which they will then try to carry out.'

There is no evidence, however, that male and female qualities as such exist. There are women, for example who lack both intuition and a sense of responsibility. Courage and aggressiveness, on the other hand, are by no means uniquely male characteristics. All attempts to generalise about the leadership qualities or abilities that women possess, as opposed to men, upon closer examination seem to collapse like a house of cards. There seems little point in labelling certain attitudes or characteristics – such as compassion, warmth, gentleness, and humility – as being 'feminine,' and other qualities as being 'masculine.' For all these qualities are to be found in both sexes in different measures or combinations.

Anita Roddick

'Be daring, be first, be different,' Anita Roddick's philosophy of business struck a responsive chord with her customers from the start. The Body Shop, her creation, first opened its doors in 1976. Ten years later her company had grown to 90 shops in Britain and 196 more in 30 countries, bringing in profits of over £5 million. More than half of her British franchisees are women. Anita Roddick encouraged young women to follow in her steps and to set up their own retail businesses. 'Promote yourself, shout about your business,' she has told them. 'And if necessary, be brilliantly devious.'

Following the example of the first Body Shop, all Anita Roddick's shops have adopted a community care project, involving hospitals, old people's homes, or handicapped children's centres. 'It is not enough to vote a chunk of money to charity,' she has said. 'What is important is to involve people in giving, in sharing, in helping.'

The Body Shop enterprise is still run like a big family. Anita Roddick and her husband Gordon – in charge of the financial side – still know most staff by name. They give Christmas parties for them and gather managers together for summer weekend meetings in their garden. 'She's a very caring person,' a franchisee of four London shops has said, 'and that feeling of caring sifts right through the company.'

Anita Roddick has set herself the target of visiting every shop at least once a year, asking questions and offering support. She has an open telephone line for anyone to contact her. 'I have nightmares of memos in triplicate,' she said.

According to her husband, Anita Roddick is a 'volcano of creativity;' her enthusiasm and concern for others is evident in the story of The Body Shop. According to her, 'We must put back into society what we have taken out. And if we don't love our staff, our neighbours, the environment, we'll all be doomed. I want to make it attractive to be good.'

Women make valuable members of the management team, it will be granted, but do they make good leaders of that team? As far as I know, ICI has yet to appoint a woman as chairman of one of its divisions! In Britain few women get to the top in large organisations. Their best route to senior leadership positions is to found and grow their own businesses, like Laura Ashley or Anita Roddick. A recent survey shows that among the thousand directors of the top United Kingdom companies, there are only eight women, and not one of them is a chief executive. And, according to the *Directory of Directors*, fewer than 3% of the directors of a further 1,500 companies are women. Yet women account to nearly 45% of the workforce. In America, thanks in part to positive discrimination, there are more female chief executive officers and directors in major companies. Europe will have to follow America's lead in the next decade.

Case-study: Margaret Thatcher

Margaret Thatcher is one of the best known leaders in the world today. Indeed she has done much to put back the concept of leadership on the political map. She emerged as leader of the Conservative Party in the mid-1970s in response to a situation which had developed in Social Capitalism in Britain. Social Capitalism, as the system that has evolved in the western world is best called, reflects four core values, each with moral undertones: money or wealth, society, the individual and nature (or the environment). Conflicts between these values, intermeshed with class skirmishing and party political struggles, had simmered down into tensions, as all the main parties became converted to Social Capitalism. But the system had failed to achieve balance in Britain. The task of getting the economy in better order by containing inflation and raising productivity defeated the Labour Government under Harold Wilson, not least because it failed to control the powerful Trade Unions. As Prime Minister, Wilson excelled at holding his team together by tactical and sometimes devious means, but he appeared to have lacked a strategy or even a sense of direction. His successor, James Callaghan, was a graduate of that school. An excellent chairman of Cabinet and an avuncular, genial man, Callaghan could make little headway. The situation, which he had both inherited and helped to create, degenerated into the famous 'winter of discontent' in 1978. It swept Margaret Thatcher into power.

James Callaghan on Leadership

'I suppose it is possible to learn from textbooks and teachers how to practise the techniques of leadership, though I can't claim I've ever done so or indeed that I've ever reflected much on the techniques. No doubt I learned unconsciously when I was a young man from observing the way in which the political giants of my youth handled the problems of the 30s and 40s, and certainly in adult life I've been continuing the process of unconscious learning by my addiction to political biography, which, speaking personally, I always find utterly absorbing. Nonetheless, I've never felt required to make a systematic study of the art of political leadership, although to be perfectly open, I might have been a much better leader if I had done so.

'I can claim only one extenuation: when Harlan Cleveland invited me to come to the Humphrey Institute to speak on leadership, I read my first and only book on the subject. It was an excellent study by James MacGregor Burns. To my amazement I found that in my imputed ignorance I had luckily, or instinctively, been doing much of what he said I ought to do.

'Many of my colleagues in the British Labour movement would say that their experience was similar, especially if they emerged from the shop floor or have come to industrial or political leadership through the Trade Union movement or have sprung into Parliament as a result of being active in local constituencies.

'We were unselfconscious when we launched out on our first fluttering leadership flights. We learned how to fly by doing it. I don't know whether a bird can learn to fly in any other way. But to most birds, as to most leaders, I think doing it comes naturally.'

From 'The Political Leader,' a talk given at the Hubert H. Humphrey institute of Public Affairs, University of Minnesota, 1982

Having been defeated in two elections in 1974, the Conservative Party introduced the practice of allowing Conservative Members of Parliament to elect their leader. For many now wanted to see a change of leader. The party had originally presented its then leader, Edward Heath, as a plain, straightforward man of integrity, contrasting him with the devious Wilson. As a grammar school boy from a middle-class family who had won a scholarship to Oxford, Heath could also be promoted as a repre-sentative of the new meritocracy. His appointment symbolised the end of the old Conservative Party's reliance on the privileged classes for its leaders. But in office, Heath revealed to his closest colleagues a lack of talent for personal relations or communication. As a chief whip – the adjutant of the Party in the Commons – he had excelled; as commanding officer, however, he somehow fell short as a leader. He saw the need for leadership, but he failed to provide it in an effective way.

A smaller group of Conservative members, headed by Sir Keith Joseph, wanted also a change in strategy. They saw the need to make Social Capitalism more task-oriented. They were not, of course, advocating a return to primitive Capitalism – that would have been impossible. But they intended to turn the helm sharply to starboard and rely far more upon traditional capitalist philosophy and monetarist techniques in order to get the ship back on course. Margaret Thatcher was not only a passionate convert to these views, she also had the courage to stand for election as leader against the formidable Heath in the first ballot.

Courage, the quality perceived in Margaret Thatcher by her sponsors in the leadership election, became her hallmark in the years that followed. Guts, nerve, pluck, resolution, backbone, all these words suggest her bold and determined attitude. Her courage is allied to her firmness, which arises from the strong belief in the moral rightness of her political position and the courses of action she advocates. She has the courage of her convictions, whatever her opponents may think about them.

> **Edward Heath on Leadership**
>
> 'The Prime Minister is above all responsible for the conduct in Cabinet. Only he can set the pace for the conduct of affairs, determining how long should be given to this or that, throwing his weight in favour of this suggestion or of that. He therefore has an inescapable responsibility for the general style and aspect of the Government, the priorities of Government action, and the impression which the Cabinet as a whole creates upon the British public and the world.
>
> 'Prime Ministers cannot boss their colleagues, let alone Parliament. But they can lead. And leadership means not saying "Do this, do that," but providing a combination of words and actions over a period of time.'
>
> Interview in *The Observer*, 21 June 1970

Senior colleagues say that they found Margaret Thatcher a feminine person, not above giving way to tears on occasion. She can use femininity to competitive advantage. It is said that she sometimes mistakes common politeness to her as a woman for signs of deference to her as a politician. Her concern and compassion for her staff and an extended family of friends and even acquaintances is evidence of the maternal side to her nature. In Denis Thatcher she found the right husband; by good luck children, in the shape of twins, arrived at one time, which shortened the time needed to rear them. She has been able to combine leadership in public office with family life successfully.

In groups or in public, Margaret Thatcher's colleagues have reported that she tended to be far more strident, aggressive and dominant than she was when in private talking to them as individuals. This may be a manifestation of that personal drive and need to win that she has had to develop in order to achieve her ambition. She is said to be a better listener in private than she appears to be in public.

Margaret Thatcher's emphasis has fallen on personal drive, self-reliance and self-help. She did not express any such strong beliefs in teamwork, nor did she show any talent for team-building. That lack, and its consequences, has been a flaw in her leadership. As a schoolgirl and at university she had no experience of leading teams in extra-curricular activities, preferring to develop her individual skills as a debater. Nor did her work as a chemist in industry or as a tax lawyer equip her for team leadership. William Whitelaw, who became her Deputy Prime Minister, saw this empty space and decided to work with her, complementing her driving sense of direction with his skills as a maintainer of at least an outward appearance of unity within the Cabinet and within the parliamentary party. Whitelaw received a peerage for his services on the bridge and within the engine room of party unity.

Margaret Thatcher and her husband Denis on the day of her re-election
as Prime Minister for a third consecutive term of office.

Margaret Thatcher on Leadership

On a visit to Bonn in 1983 Margaret Thatcher recalled that her father had been Mayor of Grantham, and said that in a democracy one needed leadership throughout society. 'Democracy is about the distribution of responsibility,' she added.

In a conversation with Max Hastings that year, reported in *The Standard* (2 June), Margaret Thatcher responded to the suggestion that it might now be time to acknowledge a greater responsibility to the unemployed. She nodded. 'We know that it is desperately depressing for a youngster not to have anything to do. But I remember when I visited Toxteth – the housing there is not bad, some of it is quite good. Yet there were weeds growing right up to some of the buildings. I said: "Surely it's possible to get a group of youngsters together and say – 'Come on and do something about this.'" But I was told: "If you do that you'll have a terrible mess the following day."

'That seems to me a very depressing attitude. What we need is more leadership at every level. You know that if you have an army, it's no good just having a general – you need leadership all the way through the system. If we have a philosophy, it is to create this leadership at every level, to say to people – it doesn't matter who you are or where you are or what you are, you have something to contribute to society. At the moment you find very good leadership in some places, and a total absence of it in others.'

Max Hastings commented on the interview: 'I was struck again, as many of us have been struck listening to the Prime Minister on the platform, by how little she refers to her colleagues in government, how much the thrust of her argument is unabashedly personal.'

Some of Margaret Thatcher's Cabinet colleagues, versed in the ways of clubbable English gentlemen, found her ignorant of the unwritten rules which they had acquired in their public schools, regiments and country houses. They complained that Margaret Thatcher did not know how to treat them properly. Behind the social snobbery there was an element of truth. Even quite senior ministers were seldom, if ever, invited to meet her on their own for a chat over a drink. She expected her senior colleagues to be able to look after themselves. If they ran into political trouble, they received little sympathy from her. She could be brutal in her application of the military maxim 'never reinforce failure.' Even at Cabinet level, however, men and women do need to feel part of a team: they need to feel that their individual contributions are valued by their leader and by their colleagues.

Whitelaw on Thatcher

As Deputy Prime Minister, William Whitelaw's influence was pervasive. It was always exercised in a calming manner – and a faithful one. He knew exactly how to get business through: when to bluster, when to cajole, when to bring out the big stick, when to produce the whisky bottle. He was good at getting people to work together and resourceful in finding solutions. His patrician and paternalist style and his open-mindedness belong to quieter political times. He did not share the Prime Minister's ideological enthusiasms, but he never tried to undermine them.

Margaret Thatcher will never become a popular politician, Whitelaw, the former leader of the House of Lords said in an interview in *Woman's Own* (April 1988): 'She ought to be more popular, because she's a much kinder, more sympathetic person than anyone knows.' He added that Margaret Thatcher appeared 'hard and ruthless' on television because she was 'crisp and determined.' He called for 'a little compassion' in the society created in the Thatcher years.

Whitelaw hinted that Margaret Thatcher was sometimes too strident. 'A certain hesitancy is not a bad thing, because people prefer it, rather than being told all the time what to do. Hesitancy is not in the Prime Minister's vocabulary. But then she gets away with it because she has been so enormously successful.' He said that, 'she has a very different sense of humour from me, but it is not quite true to say that she has no sense of humour at all.'

Whitelaw predicted that the Conservative party would get into a muddle when Margaret Thatcher left office as Prime Minister, because she has been so dominant for so long. Finally, when asked how Thatcher had changed over the years, Whitelaw replied she had gained enormously in confidence and stature.

Strong conviction, even passion, is a great asset in a leader of either sex. It generates enthusiasm, energy and single-mindedness. People like to know where they stand with a leader. But it brings the dangers of breeding inflexibility, arrogance and ruthlessness. Too much emphasis on the strong leader can be at the expense of the team. There is always a danger, too, that restraining voices are exiled and the full Cabinet becomes a rubber-stamp. Such developments may expedite the daily business, but they do not augur well for the quality of decisions in the longer term.

'The only way to safeguard yourself against flatterers,' wrote Machiavelli, 'is by letting people understand that you are not offended by the truth; but if everyone can speak the truth to you then you lose respect.' Strong leaders in particular do need colleagues of stature, who are not afraid to speak the truth in the right place and at the right time.

Will Margaret Thatcher take her place with Churchill as one of the great British political leaders of the century? To do so, she must satisfy one criterion: she must have inspired or evoked the greatness of the British nation in order to accomplish a great necessity. Though the climate within Social Capitalism in Britain had begun to change before she took office, she has presided over that change with a leader's sense of urgency. Some find that she is not inspiring as a leader. Others, however, are deeply stirred by her passionate conviction, clear and simple speech and strong sense of direction. Of her achievement, as a leader – and for leadership – there can be no doubt. It remains to be seen how Margaret Thatcher will face up to the last challenge of leadership: how to manage departure in a way that consolidates achievement.

Women As Leaders

CHAPTER REVIEW

Summary and Key Concepts.

- People tend to follow those who know the way. As Socrates pointed out in Athens some 2,500 years ago, in endeavours where women are knowledgeable – and the example used was weaving – both men and women will accept them as leaders.

- The historical accident of law of primogeniture meant that even in times and in cultures where the female sex was undervalued in contrast to the male and kept out of public life, women could still be leaders of tribes, city-states or nations. Many of these women actually showed outstanding natural qualities and acquired skills as leaders.

- Not until recent times has the door for leadership been slowly opened – or forced open – for women in almost all the areas of human work. However, there are still 'phantoms and obstacles' in the path of any woman who wishes to become the leader of a large organisation.

- At work, women leaders rightly expect to be judged by the same inexorable criteria as their male colleagues: do they enable their group or organisations to achieve its task, while building teamwork and releasing the best that is in each individual? Those requirements can be met effectively by leaders of very different temperaments and personalities. There are most probably no specifically male or female qualities of leadership.

- Women who have no paid employment can still give leadership as wives and mothers, as neighbours and citizens. A principle strand in our hope for the future must be in the awakening of women to the needs and responsibilities of leadership.

- To enable more women to attain positions of strategic leadership responsibility in industry, commerce and the public services, should be one of the aims of society.

Further Reflection

- Many women do not see Margaret Thatcher as an exemplar or role model for women as leaders. Why do you think that this is the case?

- Men and women's brains differ as well as their bodies, it has been said. Do you agree? If so, how does it affect their style of leadership?

- Like men, women have to face the issue of whether or not they can pay the price of leadership and still grow as whole people. We all want to have our cake and eat it. Many women want to be happily married and have a family, and – at the same time – pursue a successful career. Having young children means that you are always on emotional first call, however much you delegate to home-helpers. Can the demands of family be reconciled with hard work, long hours and the extra responsibility entailed in managerial leadership today?

FOURTEEN
Styles of Leadership

'These are hard times in which a genius would wish to live. Great necessities call forth great leaders.'

ABIGAIL ADAMS,
WRITING TO THOMAS JEFFERSON, 1790

It is fascinating to observe how leaders adopt very different styles, depending upon their personalities, their peoples and their times. These factors are illustrated by the four case-studies in this chapter. The first two examples – Abraham Lincoln and Charles de Gaulle – are numbered among the great political leaders of their perspective nations. Adolf Hitler is perhaps best described as a great misleader. His ruthless Machiavellian approach and lack of moral principle sets him apart from the other three leaders. Yet there are lessons to be learnt from him – 'knowledge of good bought dear by knowing ill,' as Byron wrote. Mahatma Gandhi's style was in total contrast to Hitler's corrupt and despotic rule, although he was also a man of charisma. His life reminds us of those truths buried in the teachings of Socrates, Lao Tzu and Jesus about the nature of great leadership.

Greatness

Greatness is a word that signifies a matter of degree. It can be applied separately or collectively to position and rank, knowledge or character – the three main strands of authority in leadership. In democracies there is a subdivision between great position and great rank, in so far as the highest born, or those first in the social order, do not necessarily rule the country. The people choose their supreme governor or governing body. They tend to elect those whom Edmund Burke called 'the natural aristocrats': men and women who exemplify the nation's virtues and who are perceived to have qualities of leadership. President Ronald Reagan's popularity in America stemmed in part from the nation's perception that he personified the qualities of a good American.

Abraham Lincoln. Born in a Kentucky log cabin, he was almost entirely self-educated. Having qualified as a lawyer he entered politics and was eventually elected President of the United States in 1860.

It follows that a great leader tends to hold supreme office in a nation, but may not have come from a great family (as Winston Churchill did) or even any family of rank. He or she will be seen as possessing the combined authority of knowledge and personality. But that is not enough. In order to become great in the historical sense, there must have been a really significant achievement. For greatness in history implies an accomplishment that has been critically evaluated or tested over the course of time in light of its contribution to the sum of human well-being. For this reason it is impossible to call any leader great until their accomplishment is secure. Mikhail Gorbachev *looks* as if he has the makings of a great leader in Russia today, but we cannot at present say that he is one. Nor can that be said about Margaret Thatcher. Both, however, are undoubtedly leaders of stature.

Upon whom should the accolade of greatness amongst leaders fall? Recently a selection of people from different nations were asked that question. In reply they usually nominated the leader who had won their national freedom or independence, or preserved their countries from invasion. For Americans, George Washington and Abraham Lincoln were such leaders, while the British would name great defenders of their freedom, such as King Alfred, Queen Elizabeth I or Sir Winston Churchill. The Dutch mentioned Prince William of Orange. Greeks referred even further back in time to Alexander the Great, although Eleutherios Venizelos, a Cretan who became Premier of Greece in 1911, received some votes as a leader with stature. (The Greeks, incidentally, do not apply the word 'leader' to industrialists. Aristotle Onassis, for example, was not called a leader.) Newly-emerged nations named those who led them to independence, such as Jomo Kenyatta in Kenya or Kwame Nkrumah of Ghana. In South America the name of Simon Bolivar, 'the Liberator' from Spanish colonial rule, is still pre-eminent.

Had they been asked, the North Vietnamese would have doubtless nominated a former cook at London's Carlton Hotel – Ho Chi Minh. Behind this leader's self-effacing, elusive manner was an iron will which enabled him to lead a long and bloody war against two powerful modern nations – France and the United States. Like many revolutionaries, Ho Chi Minh had suffered physically on the path to national leadership, often enduring arrest and imprisonment. In Yunnan, he was 'loaded with chains, covered in sores, put among the worst bandits, associated with the condemned, like one dead.' Ho Chi Minh, like Moses, did not live to see the final victory, but he died confident that it was an absolute certainty. Such leaders inspire a nation's lasting gratitude. They are often also seen as father-figures, personifications of the incipient nation's ideals and aspirations.

Abraham Lincoln, the subject of the first case-study, was such a figure in American history. Apart from his historic achievement of maintaining the unity of the United States, Lincoln's style of leadership – simple, direct and compassionate – has served as a model to those who came after him and aspired to lead their fellow Americans in the great democratic nation.

Abraham Lincoln

Lincoln's chief gift as a leader was his clarity of vision. Before his inauguration as President in May 1861, the outgoing Democratic government had already decided that it had no power to prevent any state from seceding from the Union. Lincoln judged that slavery was an issue which time and common sense would solve. But once the Union was gone it would most probably never return. North America could become like Europe, a continent torn with disunity, jealousy, economic rivalry and wars. He made his aim crystal-clear in a famous letter to Horace Greeley, editor of *The New York Tribune*:

> 'My paramount object in this struggle is to save the Union, and it is not either to save or destroy slavery. If I could save the Union without freeing any slave, I would do it; and if I could do it by freeing all the slaves, I would do it; and if I could save it by freeing some, and leaving others alone, I would do that.'

Thus Lincoln gave the Northern states a clear aim. His strong and dignified countenance, deeply lined and touched by melancholy, imparted a calm assurance, and a proper sense of the tragedy of this war between brothers. 'Through all the doubt and darkness, the danger and long tempest of the war,' wrote William Makepeace Thackeray, 'I think it was only the American leader's indomitable soul that remained entirely steady.'

Despite his burdens as President and Commander-in-Chief during the war between the states, Lincoln found time for individuals. There is perhaps no better expression of his tender humanity than the letter he wrote to one victim of the Civil War, named Mrs Bixby:

Dear Madam,

I have been shown in the files of the War Department a statement of the Adjutant-General of Massachusetts that you are the mother of five sons who have died gloriously on the field of battle.

I feel how weak and fruitless must be any words of mine which should attempt to beguile you from the grief of a loss so overwhelming: but I cannot refrain from tendering to you the consolation that may be found in the thanks of the Republic they died to save.

I pray that our heavenly Father may assuage the anguish of you bereavement, and leave you only the cherished memory of the loved and lost, and the solemn pride that must be yours to have laid so costly a sacrifice on the alter of freedom.

Yours very sincerely and respectfully,

Abraham Lincoln

Lincoln with the staff of the Army of the Potomac at Antietam.
The photograph shows his tallness of stature relative to the officers.

That appeal to Christian faith by Lincoln was entirely sincere. Lincoln drew deeply upon the Christian tradition in the style of leadership he chose to exercise. His simple trust of God, and humility before Him as the disposer of all things, gave him a firmness and generosity of spirit. In his second Inaugural Address, on 4 March 1865, Lincoln sounded these notes in his trumpet call to the nation:

> 'With malice towards none; with charity for all; with firmness in the right, as God gives us to see the right, let us strive to finish the work we are in; to bind up the nation's wounds; to care for him who shall have borne the battle, and for his widow and orphan – to do all which may achieve and cherish a just and lasting peace among ourselves and with all nations.'

The great accomplishment of America under Lincoln's leadership was the preservation of the Union. 'If we do not make common cause to save the good old ship of the Union on this voyage, nobody will have a chance to pilot her on another voyage.' So Lincoln had told the inhabitants of Cleveland, Ohio, at the outset of the war between the states.

An assassin's bullet killed Lincoln as the war came to its close. Alas, great leaders have so often become lightning conductors for all the hatred, malice and envy that lurks in frustrated souls. Lincoln left America a great legacy as far as leadership is concerned. He gave it an enduring example of what it means to be a great leader in a great Republic. Perhaps Lincoln's best epitaph is in his own words, which reflect the fields and farms of his boyhood days: 'Die when I may,' he said, I want it said of me by those who knew me best, that I always plucked a thistle and planted a flower where I thought a flower would grow.'

Charles de Gaulle

'We navigated by the same stars,' said Winston Churchill of Charles de Gaulle. Both statesmen were guided by a sense of their nations' historic destinies. De Gaulle was imbued with a sense of France's glorious past. Grandeur, glory, greatness – the French word *grandeur*, when de Gaulle spoke or wrote it, was sometimes translated as each of these – belonged to the essence of France. He dedicated his life to leading France back to the heights. That upwards climb would give the nation its necessary common purpose. He once said, 'France is never her true self except when she is engaged in a great enterprise.' He saw himself as personifying the enduring qualities of the French people, and his leadership role as one of stirring the spirit of France.

As an officer in the French army in the First World War, de Gaulle was severely wounded and captured by the Germans. In his *The Army of the Future* (1934) he attacked French dependence on the 'impregnable' Maginot Line, and in 1940 refused to accept Marshal Pétain's truce with the Germans, becoming leader of the Free French in England. He could never have accepted the subjection of France. 'All my life I have thought of France in a certain way,' de Gaulle wrote in the opening sentence of his wartime memoirs. He saw France as a country fated to experience either dazzling success or exemplary misfortune. 'If, in spite of this, mediocrity shows in her acts and deeds, it strikes me as an absurd anomaly, to be imputed to the faults of Frenchmen, not the genius of the land.' France was not really herself 'unless in the front rank.' Only a grand national purpose to achieve excellence among the nations, putting France in the vanguard of progress, could overcome the natural disunity of the French people. 'In short, to my mind, France cannot be France without greatness.'

In order to realise this vision France needed a great leader. 'When leaders fail,' de Gaulle told an American, Admiral Harold Stark in 1942, 'new leaders emerge upwards out of the spirit of eternal France, from Charlemagne and Joan of Arc to Napoleon, Poincaré and Clemenceau.' He then added, 'Perhaps this time I am one of those thrust into leadership by the failure of others.' Not that he doubted his place in that succession. His army marched under the flag of the Cross of Lorraine, under which Joan of Arc had rallied the French people against the English in the Hundred Years' War.

Charles de Gaulle at Bayeux in Normandy, eight days after the D-Day
landing in 1944, being greeted by enthusiastic supporters.

In 1944 de Gaulle entered Paris in triumph. He was head of the provisional government before resigning in protest against the defeats of the new constitution of the Fourth Republic in 1946. Twelve years later, when bankruptcy and civil war loomed, he was called to form a government. As Premier he put forward a constitution subordinating the legislature to the presidency, and in 1959 took office as President. Economic recovery and the eventual solution of France's colonial problems followed, but in pursuit of national interest and *grandeur* he opposed 'Anglo-Saxon' influence in Europe. In 1969 he resigned after his government was defeated in a referendum on constitutional reform, and he died the following year.

Not only did de Gaulle practise a distinctive style of leadership, but he also wrote about it. A man of character also needs *grandeur* to be an effective leader, he believed. 'He must aim high, show that he has vision, act on the grand scale, and so establish his authority over the generality of men who splash in the shallow water.' If he allows himself to be content with the commonplace, he will be looked upon by others as a good servant, but 'never as the master who can draw to himself the faith and dreams of mankind.'

Behind these words lies a tradition of thought about leadership that goes at least as far back as to Napoleon. In an interview with *The New York Times* in 1965, de Gaulle was reported to have declared, 'Men are of no importance, what counts is who commands.' As a young officer in the First World War, he had served under Marshal Ferdinand Foch, generalissimo of all the armies on the Western Front. A great exemplar of the Napoleonic tradition of leadership, Foch had written of the military commander: 'To think and to will, to possess intelligence and energy will not suffice for him; he must possess also "imperative fire", the gift of communicating his own supreme energy to the masses of men who are, so to speak, his weapon.'

This tradition is echoed in de Gaulle's short book on leadership – *The Edge of the Sword*, written originally as a series of lectures at the French War College and then published in 1932 (when de Gaulle was a forty-one year old army officer little known beyond the army). In it, he defined three key leadership qualities. To chart the right course, a leader needs *intelligence* and *instinct*; to get people to follow him along that path, he needs *authority*.

De Gaulle noted that leaders have always understood the importance of instinct or intuition. Instinct, he wrote, enables the leader to 'strike deeply into the order of things.' It is the natural analytical ability to see the essentials of a problem or situation. 'Our intelligence can furnish us with the theoretic, general abstract knowledge of what is, but only instinct can give the practical, particular and concrete *feel* of it.' Only when a leader makes proper use of both intelligence or reason and instinct or intuition, will his decisions have the hall-mark of prescience. Prescience – knowing which way to lead – is an essential element in good leadership.

It is not enough to know the uphill path, however, if no one will follow. In his lectures, de Gaulle stressed that a leader 'must be able to create a spirit of confidence in those under him. He must be able to assert his authority.'

Authority, de Gaulle believed, stems from prestige. For him, prestige is largely a matter of feeling, suggestion and impression, and it depends primarily on the possession of an elementary gift, a natural aptitude which defies analysis. It is a rare gift, one that 'certain men have, one might almost say from birth, the quality of exuding authority, as though it were a liquid, though it is impossible to say precisely of what it consists.'

De Gaulle's recipe for creating or preserving this prestige (or charisma, as it would be called now) was a modern version of the old Persian formula of establishing a proper distance between ruler and ruled. In *The Edge of the Sword*, he wrote about creation of an all-important *mystique* surrounding the leader:

> 'First and foremost, there can be no prestige without mystery, for familiarity breeds contempt. All religions have their tabernacles, and no man is a hero to his valet. In the designs, the demeanour, and the mental operations of a leader there must always be a "something" which others cannot altogether fathom, which puzzles them, stirs them, and rivets their attention…Aloofness, character and the personification of quietness, these qualities it is that surround with prestige those who are prepared to carry a burden that is too heavy for lesser mortals.

> 'The price they have to pay for leadership is unceasing self-discipline, the constant taking of risks, and a perpetual inner struggle… whence that vague sense of melancholy which hangs about the skirts of majesty.'

In cabinet meetings, de Gaulle did not engage in long discussions. He would listen carefully to his ministers, taking notes on what they said. If he wanted to exchange views with a minister, he usually requested a private meeting. After being fully briefed, he made the big decision himself, retiring into solitude in order to do so. He placed much stress upon a leader's need to have time to think, and he insisted on reserving several hours of his day for uninterrupted thought.

To maintain his personal *mystique,* de Gaulle avoided friendship with any of his colleagues. They addressed him with nothing less formal than *Mon Général.* It has even been alleged that de Gaulle deliberately transferred his personal staff after a certain period in order to reduce the risk that they would become too familiar with him. Although he did not indulge in small talk in the context of his work, at banquets or dinner-parties he was invariably a courteous host or guest. But his warm emotions were reserved for his family, and he kept them well hidden.

Field Marshal Viscount Montgomery, in his book *The Path of Leadership* (1961), wrote of de Gaulle: 'Some will say that his manner is cold and that he lacks the personality to be an outstanding natural leader. On the surface he may appear thus, giving the impression that he lacks a sense of humour and has few real and personal friends. The point is that he is shy and doesn't open up too easily. But he has a warm and generous heart, and this very soon becomes evident once you get to know him...He has those qualities of leadership which I admire so greatly – calmness in the crisis, decision, the ability to withdraw and have time to think.'

If de Gaulle possessed charisma it had eluded the British. Hence Montgomery's attempt to portray de Gaulle to his compatriots in a good light. But the personal magic that is charisma is tied to language and culture. For most of the French nation, de Gaulle was undoubtedly a great leader. In the Algerian crisis, for example, the French followed de Gaulle because in the hour of great need he seemed 'the only possible man' or 'the only one who can save France.' His subsequent performance won him deep respect and substantial popularity, but he was never adored in a quasi-religious way. During that crisis, he appeared on television – dressed in his general's uniform – in order to reassert his authority. With a calm, self-assured manner he asked the nation for its support. As he wrote later, he had to appear 'animated and spontaneous enough to seize and hold attention, without compromising himself by 'excessive gestures and misplaced grimaces.' His broadcast ended with the deeply emotional appeal: 'French people, French people, help me, help me!"

'Others made greater contributions than de Gaulle, but few had his strength of character; wrote Richard Nixon in *Leaders* (1984), in words that make a good summary. 'He was a stubborn, wilful, supremely self-confident man of enormous ego and yet at the same time enormous selflessness. He was demanding not for himself but for France. He lived simply but dreamed grandly. He acted a part, playing a role he himself created in a way that would fit only one actor. Even more, he fashioned *himself* so that he could play it. He created de Gaulle, the public person, to play the role of de Gaulle, personification of France.' A strange, shy, aloof man, but a great French leader.

Adolf Hitler

Hitler was not in fact a German. He was born in Austria, when it was part of the dual-monarchy of Austria-Hungary, Germany's principal ally in the First World War. Like Napoleon, he became the leader of a great nation which was not his own by birth.

Germany as a united nation was much younger than France. Indeed it was Napoleon who first united Western Germany in the Confederation of the Rhine (1806), and introduced to it the ideas and reforms of the French Revolution, an influence which subsequently spread eastwards to Russia. In spite of persecution, the ideas of democracy and national unity spread, and inspired the unsuccessful revolutions of 1848. The growth of industry helped to make national unity an economic necessity. Under Bismarck's leadership, after victorious wars with Austria and France, Prussia established its hegemony over a united Germany. Political, industrial and colonial rivalries with Britain, France and Russian all combined to produce the First World War. In 1918 a revolution overthrew the monarchy. The Socialists seized power and established the democratic Weimar republic. A sustained economic crisis brought Germany close to revolution and, in the reaction, the National Socialist German Workers Party manoeuvred itself into power. Adolf Hitler, as leader of the Nazis and already effective national ruler in 1933, became officially Head of State in the following year, with the title of *Führer*.

The German Minister of Propaganda, Dr Josef Goebbels, stage managed Hitler's appearances and speeches in order to create the image of the *Führer* as a powerful leader who exemplified all the German virtues. Goebbels has the dubious honour of being the first and most successful of a long line of public relations experts who address themselves to the task of invoking a charismatic response to their clients who seek the highest political offices.

Hitler did have a talent for leadership, which enabled him to climb to the pinnacle of power in his country. So there was substance behind the image. Moreover, he believed in the myth of his own superhuman powers as a leader, especially in the military field. He also required a certain awesome presence. For Hitler took pains to look and sound the part. He may well have read or heard about he concept of the 'charismatic' leader, as defined by Max Weber. Hitler quite deliberately sought to arouse a response of awe and devotion by exerting his inner powers upon people. His blue eyes, slightly protruding, seemed radiant to the Germans under his sway. Many who met him were unable to withstand his gaze; knowing this, Hitler looked people straight in the eye without blinking. His sonorous voice, punctuated by energetic gestures and mounting to a shouting crescendo, had a mesmeric effect on vast German crowds. The party rallies did much to create the phenomenon of charisma: they were theatres where audience and performer worked together to create a form of magic. To those who met Hitler it seemed almost impossible to communicate to others his personal impact upon them. 'Such could be its strength that it sometimes seemed a kind of psychological force radiating from him like a magnetic field, wrote one. 'It could be so intense as to be almost physically tangible.'

Albert Speer, Hitler's architect and later his Minister of Production, named his master's greatest strength as his uncanny ability to know men. 'He knew men's secret vices and desires, he knew what they thought to be their virtues, he knew their hidden ambitions and the motives which lay behind their loves and their hates, he knew where they could be flattered, where they were gullible, where they were strong and where they were weak; he knew all this... by instinct and feeling, an intuition which in such matters never led him astray.' This faculty gave him an extraordinary power over others (including Speer himself). Far from engendering a fellow feeling, Hitler's perceptiveness left him with a supreme contempt for his fellow men.

Adolf Hitler used photographers and film-makers in order to project himself as a charismatic leader.

After showing some flair as a generalissimo in the early days of the Second World War, Hitler was soon completely out of his depth. Despite his occasional intuitions, coupled with a phenomenal memory for statistics and a good knowledge of military hardware, Hitler lacked the Greek quality of *phronesis* which the English called prudence. He was deficient in practical wisdom or transcendent common sense. Field Marshal Manstein, one of the best of Germany's professional soldiers, who was always hostile to Hitler, did concede that he had 'a certain eye for operational possibilities,' which he said was frequently found among laymen. Manstein qualified this judgement by adding that it was an eye dimmed by a tendency to overestimate the technological resources at hand and by an inadequate assessment of possible results.

Nor would Hitler listen, another fatal weakness in leadership. The contrast with Franklin D. Roosevelt, who became Commander-in-Chief of America's forces by virtue of being President with no military experience, is especially striking. It shows how a little knowledge combined with a big faith in one's own intuitive powers can be a highly dangerous thing. For Hitler had served in the trenches during the First World War, rising to a non-commissioned officer rank. Churchill, on the other hand, who had more of a military background, always accepted the advice of his Chiefs-of-Staff in the end, if he failed to bring them round to his way of thinking.

Towards the end of the war, an atmosphere developed around Hitler which was described shortly after the catastrophe by a senior General Staff officer. He had experienced it while briefing Hitler during March and April 1945, and found it repulsive. He wrote: 'My impression – and as I determined in my conversations with others, by no means mine alone – was that a person was not merely spiritually crushed by this atmosphere of servility, nervousness, and untruthfulness, but that one could even sense it as a sort of physical sickness. Nothing was genuine there except the fear. There was fear of all shades and degrees – from being afraid of somehow provoking the displeasure of the *Führer* or annoying him by some ill-advised comment, to naked fear for life itself in view of the impending end of the drama.'

The fear felt in Hitler's presence is understandable. Like Napoleon, he could explode with anger. Signalled by finger-snapping, his rages were terrifying. They were also symptoms of Hitler's irrationality. General Guderian, who saw Hitler face to face after Stalingrad for the first time in fourteen months, reported that at this period 'he easily lost his temper and raged, and was then unpredictable.'

To those who opposed him, Hitler could be merciless. He believed that no officer had the right to disobey an order emanating directly or indirectly from him. One corps commander who did so was court-martialled and later shot. Some senior officers did find a way of dealing with him. Field Marshal Model, for example, had the advantage of enjoying Hitler's confidence and therefore was in a better position to stand up to him. He avoided making too many requests; he either came up with forceful proposals or simply reported what he had already done. Hitler's courtiers, too, found ways of manipulating their master. According to Speer, Hitler did not see through their subtle manipulation of his opinions.

Adolf Hitler with a group of young National Socialists in 1933. The photograph vividly conveys the part that a devoted audience plays in creating the phenomenon of charisma.

He had apparently no nose for methodical deceit. Among the masters of that are were Goering, Goebbels, Bormann and, within limits, Himmler. Since those who spoke out in candid terms on the important questions usually could not make Hitler change his mind, these cunning men who knew how to manage Hitler naturally increased their power. But Hitler tended more and more to hold fast and rigidly to whatever standpoint he had first taken, no matter what objections or alternatives might be urged upon him. He showed an ever strong tendency to dismiss reports that did not fit into his picture; and when he could no longer ignore them, he attributed unacceptable defeats to the inadequacy of those carrying out his orders, whether local field commanders, officers at the theatre-command level, or members of the General Staff, whose basic attitude he increasingly distrusted.

Hitler died in the supremely arrogant belief the German people had failed him; they had not proved worthy of his greatness. They had brought *Gotterdammerung* upon their own heads. He was a victim of their betrayal, whom history would one day acknowledge for the genius he knew he was.

'Mistake is an honourable thing in those following great leaders,' wrote the Roman teacher of rhetoric Quintilian in the first century AD. When it was all over, men like Alfred Speer and General Jodl came near to justifying their behaviour by a version of that idea. They could still feel Hitler's hold upon them after death, despite all that reason and common-sense now told them. They talked about themselves as if they were subjects awakening from hypnosis, apprehensive and guilty about what had happened while they were under the spell. In varying degrees of intensity, except for a hard-core of unrepentant Nazis, the German nation collectively experienced those same feelings.

Plainly Hitler was not a great leader. He accomplished nothing but the total defeat of his people, the destruction of their homes and untold misery to countless other human beings. Hitler's talent as an orator and his ability to inspire many German hearts are not in question. But charismatic powers can be used for either good or evil ends. Setting aside his charisma, Hitler's weaknesses as a leader outweigh his strengths, so that even in the more technical or functional sense of the word 'good', he fell short of the requirements of a good leader. Above all, Hitler's case tells us that there is no greatness in leadership with moral integrity and the pursuit of ends that history or God will judge as good. In that context, Hitler's story does have a significant lesson for all those who aspire to lead.

Mahatma Gandhi

Mahatma Gandhi exercised leadership through his personal example and influence rather than through power. But would his style of leadership have worked in the West? Gandhi's example, even more than those of Lincoln, de Gaulle and Hitler, reveals the extent to which leadership is bound up with culture.

For a long time the word 'culture' was used mainly as a synonym for Western civilisation – the secular process of human development. In England it acquired definite class associations. But in the late eighteenth century the German writer Johann Herder challenged this view. 'Nothing is more indeterminate than this word,' he wrote, 'and nothing more deceptive than its application to all nations and periods.' Herder attacked the comfortable assumption that the self-development of humanity had moved in a unilinear progression to flower in the European culture around him. Indeed, he attacked the European assumption of cultural superiority:

> 'Men of all the quarters of the globe, who have perished over the ages, you have not lived solely to manure the earth with your ashes, so that at the end of time your prosperity should be made happy by European culture. The very thought of a superior European culture is a blatant insult to the majesty of Nature.'

It is then necessary, he concluded, to talk of 'cultures' in the plural: the specific and variable cultures of different natures and periods, and even the sub-cultures (as we call them) of different social groups within the nation.

In India, the equivalent for 'leader' is the word *neta*. In its positive sense it is used for a person who commands respect and even awe and has charismatic qualities about him. Because of the misdeeds and misdemeanours of some of the political leaders in the post-independence era, the word has also come to be used as a taunt for those who pose as leaders but are not accepted as such. In India, the test of leadership lies in personal example, inspirational image and acceptance of the leader's qualities and attributes by the followers.

When asked, Indians tend to name Gandhi as the great leader in their nation's history. Mohandas Gandhi was born in Porbander, on India's North West Coast. In 1887, at the age of eighteen, he was sent to London, where he stayed for three years studying law. Working as a lawyer in South Africa, he experienced active racial discrimination. He led a political and religious campaign against South Africa's racist laws and was imprisoned in 1908. Returning to India in 1919, he used 'civil disobedience' to attack the caste system.

The fragile looking man, ridiculed by some, but revered by millions, advocated a simple, non-violent way of life. In 1932 he started a 'fast unto death' to demand rights for the lowest of the Indian castes – the 'Untouchables.' Later, as a member of the Indian National Congress, Gandhi was arrested in 1942 for his part in the campaign to remove India from the British Empire. Home Rule was eventually granted in 1947. During the transfer of power from the British, Gandhi toured India trying to build peace between Hindu and Muslim. At the age of 79 years he fasted for five days to try to prevent war between them. On 30 January, 1948, on his way to a prayer meeting, Gandhi was shot and killed by a fanatical Hindu, so ending a life dedicated to peace and the abolition of violence.

Such is the bare outline of this story. Through his ascetism – Mahatma means literally 'Great Soul' – and his popularity with the masses of poorer Indians, born out of his complete identification with their lifestyle and aspirations, Gandhi acquired an immense influence. He was the only one among the top leaders who adopted the dress and lifestyle of the poor masses and risked being called 'the naked Fakir' during his visit to England. This is an example which was not emulated by any of his colleagues, who appeared to show a certain degree of ambivalence towards poverty and the lifestyle of those in authority.

The image that Gandhi presented – a frail, barefooted man dressed in a *dhoti* of hand-spun cotton – may have seemed totally outside the English experience of leadership. But it echoed in one forgotten strand in the Western tradition. For Jesus had also walked barefooted (if early Arab sources are to be believed), wearing an undyed woollen robe, and practising both celibacy and a degree of ascetism.

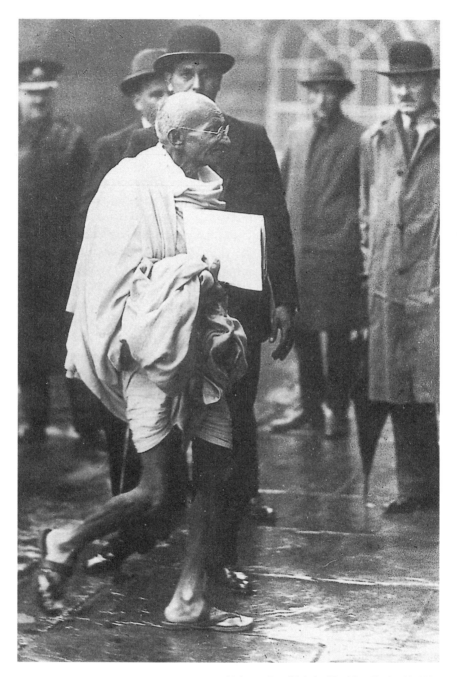

Mahatma Gandhi during his visit to England in 1931.
His appearance and lifestyle made a profound impression on his hosts.

India places spiritual life on a higher plane than material progress or even existence. Gandhi epitomised that quality of India more than any other political leader before or since. In order to lead India, he knew he must disinfect himself of ego and become as nothing. Deep in the Indian soul, too, lay a fundamental concern with right and wrong. The cultural forms in which those contrasting values are explored and defied appeared strange to the English, for the moral tradition was imbedded in the mythological doings of the pantheon of Hindu gods: *Brahma* and his associates *Vishnu*, the preserver, and *Shiva*, the destroyer and regenerator.

At the heart of the Indian experience lay the concept of spiritual quest for truth, a seeking after a state of being which is higher than the present plane of existence. Because he so manifestly followed that way, Gandhi achieved his massive popularity. His life was a spiritual quest, he maintained, and political activity came from it as a secondary mode of expression. His emphasis on right and wrong in the moral sense, in what the secularised British held to be political matters, struck a deep chord in the Indian villages. For the Indian villager also saw life in the context of an eternal struggle between good and evil.

Gandhi's quest for spiritual truth in religions other than his own, notably in the Gospels, was entirely in keeping with the eclectic tradition of Hinduism and also the primacy of the spiritual search for truth. But his search for a universal God, transcending the religions and sects of the world, also had political implications. Both before and after Independence, the most pressing issue for India was the division between those of the Hindu and Muslim religious faiths. Gandhi's search for a common God might have provided a source of unity, for in drawing near to God people draw near to each other.

Above all, Gandhi wanted to see India preserved as a unity. Like Lincoln, he saw bloodshed as inevitable: if so, let it be within India rather than between divided nations on the sub-continent. Gandhi's critics may well be right in their charge that in this respect he was naïve and unrealistic. Gandhi is also open to the criticism that he did not attempt to win over the Muslim leader, Muhammad Ali Jinnah, to his vision of India before his attitude had hardened beyond change. By the time Gandhi bestirred himself, the British, under Mountbatten's camouflage screen of charm, were beginning to wash their hands of India. Partition gave them a face-saving exit from the sub-continent.

Mahatma Gandhi surrounded by admirers. For Indians he possessed spiritual charisma or power that made many want to touch him.

As a political leader Gandhi was not great. His greatness lies more in his spiritual and moral leadership of India. His strength came from his closeness to the people. Gandhi's identification with the villagers of India led him to campaign for a restoration of traditional values. In order to stem the population drift in the already overcrowded and poverty-stricken cities, such as Calcutta and Bombay, he sought to call a halt to industrialisation.

The British had imported Indian cotton, milled it and sold back their manufactures to the Indians. As part of his rural economic programme, Gandhi advocated that the villager should keep their raw cotton and spin it themselves. As a natural leader, he led by example – spinning for at least an hour each day.

An attractive warmth pervaded Gandhi's attitude to the Untouchables, those Indians so lowly that they had no place in even the lowest of the four main caste-groups that together made up the ladder of incarnation. Gandhi gave these Untouchables a name – *Harijans*, God's people. With a clear eye, he not only saw that the caste system was the key threat in India's unity and harmony, but he took what symbolic action he could to bring that message home. Of course one man, however influential, could not alter such an integral feature of Indian social life. Perhaps the inroads of Western technology, business and secularist thought may succeed (at least in the large cities) where Gandhi failed – but in India nothing is assured.

People travelled miles to see Gandhi. In India, even looking upon a holy man from afar is believed to give the beholder a share in his *darshan* – his inner spiritual integrity or power. People wanted to touch Gandhi, too, in order to have contact with his integrity, just as the throngs reached out hands to Jesus in order to touch him. With Gandhi, as with Jesus, people touched the feet or hem of the garment, for by doing so they gave a sign that they had humbled themselves as near to the ground as possible.

Many who were friends or disciples of *Bapu* (father), or otherwise knew him well, still have about them the aura of this charming and friendly man, and embody the stoic self-discipline he inspired. Many of them still spin their own yarn on the *charkha* each day as Gandhi taught them to do, an example of his lingering message of self-sufficiency. His successor, Jawarharlal Nehru, was not of the same mould. While he had his own charisma, he was an essentially westernised politician without Gandhi's extraordinary rapport with the grassroots of India, nor his moral edge. Prime Minister Indira Gandhi (despite the name she and Gandhi were not related) knew Gandhi well. Some of her political strength came from that fact. She appreciated the need to keep in touch. India needs leaders who can combine the values of the old with the best of the new. Such political leaders will be travellers on the spiritual path that Gandhi followed.

The Gift of Equality

'He who treats as equals those who are far below him in strength really makes them a gift of the equality of human beings, of which fate had deprived them...'

Simone Weil

Nelson Mandela

A great nation in a great crisis... South Africa found in Nelson Mandela a statesman of real stature, one aptly named after that English leader of genius already portrayed in this book. His story is one of outstanding moral courage against seemingly impossible odds, of determination to destroy the evil of apartheid, and – above all – of tireless efforts to bring about reconciliation in his homeland.

Nelson Mandela reveals many of the qualities that go to make a leader, such as confidence in humanity – 'I am fundamentally an optimist' – patience and tolerance, a strong sense of justice, and an unswerving loyalty to his colleagues. But there are two qualities he personifies: *strength of mind* and *magnanimity*.

The man who has become such an inspirational figure was born in 1918, the eldest son of a Xhosa chief (the Xhosas are the next biggest tribe to the Zulus) in what is now the nominally independent homeland called Transkei. After training as a lawyer, he joined the African National Congress in 1944 and was a leader of the Congress's non-violent campaigns against apartheid during the 1950s.

After police killed sixty-nine unarmed black protesters at Sharpeville in 1960, Mandela and other Congress leaders abandoned increasingly their hopes for peaceful change. In 1961 they formed the Congress's military wing, Umkhonto we Sizwe (The Spear of the Nation).

Mandela evaded arrest, earning the nickname 'The Black Pimpernel', until August 1962, when he was jailed for five years for incitement and leaving the country illegally. In 1963 he was tried again, along with other underground leaders, and in 1964 was jailed for life for sabotage, which he openly admitted.

At his trial, Mandela spoke of 'the ideal of a democratic and free society in which all persons live together in harmony and with equal opportunities. It is an ideal which I hope to live for and to achieve, but if need be an ideal for which I am prepared to die.'

As Mandela began his long sojourn in the harsh outpost of the South African prison system, Robben Island, he resolved that he would not allow this experience to remove from him his essential dignity as a person:

> *'In and of itself, that assured that I would survive, for any man or institution that tries to rob me of my dignity will lose because I will not part with it at any price or under any pressure. I never seriously considered the possibility that I would not emerge from prison one day. I never thought that a life sentence truly meant life and that I would die behind bars. Perhaps I was denying this prospect because it was too unpleasant to contemplate. But I always knew that someday I would once again feel the grass under my feet and walk in the sunshine as a free man.'*

James Gregory, Mandela's jailer for twenty years, has written a book about his prisoner who became a friend. Soon after his arrival he had his first dramatic encounter with Mandela, then working in slave labour conditions in the searing light and heat of the Robben Island lime quarry, scene of many a fearful atrocity. Prisoners were beaten and abused and had dogs set on them. It was here that Gregory saw Mandela, standing tall, 'his ramrod back and broad shoulders prominent' in his prison shorts and sandals, amidst a group of prisoners, his whole body, says Gregory, a statement that 'I am a leader. You will not intimidate me.' Mandela greeted Gregory with a firm good morning and 'Welcome to Robben Island' and Gregory, before he knew it, slipped into the Zulu greeting he had not used since childhood, a mark of respect which left Mandela stunned.

Gradually the two men became friends. When Mandela's son Thembi was killed in a road traffic accident, Gregory, then a young man, lent him what support he could. At exactly the same age and almost twenty years later, Gregory's son was killed in a car crash, and Mandela appears to have saved Gregory from despair and even suicide by talking to him daily for weeks. Saying farewell to this prison warder whom he had known for twenty-three years, Mandela embraced him with tears in his eyes. 'The wonderful hours we spent together during the last two decades end together,' he wrote in a note, 'but you will always be in my thoughts.'

After his release from prison – 'these long, lonely, wasted years' as he wrote – Mandela showed the rare quality of *magnanimity*, which from the Latin means literally *greatness of spirit*. For the Greeks and Romans it was the sure sign of a great leader. Stemming from a well-founded high regard for oneself, *magnanimity* manifests itself as generosity of spirit and equanimity in the face of trouble or adversity.

A magnanimous leader such as Nelson Mandela lacks any kind of pettiness and rises above even justified resentment. Consider what he endured. His children were traumatically affected by those years, his first wife Evelyn was unprepared to accept his allegiance to the ANC, he was unable to pay his last respects to his mother or his son. Add to that the government's relentless persecution of his family. He says: 'To see your family, your children, being persecuted when you are absolutely helpless in jail, that is one of the most painful experiences I have had... Your wife being hounded from job to job, your children being taken out of Coloured schools, police breaking into your house at midnight and even assaulting your wife.'

Yet not once does he express bitterness towards the white community for his grim ordeal, only against the system they imposed. How typical that upon his release from prison, he called for the blacks to exhibit generosity of spirit; and on the day of the Election (27 April 1994) he spoke of the need to give the white minority 'confidence and security'.

Even when Mandela met Percy Yutar, the lawyer who led the prosecution in the trial that ended with his sentence to prison all those years ago, he smiled and placed his arm around the slender shoulders of his one-time adversary, now 84 years old, saying what had happened was now truly in the past. After this meeting Mr Yutar described the President as a 'saintly man'. And Mandela invited his jailer James Gregory and his family as guests of honour to his presidential inauguration. His natural authority and charisma are evident to all those who met him, and he possesses the gift of a winning smile. He remains courteous and attentive to individuals, whatever their age or status. He retains the common touch, greeting workers and heads of state with the same warm civility and punctilious manners.

It is such generosity of spirit that makes Nelson Mandela one of the world's most significant moral leaders since Gandhi. His moral stature stands out even more in an age so often deprived of political morality. His greatest achievement has been to create through majestic leadership a climate in which the new South Africa can collect itself for the journey that lies ahead.

Nelson Mandela showed the rare quality of magnanimity

More than anything else it is Nelson Mandela's self-sacrifice that has set him apart and no other leader in modern times has so clearly shown that even the love of one's enemy is a form of practical wisdom: to make peace with an enemy, one must work with an enemy until that enemy becomes your partner, he wrote in his autobiography *Long Walk to Freedom*.

Shortly after his election as President of South Africa, Nelson Mandela issued a message which reflected the spirit of a humble man. After a tribute to his partner in the ending of apartheid Mandela points to the greatness that is in the people of South Africa:

> *'I would like to take this opportunity to thank the world leaders who have given messages of support. I would also congratulate Mr F. W. De Klerk for the four years that we have worked together, quarrelled, addressed sensitive problems and at the end of our heated exchanges were able to shake hands and to drink coffee.*
>
> *To the people of South Africa and the world who are watching, the election has been a triumph for the human spirit.*
>
> *South Africa's heroes are legends across the generations. But it is the people who are our true heroes. The election victory is one of the most important moments in the life of South Africa. I am proud of the ordinary, humble people of South Africa who have shown such a calm, patient determination to reclaim South Africa, and joy that we can loudly proclaim from the rooftops – free at last!*
>
> *I intend to be a servant not a leader, as one above others. I pledge to use all my strength and ability to live up to the world's expectation of me.'*

With his immense moral authority gained by the patient and magnanimous bearing of adversity, Mandela shows us that it is possible to be a servant first and then a leader, one who serves by leading and leads to serve. The old mould of leadership which simply set one up above others is broken for ever.

After his release from twenty-seven years in prison Mandela experienced a personal loneliness after the brutal, public break-up of his second marriage. 'I am the loneliest man,' he said. His third marriage, to Graça Machel, widow of the ruler of Mozambique, changed the picture. 'I am blooming because of the love and support she has given me,' he said. 'She is the boss. When I am alone I am very weak.' Of Madiba – Mandela's clan name, meaning 'revered one' – Graça said recently:

> *'People say my husband is a saint, but I don't know about that. I am probably one of the few people who know him best outside politics, and to me he is just a human being who is simple and gentle. At the same time so generous and keen to give love and so eager to receive it. That is what matters to me and that's what unites us.'*

Vision, humility and vulnerability: these are the hallmarks of the leadership seen today in such leaders as Mahatma Gandhi and Nelson Mandela. These are characteristics, along with professional competence or ability, that free and equal people will look for in leaders in every field of endeavour. All leaders now need these qualities.

Styles of Leadership

CHAPTER REVIEW

Summary and Key Concepts

- To be a great leader in the historical sense there are three requirements: a great nation, a great necessity and a man or woman of great natural leadership ability.

- There are very different styles of leadership, related to individual personalities, nations and cultures. They can be equally effective in giving a strong direction for people to follow.

- As the lives of Abraham Lincoln and Charles de Gaulle show, a great leader is one who has the spirit and dignity of character which are equal to the greatness of the office.

- Some approaches – such as that adopted by Hitler – are fatally flawed. Morally unscrupulous leaders, who manage people essentially by fear and mislead them to corrupt and destructive ends, will eventually forfeit the trust of all but a few fanatically devoted followers. 'Trust being lost,' wrote the Roman historian Livy, 'all the social intercourse of men is brought to naught.'

- Gandhi's example reminds us of the importance of a leader staying close to the people and representing their greatness of spirit. Humility, in the sense of treating men and women as equals, belongs to the essence of great leadership.

- Nelson Mandela has shown the world that a lofty and courageous spirit enables a leader to bear trouble calmly, to disdain meanness and revenge, and to make sacrifices for worthy ends. It can also alter the mood of a nation.

Further Reflection

- 'Rome showed itself to be truly great, and hence worthy of great leaders,' wrote Plutarch in his biography of Cato the Elder. Nations and organisations often forget that greatness lies within themselves as much as in their leaders. Great teams and great organisations deserve excellent leaders – and often find them. Never blame your troubles on lack of leadership: put your own house in order so that you become worthy of the best leaders available.

- Some nations, in times of difficulty, are fortunate to find the great leaders they deserve; others are not. In the future, nations and organisations will have to invest more time and thought in exploring ways in which to grow leaders of calibre to face the demands of the twenty-first century. How do you think that nations can improve their stock of political and social leaders? What is your organisation doing to grow or develop leaders for tomorrow?

- Truly great leaders have a heightened moral sense to match their other attributes. Is this nobler form of leadership called for in business as well as in political life? How can business managers at all levels be encouraged to be not just good leaders but leaders for good?

FIFTEEN
Leaders for Tomorrow

'Those having torches will pass them on to others.'

PLATO

An almost universal sense of the need for good leaders has appeared within recent years. There are now many educational and training programmes specifically designed to develop leaders for today and tomorrow. Why has his happened?

The chief reason is a steady and deep shift in values, like a movement of the continental plates, a seismic change which underlies all our national cultures, shaking some more than others. The higher value placed upon the individual, fed from classical and Biblical sources, has led to much more emphasis on education. Men and women are assumed to be born, in all important aspects, free and equal. We, as individuals, are seen as ends in ourselves, not merely as means to other ends. This unique value of each person is increasingly taken for granted, and egalitarianism has been in the ascendant for some time.

Does not this affirmation of our essential personal equality lessen the opportunity and need for leadership? On the contrary, the truth has become increasingly clearer that a democratic society does need good leadership. For leaders enable free and equal people to be effective in doing what needs to be done. That principle applies to every organisation and institution within a democratic society. 'Those who are near will not hide their ability,' wrote a Taoist author, Hsun-Tzu, 'and those who are distant will not grumble at their toil…that is what is called being a leader and teacher of men.'

But can leaders be trained? The common sense conclusion of this book is that leadership potential can be developed, but it does have to be there in the first place. Most people have some degree of aptitude for getting things done with people. In this respect learning to lead and learning to swim are analagous. Most people can be taught to swim, but few will reach Olympic standards and become great swimmers.

Leadership Mentors

The word 'mentor' is derived from Greek mythology. When the hero Odysseus left Ithaca, he entrusted his son Telemachus to an old friend on the island named Mentor. The goddess Athena took Mentor's shape on more than one occasion, to help Telemachus in the difficulties that befell Ithaca during his father's absence. Under Mentor's inspired tutelage the untried youth eventually became a seasoned leader.

Telemachus appeared at first in the story as a good and dutiful son, but lacking in spark or drive: he was timid and unenterprising. Later, at the behest of Athena working through Mentor, he ordered his mother's domineering suitors to depart. When they refused, guided by Mentor he resolved to sail to the mainland and report the calamitous turn of events to his father. As the story unfolds Telemachus demonstrates ever more resolve, energy and resourcefulness. When Telemachus eventually joins Odysseus upon the latter's return to Ithaca, he acts as an intelligent and enterprising helper. He astonishes his mother Penelope, for example, by taking command in the house and leading the fight against the over-mighty suitors.

This Greek myth does illustrate a truth about leadership. Leaders are inspiring. In order to become so they need to be inspired themselves. Mentors are those who both inspire us with a vision of leadership and consciously aid our individual development as leaders. They do so as much by their examples as by their words.

Lord Slim may have sounded as if he was exaggerating when he said in words already quoted above: 'There is nobody who cannot vastly improve his or her powers of leadership by a little thought and practice.' But young people in particular need that voice of encouragement from one of the great leaders of our times. For many of us do have hidden potential for leadership which too often only emerges in times of crisis, such as wars. Yet the problems and opportunities of our troubled peace call for leadership on an unprecedented scale.

Leadership is probably more caught than taught. The example of a few good leaders ignites in us the spirit of leadership, and we in turn have the responsibility of passing on the torch to those who are ready to receive it. But the leaders of tomorrow will need a personal greatness as leaders which does not characterise many leaders today. Hence this book, which is in part an appeal from history over the heads of this generation to the leaders of tomorrow, showing the way to a new excellence in leadership.

The Leader as First Companion

John Hunt, now Lord Hunt, led the British expedition that first climbed Everest in 1953. These words are from a talk he gave in 1959, entitled 'Leadership in the Modern Age.'

'Firstly, I will give you my definition of leadership, as applied to someone to whom other people are entrusted. To me, it is best described as the art of inspiring others to give of their best, and the courage to use this art. This is what leadership means to me: it demands that the leader operates from inside his group, not from above it; that in setting a good example, he does not steal the initiative of the others; in other words that he takes his full share – but no more than his share – of the job in hand. This implies a willingness not merely to decentralise, or apportion the burden, but an ability to persuade each other member of the group that his is an equally essential job, and that each has his own liberty as well as responsibility to develop that part as a whole.

'Good leadership derives from a right attitude to the job of leading; that this is only one of the jobs to be done. A leader has been well described as a "first companion." Then, of course, it is the art of blending the efforts of everyone concerned to produce a combined result.'

Not Followers But Companions

Leadership as a concept, however, has one questionable assumption, caught like a fly in amber, within the image behind. A leader seems to imply a follower. The basic metaphor leadership – a leader on a track or journey going ahead and showing others the way – does give us a picture of followers. Indeed a leader has been defined as 'a person who creates followers.' Now sheep are programmed to follow, which is why they are so easy to lead. Men and women are inclined to follow, too, but being rational, they ought always to exercise their reason or judgement before doing so. Alexander the Great found that he could not lead his Greeks against their better judgement. Discriminating and determined colleagues are as important as good leaders.

Educated, intelligent, highly technically competent people today are not likely to see themselves as followers. When the Germans allowed themselves to become a nation of followers, with a demagogue as their misleader, they did so with disastrous results. Good leaders today will tend to see people as colleagues, companions or partners, not followers. As one progresses through levels of leadership, of course, many of those colleagues will be leaders in their own right. Apart from the Taoist teachings, there are examples in the Western tradition of how leaders can transform subordinates or followers, giving them a sense of being co-equal partners in the common enterprise. 'No longer do I call you servants, for the servant (or slave) does not know what his master is doing,' said Jesus to his disciples, 'but I have called you friends, for all...I have made known to you.' Nelson saw his captains as a 'band of brothers' and treated them as such. True leaders want equals, not subordinates.

An Invitation to Greatness

'Be not afraid of greatness,' wrote Shakespeare. Greatness in leadership is possible to many more people now. Historical greatness in politics, of course, is restricted to few men and women, because it depends not only upon a person's gift for leadership but also their headship of a great nation or group of nations in a time of great necessity. But more politicians will become world leaders, if not great statesmen, as they learn to transcend party and national interest, taking a much broader view of what is good for the world and developing the leadership skills needed to move in that direction. 'The leadership of the privileged has passed away; but it has not been succeeded by that of the eminent,' wrote Winston Churchill in *Great Contemporaries* (1937). 'Nevertheless, the world is moving on; and moving so fast that few have time to ask – whither?' In a period when politicians have become even more dominated by short-term issues, Churchill's words are still apposite.

One man who personified the leadership needed in tomorrow's politicians was Dag Hammarskjöld, Secretary General of the United Nations. Son of a Swedish prime minister, he became the world's leading civil servant in 1953 and held that job until his death in a plane crash in 1958 while attempting to solve the crisis in the Congo. After his death a book of his reflections was published under the title of *Markings*. That word translates the Swedish phrase *Väg märken*, the waymarks or stone cairns that are found beside mountain paths. One of Dag Hammarskjöld's 'markings' underlines a message that has emerged as one of the central themes of this book. Speaking to himself when alone one evening, he wrote: 'Your position never gives you the right to command. It only imposes on you the duty of so living your life that others can receive your orders without being humiliated.'

Other leaders, at all levels and in all fields, can and should aspire to that ideal. For it is the only kind of leadership that will really work over a long period of time among free and equal people.

Thus greatness now is more a matter of quality rather than degree. It is possible to be a great leader as a supervisor or hospital sister, as the head of a university department or as a school teacher, as the chief executive of a company or as the director of a government department. Such greatness in the 'ordinary' roles of leadership is what helps to constitute a great nation in the spiritual and moral sense of that word.

Perhaps an example will illustrate what is meant by personal greatness in leadership. The Academy Sergeant Major at Sandhurst during the 1950s and early 1960s was a man called John Lord.

Not Rulers but Leaders

The celebrated Dutch historian John Huizinga concluded his chapter on 'The Spirit of the Netherlands', in *Dutch Civilisation in the Seventeenth Century* (1968), with these words:

'A wondrous destiny has helped to create our nation, to set us apart from the original stem, and to make us a noble part of Western Europe. Through Delfzijl and Vaals runs the border between Western and Central Europe. In our Western character lies our strength and the reason for our existence. We belong to the Atlantic; our centre of gravity is in and across the sea. Our company is that of Western nations and above all of that great British people who created the modern democratic state and continue as a bastion of liberty.

'Authority, yes, provided it is understood aright – authority based not on brute force but on the subordination of authority itself to the highest law and bound by legal principles that draw their inspiration from it.

'Leadership, gladly, provided our leaders are guides and not dictators. We do not wish to be led like Breughel's blind or like a bear on a chain. Our leaders must be men who summit to a higher wisdom, to wisdom that sets its sights beyond the limits of national and state interest, just as the helmsman steers by the stars.

'To keep trust, to point the way, to care, to direct – those are the ancient virtues by whose presence St Augustine distinguished the true political task from the evil appetites for power and domination. Political thinking aware of the commands of justice and the limits of human power must always come back to the old images of the steersman who, knowing his own human frailty holds the oar steady in the storm, of the fallible shepherd who humbly tends his flock. A poet put it into the mouth of him, but for whose labour there would have been no Dutch nation and no Dutch state:

"You shepherd never sleepeth
albeit you have strayed."'*

*From the national anthem.

Unlike the stereotype of a Guards Regimental Sergeant Major, Lord was a slim man who did not swear or raise his voice when he was not on the parade ground. In mass meeting he practised Seneca's dictum: 'To make another silent, first be silent yourself.'

Captured at Arnhem in 1944 while serving with the Parachute Regiment, Lord found himself incarcerated with about 2000 other ranks from the British Airborne Division in a German prisoner-of-war camp called Stalag XIB. There were only 20 or 30 British soldiers among the 17,000 Russians, French, Belgians, Yugoslavs, Poles, Dutch and Serbs. He found the prisoners in conditions of chaos and misery. They had tended to succumb to the lethargy that hunger, boredom and squalor can so easily induce. They lived in decay and wretchedness, and when they died their bodies were taken unheeded to their graves in an old cart. In just over six months John Lord transformed this situation. By the authority of his personality he brought order and gave direction to the whole camp. Major Ralph Cobbold was the first to visit the camp on the day of liberation, as *The Times* reported on 2 May 1945:

> 'At the gate was an impressive guard in maroon berets. "We thought that the 6th Airborne Division must somehow have got there first." said Major Cobbold, "but when I asked the guard commander when he'd arrived his answer was, "Just after Arnhem, Sir." It was faultlessly turned out, that guard. It could have gone on duty at Buckingham Palace."

> 'Then a majestic figure appeared, the Regimental Sergeant Major himself, with gleaming brass, immaculate webbing, razor-edged trouser creases, dazzling boots, a spectacular salute. As the officers walked with him to his office hundreds of prisoners, though wild with the joy of liberation, saluted with precision. In the office he produced chairs and offered cups of tea. Asked for numbers and particulars of prisoners in the Stalag, RSM Lord rang a bell. "Bring me the personal files, corporal," he ordered when the door opened, and the fullest details were handed to Major Cobbold.

> 'Passing through the camp, the officers were able to judge the magnitude of the task performed by RSM Lord and this team of Warrant Officers and Non-commissioned Officers, several of them ex-guardsmen. In place of the lifeless confusion of six months earlier they saw everywhere evidence of the highest morale and discipline. A smoothly running organ-

isation had been worked out and maintained. Daily inspections and guard-mounting, most unpopular when introduced, had restored the prisoners' self respect and revived their military bearing: and all had been accomplished amid appalling conditions of over-crowding and undernourishment.

'Four hundred men were crowded into each hut, which had bunks for only 250. To each man only one blanket was allowed, even in the depth of winter. In the cookhouse the RSM showed the officers the daily meat ration for nearly 5,000 men – 2 coal buckets full of horse-flesh. All who could had to parade for physical training and this drastic effort of RSM Lord to build up their sinking reserves of strength must have saved the health of hundreds and perhaps the lives of some. When a prisoner died he was given a military funeral with a bearer-party, a slow march through the camp, and a Union Jack on his coffin. National flags could not be displayed in prison camps, but the RSM always had a Union Jack to cover the coffin as soon as the bearers had borne it outside the compound.

'Three times RSM Lord could have given up his task. He and his team were offered a transfer to a Non-Commissioned Officers' camp, where conditions were far better. In a body they refused. As British spear-heads drove east from the Rhine a large number of priority prisoners were marched off eastwards. RSM Lord's name was high on the list, but he did not go. He hid himself under the floor of a hut and was fed through a hole in the floorboards for five days while search parties hunted him. Then he emerged to resume his leadership of the Stalag until he could hand over to an officer of the advancing British armies. Even when he had done that he did not leave for England on the first of the aeroplanes to fly the liberated prisoners back, as he could easily have done. He volunteered to stay instead and organise the evacuation of his men. "I wanted to see them all out," he said.'

Unlike many senior warrant officers, John Lord did not take a commission after the war. He became Academy Sergeant Major at Sandhurst for fifteen years, where he exerted a considerable personal influence by his example as a leader on several generations of staff and officer cadets. He also lectured with great effect upon such subjects as leadership, morale and discipline, revealing a depth of thought and sureness of principle.

He stayed among the other ranks, but he led the leaders of today's and tomorrow's army in understanding the true nature of their responsibilities. He handed on the torch.

In peace, as in war, there are now many situations that call for personal greatness. The first step towards it is always the willingness to take responsibility. 'The price of greatness is responsibility,' wrote Winston Churchill. Position is really secondary. True, people who occupy the major roles or positions of leadership *ought* to lead and be trained to lead. But it is possible for those in much humbler positions – or even those with none, like John Lord in Stalag XIB – to achieve a degree of excellence in leadership and teamwork. Lord Hunt, of Everest fame, made that very point in the talk already quoted: 'In its true sense, leadership should mean giving a lead by example, even without a position of authority. True leadership is simply an expression of human greatness. Some of the finest examples of this aspect of leadership are displayed by men who have no high position or reputation at stake, but with much to lose in security, in comradeship and convenience, who stand up for what they know, from their conscience, to be right.'

Our greatness lies in our ability to transcend ourselves in the service of that which has greater value to us than ourselves. There is not a single man or woman who has not had great moments, who has not risen to rare occasions. It is true that we need situations which call out the best in us as leaders, but all leaders can prepare themselves for such a time. Nor will opportunities be lacking. For as Walt Whitman writes: 'It is provided in the essence of things, that from any fruition of success, no matter what, shall come forth something to make a greater struggle necessary.'

Leaders For Tomorrow

CHAPTER REVIEW

Summary and Key Concepts

- A leader should be able to place himself or herself on an equal footing with the others involved, relying upon their authority of knowledge and personality to gain respect. Such a stance does require considerable inner confidence; people will soon sense if it is there. They will soon sense, too, if a leader can show them the way forwards and lead them on their journey.

- Leadership exists on different levels – team, operational, strategic, national and global. The philosophy of leadership in this book applies to *all* those levels. It transcends colour, race, gender, time and space. Why? Because underlying human nature is more or less the same.

- Leadership comes into its own when people are free and equal. Leaders create not followers but partners in the common enterprise.

- 'Smith is not a born leader yet,' one manager read in his annual appraisal. Given some natural aptitude for leadership – much more widely distributed than was once supposed – everyone can develop leadership ability. You have no excuse! But tomorrow calls for a new standard of quality of leadership within you, one only glimpsed in times past in the very best of natural leaders. Now the world calls for many more such great leaders. Will you be among their number?

- The author Graham Greene was once asked if he considered himself to be a great novelist. 'Not great,' he replied, 'but one of the best.' It may be that personal greatness in leadership may elude most leaders, dependent as it is upon situations which evoke it as well as one's gifts as a leader. But you can and should aspire to being 'one of the best'.

- Real excellence goes hand in hand with humility, that unlikely leadership virtue. Humility includes both seeing the truth about oneself and also being open to learning more about good leadership. It suggests, too, that necessary sense of greatness in others. For in John Buchan's words: 'The task of leadership is not to put greatness into humanity, but to elicit it, for the greatness is there already.'

Picture Acknowledgements

The publishers would like to thank the following for supplying photographs or allowing them to be reproduced:

P248 Anglia Television.

P174 Authors Collection.

P13, 60 British Museum, London.

P31, 87, 131, 310, 324 Camera Press.

P17, 65 J. Allan Cash Photo Library.

P286 Courtauld Institute of Art, London.

P202 E. T. Archive.

P177, 181, 278 Mary Evans Picture Library.

P10 Graeco-Roman Museum, Alexandria.

P38 Sonia Halliday Photographs.

P15, 48, 54, 69, 73, 141, 259, 265 Robert Harding Picture Library.

P27 Alan Howard, BBC Norwich.

P5, 91, 98, 183, 196, 212, 226, 229, 238, 272, 288, 304 Hulton Picture Collection.

P199 Huntington Gallery, San Marino, California.

P123, 125, 127 Imperial War Museum, London.

P46, 49, 82, 113, 140, 224, 307 Mansell Collection.

P41 MOA Museum of Art, Atami, Japan.

P192, 269, 280 National Portrait Gallery, London.

P331 PA Photos Ltd.

P85, 117, 209, 236, 297, 317, 319, 326 Popperphoto.

P149, 153 Ronald Sheridan Photo Library.

P217 Royal Geographical Society, London.

P266 Roger Viollet, Paris.

P101, 150, 167, 257, 290 Weidenfeld and Nicolson Archives.

Select Bibliography

Aristotle, *The Politics and Ethics*, Penguin Classics, 1981 and 1976.

Asser, *Life of King Alfred*, Penguin Classics, 1983.

Barnard, C.I., *The Functions of the Executive*,
Harvard University Press, 1938.

Blondel, J., *Political Leadership: Towards a General Analysis*, Sage, 1981.

Bosworth, A.B., *Conquest and Empire: The Reign of Alexander the Great*, Cambridge, 1988.

Burns, J. MacGregor, *Leadership*, Harper & Row, 1978.

Carlyle, T., *On Heroes, Hero Worship and the Heroic in History*, 1841. (Oxford University Press ed., 1904).

Carpenter, H., *Jesus*, Oxford University Press, 1980.

Crozier, B., *De Gaulle*, Eyre Methuen.

De Gaulle, C., *The Edge of the Sword*, Greenwood Press, 1932.

Emmet, D.M., *Function, Purpose and Powers*, Macmillan, 1958.

Fest, J.C., *Hitler*, Penguin, 1977.

Greenleaf, R.K., *Servant Leadership: A Journey into the Nature of Legitimate Power and Greatness*, Punlist Press, 1977.

Hamilton, N., *Monty: Master of the Battlefield 1942-1944*,
Hamish Hamilton, 1983.

Hammarskjöld, D., *Markings*, Faber, 1964.

Harvey-Jones, J., *Making It Happen: Reflections on Leadership*,
Collins, 1988.

Heider, J., *The Tao of Leadership*, Wildwood House, 1986.

Hsun Tzu, *The Art of War*, ed. J. Clavell, Hodder & Stoughton, 1981.

Huntford, R., *Scott and Amundsen*, Hodder & Stoughton, 1979.

Huntford, R., *Shackleton*, Hodder & Stoughton, 1985.

Jay, A., *Management and Machiavelli*, Hodder & Stoughton, 1967.

Kennedy, L., *Nelson and His Captains*, Collins, 1975.

Lane-Fox, R., *Alexander the Great*, Allen Lane, 1973.

Lawrence, A.W. (ed.), *T.E. Lawrence by his Friends*,
Jonathan Cape, 1937.

Lewin, R., *Slim the Standard Bearer*, Leo Cooper, 1976.

Mant, A., *Leaders We Deserve*, Martin Robertson, 1983.

Montgomery, B.L., *The Path to Leadership*, Collins, 1961.

Needham, J., *Science and Civilisation in China*, Vol. 2.
Cambridge University Press, 1956.

Nixon, R., *Leaders*, Sidgwick & Jackson, 1982.

Oman, C., *Nelson*, Hodder & Stoughton, 1947.

Plutarch, *The Rise and Fall of Athens, Makers of Rome, Fall of the
Roman Republic*, Penguin Classics, 1960, 1965 and 1972.

Pollard, S., *The Genesis of Modern Management*, Edward Arnold, 1965.

Raab, F., *The English Face of Machiavelli*,
Routledge & Kegan Paul, 1964.

Schram, P.E., *Hitler: The Man and the Military Leader*, Allen Lane, 1972.

Scott, J.M., *Gino Watkins*, Hodder & Stoughton, 1935.

Slim, W., *Defeat into Victory*, Cassell, 1956.

Stewart, D., *T.E. Lawrence*, Hamish Hamilton, 1977.

Tead, O., *The Art of Leadership*, McGraw-Hill, 1935.

Tendulkar, D.G., *Mahatma*, Greenleaf Books, 1983.

Thucydides, *History of the Peloponnesian War*, Penguin Classics, 1954.

Tinker, H., *Men Who Overturned Empires: Fighters, Dreamers and
Schemers*, Macmillan, 1988.

Thomson, R., *After I Was Sixty*, Hamish Hamilton, 1975.

Warner, O., *A Portrait of Lord Nelson*, Chatto and Windus, 1958.

Watt, E.D., *Authority*, Croom Helm, 1982.

Watts, A., *Tao: The Watercourse Way*, Jonathan Cape, 1976.

Willner, A.R., *The Spellbinders: Charismatic Political Leadership*, Yale
University Press, 1984.

Xenophon, *Memorabilia and Oeconomicus*, ed. E.C. Marchant and O.J.
Todd, 'Xenophon in Seven Volumes,' Vol. IV, Harvard University Press
and Heinemann, 1923.

Xenophon, *The Persian Expedition and A History of My Times*, Penguin
Classics, 1972 and 1979.

Index

Abbot, George   157, 158

Abbot, Maurice   157

Abbot, Robert   157

Abercrombie,
General Sir Ralph   201

Aboukir Bay   189, 199, 201

absolute rule   169, 170, 260

accountability in leadership   77

accounts   246

achievement   213, 256, 262, 300,
305, 306, 308

Adam, Sir Ronald   237

Adams, Abigail   184

Agamemnon, HMS   189, 197

aggressiveness   118, 291, 296

aim in leadership   74, 80, 109,
210, 218, 306, 311,
also *see* common task

Alamein, battle of   124

Alanbrooke,
Field Marshal Lord   101

Albermarle, HMS   190

Alexander the Great   58, 67-72,
111, 132, 142, 189, 194, 254,
258-264, 267, 305, 338

Alfred the Great   148-154,
156, 305

Algerian crisis   314

Allenby, General   269

America   285, 293, 304-306,
308, 309, 318,
also *see* USA

American
Civil War   100, 143, 306

American War of
Independence   182, 184

Amundsen, Roald   208, 209, 213

analytical thinking   94, 95

Anglo-Saxon kings   150

An Tanaiste   146

Antarctic, the   208, 211, 215

Anthony, Mark   258

Antisthenes   25

anxiety   99, 100, 103, 106, 115

Apostles   44-47

aptitude tests   238

Aquino, Cora   276

Arab Revolt   268, 270, 271

Arctic, the   208, 213

Aristophanes   6
   The Clouds   6

Aristotle   47, 78, 79,
160, 162, 167
   Ethics   78

Arrian   67, 71, 72, 264

Artaxerxes II   12

Artemisia, Queen   277

Arthur, King   154

Arundel, Lady   284

A Soldier Looks Ahead   234

Ashley, Laura   293

Asser, Bishop of Sherborne 151
   Life of King Alfred   151

assessment centres   237, 239

Assyria 264

Athens and the Athenians 5, 7, 11, 24, 27, 31, 36, 79, 80, 83, 84, 112, 138, 157, 158, 178, 301

Attila the Hun 260

attitude to leaders 234

Attlee, Clement 77, 90-92, 243

Austin, Herbert 231

Australia and the Australians 121, 243, 245, 246

Austria-Hungary 315

authority:

    bureaucratic 255

    charismatic 255

    of knowledge 11, 12, 13, 20, 27, 33, 47, 55, 187, 194, 213, 225, 230, 277, 284, 303, 305

    of personality 11, 50, 55, 146, 184, 187, 199, 215, 255, 267, 273, 303, 304

    of position 11, 12, 55, 80, 187, 303, 342

    religious 37

Babylon 12, 71, 265

Bader, Douglas 241

bad leadership 16

Ball, Sir Alexander 193

Bandaranaike, Sirimavo 276

Bankes, Lady 284

Barfleur, HMS 190

Bar Lev, General 95

Barnard, Robert 172

Bastille, storming of the 279

Baxter, Richard 159

Bede, the Venerable 152

    Ecclesiastical History 152

Bedouins, the 146, 215, 268-270

Belleisle, HMS 202

Bellerophon, HMS 268

Benedetti, Carlo 254

Beni Howeitat tribe 270

Bevan, Aneurin 90, 92

Bevin, Ernest 90, 92

Bible 52, 62, 64, 138, 158, 199, 279, 281

Bion, W.R. 237

Bismarck, Prince Otto von 315

Bixby, Mrs 307

Blunt, Lady Anne 146

    Bedouin Tribes of the Euphrates 146

Bochkareva, Mariya 279

Body Shop, The 292

Bolivar, Simon 305

Boeotia 11

Bolsheviks 226

Bonaparte, Napoleon 107, 111, 132, 190, 254, 267, 268, 309, 311, 315, 318, 321

Bonham-Carter, Lady Violet 53

Boone, Daniel 58, 180-182

Boreas, HMS 200

Bormann, Martin 320

Boudicca 278, 279

Braley, Bertram 233

Brearley, Mike 273, 274

    Art of Captaincy 273

Brinsley, John 160
A Consolation for our
Grammar Schools 160
Britain,
invasion of 125, 126, 145
British Army 193, 234, 237,
239, 242
British colonies 175, 176
British Empire 138, 221
British Expeditionary
Force 234
British Institute of
Management 233
British Railways 243
British tribes 139, 145
Brunel,
Isambard Kingdom 228, 229
Brunel, Marc 228
Buchan, John 4, 271, 344
Buckingham, Duke of 52
Bunker's Hill, battle of 182
Burghley, Lord 164, 169, 186
Burke, Edmund 175, 304
Burma 115, 118, 121
Burns, James MacGregor 294
Butler, Josephine 289
Byrhnoth 148
Byron, Lord 303
Byrtwold 148

Cabinet, running the 90-93,
102, 293, 297, 298
Cadbury family 231
Cadiz 194, 195, 197

Caesar, Julius 36, 139-144,
150, 154, 160
Callaghan, James 293, 294
Callaway, Colonel 180
calmness in
leadership 99-102, 210, 218,
219, 241, 299, 314
Cambridge University 159, 188
Camulodunum 279
Capernaum 45
Cape St Vincent,
battle of 190, 195, 200
Captain, HMS 195, 200
Carduci 17-21
Carlyle, Thomas 225, 227,
230, 256, 258
Signs of the Times 230
On Heroes, Hero –
Worship and the Herioc
in History 225, 256
Carnegie, Andrew 231
Carrel, Alexis 94
Reflections upon Life 94
Carthaginians 104
Cecil, Lord 172
change and
leadership 220-250, 289, 300
charisma 134, 241, 254-257,
317, 321, 322, 327, 330
Charlemagne
(Charles the Great) 309
Charles I, King 175, 285
Cheshire Homes 242
Cheshire, Leonard 241, 242

chief executives,
women as 293, 294

China 39, 43, 109, 223

Chirisophus 18, 19

Christian beliefs 39, 48, 49,
138, 148, 149, 152-154,
157-159, 170, 171, 254, 269,
274, 281, 282, 308

Christian ideals of
leadership 154, 156, 169, 171

Chuang Tzu 40

Churchill,
Sir Winston 53, 81, 85-88,
103, 129-131, 143, 242,
269, 271, 300, 305, 309, 318,
321, 339, 343
Great Contemporaries 339

Church of England 171, 281

Cicero 36, 72, 105

civil disobedience 323

Civil Service 239

Clarendon, Earl of 172, 173
*History of the Great
Rebellion* 173

Clark, William 197

Clarke, William 182

Clearchus 12-15, 83

Cleitus 262

Clemenceau, Georges 309

Cleveland, Harvey 294

coal mines 230, 232

Cobbett, Willaim 208

Cobbold, Major Ralph 341

Coenus 263

Colet, John 158

Collier, John 108

Collingwood, Admiral 200

Colville, Sir John 143, 321
The Fringes of Power 321

common task 21, 28, 29,
34, 58, 66, 75, 108, 111,
116, 206, 230, 241, 247,
273, 294, 301, 338

communications
in leadership 108-133, 166,
195, 240, 243-245, 295

Communism 223-225

Companion Cavalry 262

Congo, problem of 318

Conrad, Joseph 205

Conservative Party 293, 295

Corfe Castle 284

Cornwall, King of 154

coronation service 152, 153

Corsica 189

cotton mills 230

courage in leadership 69, 75,
122, 164, 169, 184, 194, 210,
241, 256, 262, 270, 291, 295

courtesy in leadership 167-169,
185, 186, 299

Crimean War 287

Cripps, Sir Stafford 233

crisis situation 11, 12, 68, 83,
93, 102, 150, 210, 216,
217, 247, 314, 336

Crockett, Davy 177-182

Cromwell, Oliver 82, 175, 285

Cromwell, Thomas   169, 172

Cross of Lorraine   309

Crystal Palace   221

culture   322

Cunaxa   12, 13, 15, 71

Cyrus the Great 30, 72, 261, 265

Cyrus the Younger   12, 16

Damascus   269

dams, raids of   241

Danes, the   145, 148, 149-152

Darwin, Charles   223

David, King   63, 152

Davout, General   267

Dayan, Moshe   95

D-Day   240

decision-making   77-83, 218,
       291, 300, 313

decisive action   84, 218, 261

de Gaulle, Charles   61, 303,
       309-315, 322, 333

   The Army of the Future   309

   The Edge of the Sword   311

de Guingand, General   127

deification of leaders   260-263,
       265, 267, 268

Deioces   264, 265

democratic leaders   234-242

democratic society   1, 36, 133,
       178, 179, 214, 235, 242, 249,
       260, 265, 298, 303, 315, 335

Demosthenes, general   83

Demosthenes, orator   109

Derby, Countess of   284

Diades   70

Dickens, Charles   53

   David Copperfield   53

Dill, General Sir John   143

Diogenes   158

Dionysodurus   7, 8

directors   246, 247, 292, 293

Directory of Directors   293

discipline   14, 121, 140, 197,
       211, 214, 241, 342

Discovery, HMS   208

divisiveness   64

divorce   283

Dole, Senator Robert   132

Dolphin, HMS   188

Drake, Sir Francis   164, 166,
       167, 186

Dunkirk   234

Durham, Bishop of
see Henson, Dr Hensley

East Indies   188

Eden, Anthony   102

Edgar, King   153

Edge Island   213

education for leadership
also *see* training   158, 159

Edward VI   158

Egypt   267

Egyptian Canal Corps   270

Eighth Army   114, 124, 126,
       235, 240

Einstein, Albert 94

Eisenhower, General 81, 86-88

Elephant Island 212

Elizabethan society 156-160, 163

Elizabeth I 156, 158, 164, 169,
171, 172, 280-282, 305

Elyot, Sir Thomas 161, 162-164,
167, 168, 172, 176, 198, 287

The Governor 162, 163

encouragement, leading by 20,
29, 30, 67, 261

Endeavour, HMS 211

Endurance, HMS 211

energy, generating 111, 112,
124, 300, 311

engineers 227-229, 246

English Civil War 172-175, 221,
284, 287

entrepreneurs 228-230, 232, 246

equality 184, 327, 335

Erasmus, Desiderius 158, 222

Essex, Earl of 163

Essex, General 285

estate management 30-32,
79, 261

Europe, invasion of 86, 121, 234

Everest expedition 337, 343

evoking charismatic
response 259

example, leading by 19, 20,
67, 141, 152, 154, 175,
184, 202, 203, 217, 227,
239-242, 326, 338, 342

factory reforms 230

Fairfax, Sir Thomas 52

Falkland Islands 188

family life, leadership in 296

Fascism 271

Fascists, British 271, 272

favouritism 45

Fayol, Henri 232, 233

*General and Industrial
Administration* 232, 233

Feather, Vic 242

feminist movement 279

Feuerbach, P.J.A. 256

Finch, Lady Anne 285-287

Finch, Sir John 285

First World War 220, 227,
231, 232, 242, 268, 290,
291, 309, 311, 315, 318

flaws in leadership 16, 86, 262,
296, 300

arrogance 37, 39, 55, 81, 168,
271, 300, 320

Florentine Republic 170

Foch, Marshall Ferdinand 311

Ford, Henry 231

Fortescue, J.W. 79

Fourteenth Army 115, 118,
120-122, 240

France and the
French 189, 190, 194, 195,
197, 198, 200, 228, 267,
309, 311, 314, 315, 341

Franciscans 255

Frederick the Great 13

Free French	309
French navy	228
French Revolution	315
Fry family	231
Fuller, Thomas	157
functions of leadership	24-29, 34, 54, 67, 233, 237, 277
future leaders	327, 335-344
Galland, Adolf	241
Gallipoli campaign	243
Gandhi, Indira	276, 327
Gandhi, Mahatma	303, 322-327
Gaul	139, 141
Gedrosian desert	67, 68, 70
General Election 1945	242
General Strike	234
gentleman-leader, the	155-186, 207, 227
George III	204
German tribes	142, 145
Germany and the Germans	87, 94, 142, 197, 309, 315, 316, 318, 320-322, 338
Getty, J. Paul	95
Gettysburg, battle of	100
Ghana	305
Gibson, Guy	241
Gilbert, Martin	103
giving direction in leadership	47, 58-76, 108, 187, 218, 300, 341, 342
Gorbachev, Mikhail	305
Goebbels, Dr Josef	315, 320

Goering, Herman	320
Gordon, General	36, 143
Gorgias of Lentini	15
Grahame, Kenneth	99
The Wind in the Willows	99
grammar schools	158-160
Gray, Thomas	176
Great Depression	233
Great Exhibition	221
Great Western Railway	228
Greece and the Greeks	12, 14, 18-21, 24, 29, 34, 36, 37, 47, 62, 68-72, 75, 78, 79, 105, 138, 156, 160, 168, 258, 260, 263-267, 275, 305, 330, 338
Greek leaders	6-12, 42, also *see* Socrates, etc
Greeley, Horace	306
Greene, Graham	344
Greenland	213
Gregory, Pope	152
Cura Pastoralis	152
Guderian, General	318
Guildford Grammar School	158
Guinevere, Queen	154
Halifax Grammar School	159
Halicarnassus	277
Hamada	53
Hamilton, Alexander	179
Hamilton, Lady Emma	189, 195, 204
Hamilton, Sir William	204

Hammarskjöld, Dag 339
Markings 339
Hampden, John 173-176
Hannibal 104
Hargood, Captain 203
Harrow School 160
Harvey-Jones,
Sir John 247, 248, 291
Making it Happen 291
Hashemites 268, 270
Hastings, Max 298
Heath, Edward 294, 295
Hebrew tradition 221
Hejaz 268
Henry VIII 169
Henry, Patrick 184
Henson, Dr Hensley 4
Hephaestion 70
Heracles 258, 260, 262, 265
Herbert, Sidney 288
Herder, Johann 322
Hermocrates 110
Herodotus 70, 260, 264, 277
hero worship 255, 259
hierarchy 47
Hillary, Sir Edmund 211
Himmler, Heinrich 320
Hinduism 325
Hitler, Adolf 4, 85, 87, 94, 111,
171, 272-274, 303, 315-321, 333
Ho Chi Minh 305
Homer 7, 62, 70

Hood, Lord 189, 190
hospice movement 291
House of Commons 157, 173
Houston, Sam 182
Howe, Lord 197
Hsun-Tzu 50, 109, 335
The Art of War 50, 109
Huizinga, John 340
*Dutch Civilisation in
the 17th Century* 340
human needs 28, 29
humility in leadership 34, 42-47,
49-57, 71, 88, 124, 171, 193,
205, 308, 333, 334, 344
humour 103-106, 214,
215, 241, 299, 314
Humphrey Institute, USA 294
Hundred Years' War 309
Hunt, Lord John 337, 343
hustings 145
Hutchinson, Anne 285

Iacocca, Lee 254
Iceni, the 279
I.C.I. 243, 291, 293
idiosyncrasy credit 204
imagination in
leadership 77, 94, 97, 98, 99,
105-107, 111, 143, 195
India 115, 118, 120, 130, 180,
191, 263, 322, 323, 325-327
Indian National Congress 323

industrial
entrepreneurs   228-233, 305
Industrial Revolution   27, 221,
230, 231
industry, changes in   113, 242
industry, leadership in 232, 233,
242-250, 254, 276
information,
need for 109, 110, 114, 133, 245,
and see communications
in leadership
inspiration in leadership   32,
105-135, 175, 195, 205, 215,
233, 241, 255, 256, 261, 293,
308, 309, 321, 327, 338
integrity in leadership 152, 171,
172, 185, 186
interviews   237
intuition in
leadership   66, 93-97, 105, 262,
270, 291, 312, 316-320
invoking charismatic
response   258, 265, 267, 268
Ireland   146
Ismay, General   143
Italy   139, 170

Jackson, General Stonewall 143
Japan and the Japanese 53, 115,
118, 120, 121
Jefferson, Thomas   184, 303
Jerusalem   265
Jesus of Nazareth and
his disciples   28, 37-52, 65, 158,
303, 323, 327, 338

Jews   148, 279
Jinnah, Muhammed Ali   325
Joan of Arc   279, 309
Jodl, General   320
Jones, Jim   255
Jonestown   255
Joseph, Sir Keith   295
Judaea   62, 64, 138
Judaeo-Christian
religion   223, 254
Judas Iscariot   45
judgement in leadership 77, 88,
90, 210, 241, 270
judo   40

Kangerdlugsuak   216
Keats, Captain   195
Kempis, Thomas à   42
Kennedy, President John   313
Kenya   305
Kenyatta, Jomo   305
king-gods   267
also see deification of leaders
knowledge, leadership
through   4-23, 33
Kurdistan   17

Labour Party   293, 294
Labrador   213, 214
Lafayette, Marquis de   184
Lambert,
Major-General John   175
Lannes, Marshal   267

Laomedon 70

Lao Tzu 39-41, 43, 49, 51, 53, 56, 303

   Tao Tê Ching 39

Lathom House 284

Lawrence, A.W. 273

Lawrence, T.E. (of Arabia) 107, 239, 254, 268-273

   Seven Pillars of Wisdom 271, 273

Leach, Bernard 53

leader, born 4, 33, 34, 239

leader, derivation of word 59-61

Lee, Laurie 254

Lee, General Robert E. 100, 101

Lenin 223-226

   What is to be Done? 226

Leverhulme, William H. 231

Lewin, Ronald 124

Linacre, Thomas 158

Lincoln, Abraham 182, 303-308, 322, 325, 333

   Inaugural Address 308

listening in leadership 56, 109, 110, 114, 133, 209, 318

Livy 144, 333

Locker, William 194

Londinium 152, 279

Long Parliament 173

Lord, John 340-343

Lowestoffe, HMS 194, 200

loyalty to leaders 260, 264, 273

Luddites, the 231

Luther, Martin 222

Lyon, John 160

majesty in leadership 167, 168

Macedonians, the 71, 262

Machiavelli, Niccolo 156, 169-173, 185, 267, 270, 300, 303

   Discourses on Livy 171

Macmillan, Harold 102

MacNeice, Louis 231

Malham, Salyam Bint 279

Malory, Sir Thomas 154

management of change 74, 249

management through leadership 232, 233, 243, 247

manager-leaders (women) 291-293

managers 14, 32, 53, 61, 119, 246-249, 255

Manstein, Field-Marshal 318

Mao Tse-tung 223

Marduk 265

Marius, General 142, 143

Marlborough, Duke of 79, 102

Marmont, Marshal 267

marriage, leadership in 282-285, 287

Married Women's Property Act 289

Marx, Karl 220, 223, 225, 226, 289

   Das Kapital 225

Mayflower Compact 182

Medes, the 261, 264

Medina 269

meeting needs in
leadership 14, 25, 28, 29, 37,
47, 48, 55, 58, 66, 67, 70, 71, 74,
108, 109, 120-122, 197, 198, 215,
216, 238, 239, 273, 277

Meir, Mrs Golda 95, 96, 276

mentors 189, 194, 336

Menzies, Sir Robert 130

Mercia 150, 152

Mercurius Aulicus 285

Mericourt, Theroigne de 279

meritocracy 294

military leaders,
qualities of 7, 8, 12-16, 83,
100, 114-129, 175, 187, 279

Milton, John 144, 221, 223,
282, 284, 287

Model, Field-Marshal 319

monarchy 260, 265

monasteries, privatised 159

Moncrieff, Jock 241

Mond, Alfred Moritz 231

Montgomery, General 5, 114,
115, 124-128, 132, 134, 240,
242, 249, 314, 321

The Path of Leadership 314

Moore, Trooper 270

Moorehead, Alan 235

The Desert War 235

moral climate 37, 282, 326, 327

morale and leadership 60, 74,
111-127, 166, 199, 211, 342

More, Sir Thomas 158, 282

Morrison, Herbert 90

Moses 305

Mosley, Sir Oswald 271, 272

motivation in leadership 74,
79-81, 111, 115, 218, 261

Mountbatten,
Admiral Lord 86, 121, 325

movement organisation 227

Mulberry harbours 86

Murray, General Wolfe 103

Muslims 323, 325

mystique 312-314

Nansen, Fridtjof 209

Napoleon – *see* Boneparte

Nationalist Socialist German
Workers' Party 315

natural gifts as leader 261

natural succession 146, 277

Nazi invasion 129

Nazi party 315, 320

Nehru, Jawarharlal 327

Nelson, Horatio 132, 185,
187-206, 228, 247, 338

Nero, Emperor 170, 279

Netherlands, the 164, 281, 340

Newcombe, Silas 180

New Guinea 121

New Israel 221

New Model Army 52, 175

New Zealand 211

Nicholas, Paul 202, 203

Nicomachides 25-28

Nietzsche,
Friedrich Wilhelm 256

Nightingale, Florence 287-289

Nile, battle of the 189, 190, 193,
195, 197, 198

Nimrod, HMS 211

Nixon, President
Richard 313, 314
   Leaders 313, 314

Nkrumah, Kwame 305

Normandy, invasion of 86

North Africa 143, 235, 240

North American
Indians 180, 181

Norway and the
Norwegians 210

Oates, Lawrence 210

obedience and
leadership 8-14, 30, 37, 42,
151, 159, 167, 168, 188, 201,
208-210, 255-261, 282, 318

officer selection 236-240

Officer Training Corps 269

oligarchy 260

Olympus, Mount 30, 257

Onassis, Aristotle 305

Orient, the 222

Orosius, Father Paulus 152

Owen, Lt. John 203

Owen, Robert 230, 231

Ovid 72, 204

Heroides 204

Oxford University 153, 158,
159, 269, 271

Palestine 269

Pankhurst, Emmeline 289-291

Pankhurst, Richard 289

Parker, Matthew 171

Parliament 157

Paulinus, Suetonius 279

Peloponnesian War 79, 83

People's Army 239, 240

People's Temple Sect 255

Pericles 11, 36, 79, 80, 83, 84,
110, 112, 113, 150

Peron, Isabelita 276

Persia and the Persians 12, 15,
17, 19, 47, 59, 70, 71,
261-267, 275, 277, 312

personal drive 124, 296

persuasion, leading by 81, 112,
154, 241, 338

Pétain, Marshal 309

Philip of Macedon 69, 109

phronesis 79, 80, 105, 162, 318

physical characteristics
of leaders 258, 261, 268,
273, 306, 316

pioneers in
America 180-182, 185

Pitt the Elder, William 133

Plato 6, 7, 11, 21, 22, 36, 112, 160, 335

   Dialogues 6

   The Republic 6

Plutarch 36, 79, 83, 104, 112, 139, 141-144, 260, 334

polar explorers 207-219

Polar Medal 213

political leaders 24, 90, 91, 128-132, 144, 303-306, 315, 322, 325, 327

political leadership 293, 294

Pope, the 48, 152, 159

potential for leadership 33, 34, 132, 158, 239, 245, 246, 276, 335-337

Powell, Mary 282

power in leadership 37-42, 79, 139, 144, 169, 223, 241, 262, 316, 322, 327

practical reasoning 77-84, 95, 105, 316

Prasutagus, King 279

presidents 132, 184, 304-308, 313, 332

pressure groups 89

prime ministers 90, 92, 93, 95, 102, 129, 130, 132, 143, 243, 276, 293, 295, 299, 321, 327, 339

progress chasing 85

prostration 153, 264, 265, 275

Proxenus 15, 16

public relations 132, 189, 315

punishment 14, 19, 25, 32

Puritans 159, 171, 173, 176, 179, 221, 284, 285

Pym, John 173, 175

Quaker families 231

qualities in leadership 7, 20, 67, 77, 146, 162-169, 187, 204, 210, 218, 228-230, 241, 274, 277, 287, 291, 292, 295, 300, 301, 304, 311, 312, 314, 322, 328, 338, 343, also *see* Christian ideals

Quintilian, Marcus 320

racial discrimination 323

Raffles, Stamford 221

railways 227, 243, 290, also *see* British Railways

Reagan, Ronald 132, 304

Regan, Donald T. 132

Reformation, the 158, 159, 222, 282

religion 256, 258, 261, also *see* Christianity, Hinduism etc.

Renaissance, the 12, 36, 156, 158, 162, 163, 169, 185, 222, 281, 282

respect for leaders 16, 20, 21, 264, 314, 322

responsibility in leadership 81, 85, 86, 238-240, 247, 291, 338, 343

rewards 25, 29, 30, 35, 37, 42, 44, 45, 47, 147, 261

rhetoric 112, 129, 130, 132, 320

Rhine, Confederation of the 315

Rhode Island   179

Robertson, George   182

Robertson, James   182

Rochefort   268

Rockefeller, John Davidson 231

Roddick, Anita
and Gordon   292, 293

Rome and the Romans   37, 42,
    47, 50, 72, 104, 112, 138-145,
    148, 149, 152, 160, 171, 222, 258,
    260, 267, 275, 279, 320, 330, 333

Rommel, General   126

Roosevelt, Franklin D. 129, 318

Roosevelt, Theodore   81, 89

Rose, Kenneth   130

Roseberry, Lord   133

Round Table, the   153, 154

Roundway Down   285

Rowntree family   231

Royal Air Force   241, 242, 270

Royal College of Physicians 158

Royal Geographical Society 213

Royal Marines   202

Royal Navy   13, 27, 187, 198,
                    204-206, 211, 268

Ruskin, John   51
    Modern Painters   51

Russia   223, 225-227, 305, 315

Russian Revolution 226, 227, 229

Sainsbury, John   97

St Andrews University   4

St Francis   255

St Paul   42, 61, 158, 273, 274

St Paul's School   158

St Peter   45

St Vincent,
Admiral Lord   187, 189, 197

Salamis, battle of   277

Samarkand   262

Sandhurst   340, 342

San Francisco   255

San Joseph, the   200

Santa Cruz   194

Sassoon, Siegfried   271

Saunders, Dame Ciceley   291

Saxons   59, 145

Scott, J.M.   213

Scott, Capt. Robert
Falcon   207-211,
                        213, 218, 219

Scutari   287, 289
    death rate at   289

Seal, Eric   103

Second World War   114-128,
    143, 220, 233, 234, 249, 291, 318

security, personal   267

selection of leaders   29, 220,
                        237, 238

selection of personnel   29, 90

self-development   33, 34

Seneca   169, 339

Sertorius, General   260

servant-leader   37-57

service in leadership   28,
                        37-57, 221

Sevier, John   182

Shakespeare, William –
quotations from   81, 115, 124,
            156, 157, 160, 168, 172,
                282, 284, 338

Shackleton,
Sir Ernest   207, 211-213,
                        218, 219

Shannon, Dave   241

Shelbourne, Thomas   175

shepherd as leader, the   61-65

Ship Money   173

shop floor, starting on   237

Siberia   226

Sidney, Sir Philip   163-165

Sigebert of the East Angles 153

Singapore   221

617 Squadron   241

skills in leadership   11, 24-36,
                74, 81, 93, 293, 316

slavery   47, 279, 306

Slim, General
Sir William   22, 24, 114-124,
                128, 134, 234, 240,
                242-246, 249, 337
    Defeat into Victory   114

Smiles, Samuel   227
    Lives of the Stephensons 227
    Self-Help   227

Social Capitalism   130, 131,
                        293, 300

social change   242

social classes   47

Socialism   234, 235

social reformers
(women as)   287-291

Socrates   5-9, 11, 12, 15, 16,
        20-22, 24-29, 33, 34, 37, 41, 47,
        62, 78, 138, 158, 277, 301, 303

Sohm, Rudolf   256

Soteridas   18, 19

South Africa   323, 328,
                    329, 331, 332

South America   305

South-east Asia   121, 240

South Georgia   212

South Pole   207-211, 218

Soviet government, first   227

Spain and the
Spaniards   139, 166, 188,
                    197, 260, 281

Spanish Armada   281

Sparta and the Spartans 12, 13,
        18, 24, 83, 110, 112, 143, 265

Spartacus   47

speech-writers   128

Speer, Albert   316, 319, 320

spiritual path   325-327

Springfield, Massachusetts 179

Sri Lanka   276

Stalag XIB   341-343

Stalingrad   318

Stark, Admiral Harold   309

Statistical Society   289

Steffens, Lincoln   89
    The Shame of the Cities   89

Stephenson, George   227

Stirling, W.F.   270, 271
    *T.E. Lawrence by
    his Friends*   270

stress 238, 270

styles of leadership 303-334

Suckling,
Capt. Maurice 188, 189, 194

Suez Crisis 102

suffragettes 289, 290

Sutton Hoo mask 60

Sykes, John 194

Tacitus, Pulius 77, 99, 145-147,
156, 279

tank regiments 235, 240

Tantalus 241, 271

Taoiseach 146

Taoist teachings 40, 44, 48, 55,
335, 338

Taya, Abu 270

Taya, Auda Abu 270

Tead, Ordway 89
   The Art of Leadership 89

team building 28, 29, 34, 35,
52, 55, 69, 70, 74, 108, 120, 125,
166, 180, 187, 197, 206, 210, 225,
262, 274, 275, 291, 293, 296, 301

technology 221, 227, 241, 245

telecommunications 129, 130,
132

television 128-130, 132, 267,
273, 275, 299, 314

Tenerife 189

Tennyson,
Lord Alfred 218, 221-225
   Locksley Hall 225

Tenth Legion 139, 142, 145

Ten Thousand, the 12, 17, 19

tests of leadership 273

Thackeray, W.M. 306

Thames tunnel project 228

Thatcher, Denis 296

Thatcher, Margaret 276, 293-300,
302, 305
   family life 296

Themistocles 82, 84

Thesiger, Wilfred 146
   Arabian Sands 146

Third Reich 171, 234

32nd Regiment 268

Thomas, Lowell 271

Thomson, Roy 78, 96, 97, 105
   After I was Sixty 78, 96, 97

three circles model 35, 66, 67,
75, 134, 238

Thucydides 83, 84, 110, 112

Times, The 78

Tissaphernes 18, 19

Toxteth 298

trade unions 230, 232, 234,
242, 293, 294

Trades Union Congress 242

traditions of leadership 5, 11,
12, 138-155, 208, 221, 224, 225,
231, 249, 277, 279, 281,
282, 323, 325

Trafalgar, battle of 194, 195,
200-202, 206

training of leaders 4, 33, 34,
220, 336, 337

transferability of leadership
functions 25, 29

tribal society 55

tribal traditions of
leadership 145-148, 277, 279

Tudors, the 158

Tu Mu 50

Turks, the 268

Tweedsmuir, Lord
see John Buchan

Twentieth Legion 279

Tyre 261

Ulyanov, Vladimir Ilyich
see Lenin

unemployment 298

United Nations 339

unity, creating 50, 63-65, 69-72,
74, 75, 118, 139, 166, 182, 194,
195, 233, 261, 264, 296, 298,
306, 315, 325, 337

Untouchables 323, 326

Urwick, L.F. 233

*The Elements of
Administration* 233

USA 138, 184, 185, 255, 305, 306

Uther Pendragon 154

Venizelos, Eleutherios 305

Verulamium 279

Victorian era 221, 222, 228

Victory, HMS 195, 200

Vikings 145-152

Virgil 139, 144

Aeneid 139

vision in leadership 110, 111,
133, 180, 270, 306, 309, 311

Voltaire 102

votes for women 289-291

Walker Trust 4

Waller,
General Sir William 284, 285

Waller, Lady Anne
see Finch, Lady Anne

Walsingham, Sir Francis 171

Wardour Castle 284

War Office Selection Board
(WOSB) 237-239

Washington,
George 182-185, 305

Waterloo, battle of 191, 268

Watkins, Gino 207, 213-217

Wavell, Field Marshal Lord 5

Way, the see Christian beliefs

Weber, Max 255, 256, 316

Wehrmacht 13

Weil, Simone 327

Weimar republic 315

Wellesley, Sir John
see Duke of Wellington

Wellington, Duke of 79, 190,
191, 193, 196, 198

Wessex 150, 152

Western Germany 315

West Indies 188, 197

Whitelaw, William — 296, 299

Whitman, Walt — 343

William of Orange — 305

William, Prince — 190, 197

Williamson, Henry — 271

Wilson, Harold — 293, 294

Wilson, Woodrow — 89

Winthrop, John — 176

Wolfe, General — 86

women as leaders — 276-302

Women's Battalion of Death — 279

Women's Social and Political Union — 289

Woolf, Virginia — 276

Wordsworth, William — 258

Worsley, Frank — 211

Wright Brothers — 222

Wu Ch'I — 50

Wu Wei principle — 40

'X' Captain — 234-237, 239, 240

A Soldier Looks Ahead — 234

Xenophon — 6-21, 24, 28, 30, 32, 33, 35-37, 47, 67, 71-73, 110, 138, 162, 201, 261, 265

Cyropaedia — 21, 30, 72, 162

Memorabilia — 6

Oeconomicus — 30

Persian Expedition, The — 12

Xerxes — 277

Yom Kippur — 95

Yunnan — 305

'Zadok the Priest' — 153

Zutphen — 163